The Reformation and the English People

To
N. A. S.

The Reformation and the English People

J. J. Scarisbrick

Basil Blackwell

C 51, 954 /274.2d

£14·50

First published 1984
Basil Blackwell Publisher Limited
108 Cowley Road, Oxford OX4 1JF, England.

British Library Cataloguing in Publication Data
Scarisbrick, J. J.
   The reformation and the English people.
   1. Reformation — England
   I. Title
   274.2'06   BR377

   ISBN 0-631-13424-7

Typesetting by System 4 Associates, Gerrards Cross, Bucks.
Printed in Great Britain by Billing and Sons Ltd, Worcester

Contents

Preface

This book began its career as the Ford Lectures for 1982. So I must begin this preface by thanking the University of Oxford for conferring on me the highest honour that can befall an English historian (i.e. a student of English history) with their invitation to join that long and distinguished line of scholars who have given these annual lectures. I also thank (again) the friends and colleagues who entertained me royally on my weekly pilgrimage to their university during the Hilary term 1982.

I have reworked the material used in those lectures and made considerable additions and excisions. Six lectures have thus evolved into eight chapters. But essentially this is the book of the lectures.

It is not another general study of the English Reformation. It is an essay which attempts to trace some of the ways in which and some reasons why English society at large underwent and responded to the profound changes in religious loyalties, attitudes and practices during the sixteenth century which were officially implemented from 'above' by statute, proclamation and royal commission. So it is much more about *mentalités* than events. Even so, I am conscious of how much I have not tackled adequately -- the spread of English Protestantism, for example -- partly because there is much more local study to be done before a national picture can be drawn, partly because a thorough account would require a much bigger book than this one.

I have deliberately tried to keep footnotes lean and to avoid long bibliographical excursions therein, which, given the vast accumulation of writings on the English Reformation, would have been very easy. Hence footnotes go beyond immediate reference for statements in the text only when the matter in hand is contentious and requires additional support, or when recent important revision of former views demands that the works concerned be cited. If I have borrowed ideas without due acknowledgement I apologise humbly to the victims. If some major works do not get a mention this, I hope, is only because of the operation of the criteria just noted.

I am most grateful to the University of Warwick for granting me study leave during 1981–2 to complete research for this book. In the course of that leave I visited a number of local record offices up and down the country (listed in the bibliography). They proved to have one remarkable feature in common: astonishingly kind, patient and helpful staff. It was a continual pleasure to be greeted by city and county archivists so ready to help a newcomer and produce the 'goods' that more could be accomplished in a day or two than would have been thought possible. No wonder those search-rooms are crowded.

I thank those kind archivists and their colleagues. I also thank Mrs Myrna Harwar for typing the final draft of this book excellently and expeditiously.

J. J. S.
University of Warwick

Abbreviations

Arch. f. Ref.	*Archiv für Reformationsgeschichte*
BL	British Library
CPR	*Calendar of Patent Rolls*
CRO	County Record Office
CRS	Catholic Record Society Publications
CSP	*Calendar of State Papers*
Foley	Foley, H. (ed), *Records of the English Province of the Society of Jesus* (1877–83)
LP	*Letters and Papers, Foreign and Domestic, of the Reign of Henry VIII*, edited by Brewer, Gairdner and Brodie (1862–1932)
LRS	London Record Society
PS	Parker Society
RO	Record Office
SP	State Papers (Public Record Office, London)
TRHS	*Transactions of the Royal Historical Society*
VCH	*Victoria County History*

Unless otherwise noted, all manuscripts cited here are in the Public Record Office, London.

All references to *LP* refer to document numbers, not pages.

1

Layfolk and the Pre-Reformation Church

This book is about a supreme event in English history, the Reformation. Its theme could be summarised thus: on the whole, English men and women did not want the Reformation and most of them were slow to accept it when it came.

The English Reformation was in only a limited sense popular and from 'below'. To speak of a rising groundswell of lay discontent with the old order, of growing 'spiritual thirst' during the latter Middle Ages, and of a momentous alliance between the crown and disenchanted layfolk that led to the repudiation of Rome and the humbling of the clerical estate is to employ metaphors for which there is not much evidence. They derive partly from the fact that modern tastes have tended to prefer the grand, long-term explanations of big events (especially if they give pride of place to impersonal changes in social structures or aspirations) and partly from the fact that a basically Whiggish and ultimately 'Protestant' view of things is still a potent influence on our thinking. Diluted, residual and secularised that influence may now be. But we still find it difficult to do without the model of late-medieval decline and alienation − followed by disintegration and then rebirth and renewal − just as we still find it difficult to believe that major events in our history have lacked deep-seated causation or have ever run fundamentally against the grain of the 'general will'.

The only valid reason for challenging a widely held view on how the English Reformation 'happened' is that the evidence (whether new evidence or the old looked at afresh)

no longer seems to accord with it. We have hitherto been
content with the image of the Tudor regime unleashing and
then riding the back of the tiger of popular anticlericalism,
anti-papalism, patriotism and so on. If that is now suspect,
this is because one can no longer find much of a tiger.[1]

The wills written by English men and women in the first half
of the sixteenth century are the first evidence. Thousands
survive. Quite a number have now been printed. Most can
only be read in the manuscript collections in the Public
Record Office and in the diocesan and county archives
around the country. An admittedly (and inevitably) limited
skimming and sampling — but, it is hoped, one sufficiently
random and on a sufficient scale to be reliable — produces
the following conclusion: up to the very moment when the
traditional medieval religious institutions and practices were
swept away, English layfolk were pouring money and gifts
in kind into them. Wills are a source which, quite rightly,
has attracted plenty of attention recently — because so many
survive and because, since quite humble folk as well as those
at the top wrote them, they provide opportunities to make

[1]   I must quickly add that several other people have recently been moving to
similar conclusions: see (e.g.) M. Bowker, *The Henrician Reformation. The diocese of Lincoln under John Longland, 1521—1547* (Cambridge, 1981); C. Haigh,
Reformation and Resistance in Tudor Lancashire (Cambridge, 1975); S. Lander,
'Church Courts and the Reformation in the Diocese of Chichester, 1500—58' in
R. O'Day and F. Heal (eds), *Continuity and Change: Personnel and Administration of the Church in England, 1500—1642* (Leicester, 1976), pp. 215—37. Other
(and older) authorities are cited later in this chapter and in chapter 3. For a full
review of recent writings see C. Haigh, 'Some Aspects of Recent Historiography
of the English Reformation', in W. J. Mommsen (ed.), *The Urban Classes, the
Nobility and the Reformation* (Publications of the German Historical Institute,
London, 5, 1980), pp. 88—106. Similar revisionism is to be found among historians of the continental Reformation. G. Ritter, 'Why the Reformation occurred
in Germany', *Church History*, xxvii (1958), 99—106, and B. Moeller, 'Frömmigkeit in Deutschland um 1500', *Arch. f. Ref.*, lvi (1965), 5—31, have challenged
theories of pre-Reformation 'seething discontent' and 'spiritual thirst', Hesko
Oberman has also greatly enriched our appreciation of pre-Reformation religious
life and thought. See R. Crofts, 'Books, Reform and the Reformation', *Arch. f.
Ref.*, lxxi (1980), 21—35, for interesting new evidence and a survey of some of
the literature. Though England still seems a case apart, the 'objective' criteria (to
use Crofts' adjective) — bequests, church attendance, etc. — which German historians have been invoking to illustrate the vitality of Christian life in pre-Reformation
Germany yield remarkable parallels to the evidence which I present below.

some acquaintance with 'ordinary' men and women who make no other appearance in history. And, it seems, they show a society committed to the old religion until the moment when it was supplanted.[2]

Donations to the religious orders may have declined in pre-Reformation decades. But Observant Franciscans, the Carthusians and a surprising number of nunneries were still being remembered in wills up to the dissolution of their houses. Despite what the textbooks say about the friars having fallen particularly low in public esteem by the time of the Reformation, there were still a large number of legacies to them (albeit usually small ones) and frequent requests that they should attend the funerals of testators.[3]

Above all, wills of the first decades of the sixteenth century (up to the 1540s) show English men and women — particularly women, perhaps — pouring into their parish churches gifts of money, sheep, cattle, timber, crops of wheat, rye and beans, bushels of malt and loads of stone, beehives and barrels of salt and fish, jewels and rings, silver and pewter plate, gowns of silk, satin and sarsenet, sometimes quite humble household objects or the implements of husbandry or village crafts. Gifts in kind were usually sold by the recipients. Gifts of livestock were commonly rented out to parishioners and provided an income. Gifts of plate and cloth were kept for immediate liturgical use or for conversion into vestments. Gifts of gems and the like might adorn statues and shrines. So, all these legacies went to parish churches and chapels of ease to embellish and repair them, and to endow high altars and side altars dedicated to various saints and what are often called 'services' (Our Lady's service, Holy Trinity service, and so on), which were effectively chantries that a number of folk could endow and which would normally be served by a stipendiary priest — an unbeneficed priest

[2] This conclusion is based on sampling of wills in the county record offices in Gloucester, Huntingdon and Northampton, as well as the PRO (Prerogative Court of Canterbury) and BL. Wills of the first half of the sixteenth century from Bedfordshire, Lincolnshire, London, the 'North', Somerset and Sussex, printed in extenso, have also been used. See especially notes 4, 8, 12, 20 below and bibliography for details. I reckon that, in all, I have read over 2,500 wills. Though the majority come from the Midlands, I believe there is sufficient geographical spread and that the sampling was sufficiently random to permit general conclusions.
[3] D. M. Palliser, *Tudor York* (Oxford, 1979), p. 227.

hired to say mass for the founders. Above all, layfolk (especially the humbler ones) were giving money and donations in kind to 'find', that is, to support, the thousands of lights and lamps which burned before high altars, roods, statues, paintings, altars (particularly the Easter altar of Repose used on Maundy Thursday) and shrines of Our Lady and saints.

They left money and goods for repairs and new buildings, for church furnishings, for organs, clocks and especially church bells. They left their worldly goods to religious confraternities, to choirs, and for the upkeep of churchyards. Many testators endowed more than one church. The wealthy might endow at least half a dozen. One man endowed sixteen.[4]

It may be that there had been a decline in the volume of masses which testators asked for at their death, their 'month's mind' and obits (i.e. one month and then annually after death). Many testators showed a strong concern for the poor, education, and the upkeep of bridges and highways — and all the other this-worldly causes to which the label 'secular' has been attached — which, however, is a suspect word because it suggests a false antithesis.

But — and this is the point — there was still an intense preoccupation with expiatory bequests, that is, bequests which, directly or indirectly, resulted in masses, prayers and sacrificial offering to Heaven of earthly possessions for the repose of the souls of the benefactor and his or her kin. Moreover what at first sight looks like a 'secular' benefaction may turn out to be strongly religious in the most obvious sense of that word. For example, when Sir William Shaw, sometime lord mayor of London, founded a chantry and a grammar school in his home town of Stockport in 1488, he might be thought to have been showing a typical concern for the practicalities of this world and the exigencies of the next, i.e. to be balancing the secular and religious nicely — except that the statutes of the school required the boys to forgather every Wednesday and Friday at the family grave in the parish church and recite the *De Profundis* and other

---

4 He was John Rayns of Donington (Lincs.), who wrote his will in 1531. See C. W. Foster (ed.), *Lincoln Wills III, 1530–32*, Lincs. Rec. Soc., 24 (1930), 225–6.

prayers for the Shaw family.[5] Here as elsewhere, the boys were auxiliary intercessors alongside the chantry priest and his daily mass. The school itself was a lesser chantry. Again, when someone founded an almshouse he usually required the inmates and their chaplains to pray steadily for the souls of the benefactors and his or her relatives. An almshouse was indeed a beadhouse, a form of chantry; the almsmen and women were a perpetual prayer-force. Similarly (as we shall see), a bequest to a religious guild, though it might also promote its secular purposes, was always a means of ensuring masses and other intercessory prayers in perpetuity after death for the testator and relatives.

Patterns of giving change with needs and religious fashions (if that is the right word). There may have been more concern in the early sixteenth century with poverty, with the upkeep of hospitals, bridges and roads, and with education — and less with monasticism. But this does not indicate that the basic motives had altered. Folk were still giving, as far as one can see, because they wanted to do good for themselves and their families in the next world, and good for their neighbours and perhaps their own reputations in this. There is no evidence that any less was being done for the glory of God. There was no decline in the zeal for posthumous prayer and propitiation. We must always remember that many bequests indirectly guaranteed requiem masses and a regular stream of intercession for the faithful departed until, it would have been presumed, the end of time. Finally, the flow of unequivocally religious bequests — now directed mainly towards the secular clergy and parish churches — remained huge.

It is not easy to give reliable global statistics. But we can try.

Leaving aside the occasional wills which are so short that the lack of religious bequests proves nothing (the authors may have had little or nothing to give), even in the mid-1530s two testators out of three were still asking explicitly for prayers at their death.

Now, that figure is not the whole truth, because it is likely that many of the remaining one-third took it for granted that there would be not just a Christian burial with requiem mass,

5   *VCH, Cheshire*, iii, 249.

but also subsequent prayers for them even though they made no provision for this in their wills. We know this because not infrequently testators left money (often at the end of their wills) for doles of cash and food or clothing to be made to the poor at their month's minds and obits, even though they had previously made no mention of requiem masses on these occasions. They had presumably taken them for granted. So the fact that two out of three asked for prayer for the repose of their souls, and especially for mass, does not imply that one out of three did not want them.

On average at least one in five left money to friars; and over half of these endowed all four orders of friars (in their home or nearby towns). On the eve of the dissolution, one in six were still giving to monks and nuns. Some houses commanded special respect. For instance, the 350-odd Lincolnshire wills proved in the years 1530—32, though otherwise fairly normal in their volume of bequests to the religious, produced no less than eighty-seven donations (albeit small ones of a few pence apiece) for St Katherine's Priory by Lincoln, which ran an orphanage.[6] Finally, about three testators out of every five left bequests for local church building and repairs, furnishings, lamps and lights.

There were regional variations, no doubt. For example, there was the extraordinary phenomenon of Buckinghamshire, whose Lollardy, deep-rooted upland semi-paganism, not to mention its lack of religious houses, account for the remarkably non-religious tone of its surviving wills. There was certainly an upsurge of Protestant wills, with a full-blown non-Catholic preamble and absence of traditional religious legacies, in London from the mid-1530s. There was a sprinkling of similar wills in the south-east; and Protestant wills started appearing all over the place in the next decade.

But the important thing is this. Before that time the number of wills which deliberately made no religious bequests was a tiny proportion of the whole — perhaps three or four per cent. And when Protestant wills did begin to appear they were but a few prophetic voices in the wilderness. Through the 1530s and 1540s the overwhelming majority of folk were still pouring bequests into the old religion.

6   Foster (ed.), *Lincoln Wills III, passim.*

From global figures and national averages let us descend to particular examples. First, consider what bequests could mean to an individual parish. In the year 1531 the church-wardens of Wimborne Minster in Dorset received twelve legacies, consisting of two lots of cash, five sheep, one cow, two donations of timber (one of 100 laths), a candle and three rings.[7] There could presumably have been other bequests to the clergy and to various 'services' which were not recorded in the churchwardens' accounts. So here is a parish church in a small market town which clearly enjoyed the support of the local community. Here were at least twelve families, perhaps several more, who, by virtue of these bequests, had a heightened sense of involvement in their church, perhaps a proprietory attitude to it -- because every benefaction to some extent implicated the rest of the immediate family.

Then, consider the wills of individuals — a random sample: first, that of Lady Jane Hastings, written early in the century (1505). As well as remembering parish churches, secular clergy and her chaplains, she made bequests to one confraternity, two of London's anchoresses and one anchorite, all four orders of friars in London (plus the house of 'crutched' friars), the nunnery at Clerkenwell, the Carthusians of Sheen and London, and the Bridgettine house at Syon. She also left legacies for the friars of Northallerton (Richmond) and York — all four orders — and the Carthusians of Mountgrace.[8]

Twenty-six years later, a London dyer named William Bowden left bequests to three parish churches and four religious confraternities. He left £10 to the 'crutched' friars of London to pray for his parents, his children and 'all Christians', and £3 6s. 8d. for their church-building pro-gramme. He gave legacies to all the other friaries of London (and to the Observants of Richmond and Greenwich), to four leper houses and to poor prisoners. He provided for a priest to say mass daily for his family for seven years at £6 13s. 4d. per annum. Finally, he left a chalice and corporal to the church in Northumberland where his father and mother were buried. The will was written in 1531, but not proved until

---

[7] Dorset CRO, P 204/CW, fo. 80.

[8] C. W. Clay (ed.), *North Country Wills I*, Surtees Soc., 116 (1908), 73–5.

February 1535. By the time he died, some of the institutions which he endowed, namely, the Observants, were already under attack.[9]

A few days before that will was proved, a man much lower down the social scale, John Nichols of Boddington in Northamptonshire, was disposing of his earthly goods. He left 2s. to the Rood light, to Our Lady's and St John's lights, 2s. to other 'torches' and 2s. to the bells in his parish church. He bequeathed fourpence apiece to all four orders of friars in Northampton and no less than 26s. 8d. to the prioress of Catesby, a nearby nunnery, 'to be praied for' and for 'the maytenaunce of her house'. Altogether he gave almost £2 to pious causes. He had only £5 left for his son and heir (and that was conditional upon the son staying with his mother and looking after her). Catesby priory was suppressed a mere eighteen months later.[10]

George Earl of Shrewsbury, a no-nonsense Tudor aristocrat if ever there was one, wrote his will in August 1537 while 'in good helthe' and shortly after he had played a conspicuous part in putting down the Pilgrimage of Grace for his king. He left money for a thousand priests to say mass once and for three priests to say mass daily for twenty years — for himself, his wife, parents and ancestors. He left 40s. each to three charterhouses and £1 each to the friars of Nottingham and Derby. He also bequeathed clothes and vestments to Worksop Abbey. He may have been in good health, but he was not in good foresight — because the religious houses he endowed had been suppressed by the time his will was proved in early 1539.[11]

So here is a tough Tudor peer, a man sufficiently involved in national affairs to have known (one would have thought) which way the wind was blowing, distributing his worldly possessions exactly as his most pious predecessors had done, and endowing friars and Carthusians and nuns even as friaries and charterhouses were about to be finally razed and just a few months before his chosen nunnery was obliterated.

The will of one Robert Burgoyne may also be cited. If the

---

9   PCC, 26 Hogen, fo. 161v.
10 Northampton CRO, Wills, 1st ser., vol. E, fo. 168.
11 Clay, *North Country Wills I*, pp. 144—51.

earl of Shrewsbury failed to read the signs of the times, what should we make of Burgoyne? He was an auditor of the Court of Augmentations, the government agency in charge of the dissolution of the monasteries and the disposal of their former possessions, and had himself made a fortune out of the spoliation of the religious houses. Here, surely, would be the ultimate in flint-faced Tudor secularism. But he left legacies to several churches for a huge number of masses — of the Holy Trinity, Holy Spirit, Blessed Virgin and (intriguingly) the Five Wounds — as well as bequests of vestments (some of them perhaps acquired from religious houses?). Most remarkably, he provided for a chantry to be set up in his native parish in Bedfordshire, with a priest who could sing 'playne songe and deskante well', and teach grammar.[12]

His will is dated October 1545. It is as pious and traditional as they come — except, of course, that there cannot now be benefactions to religious houses (thanks not least to his own endeavours). It was written but a few *weeks* before the first act for dissolution of chantries was passed: yet here is a 'compleat' Tudor bureaucrat, working in Westminster itself, founding a chantry, with its attendant school. Of course, that first act merely permitted the king to dissolve those chantries which had fallen into decay or been despoiled by their own founders. But a man of Burgoyne's experience should have been able to perceive what was intended. The message, that this was but a disarming first step, was not all that difficult to decode! Apparently, however, it passed him by. Could there be more eloquent testimony to the presumption (of even the most worldly-wise) that the old order would somehow trundle on till Kingdom come than the abortive Burgoyne chantry of 1545?

Of course, wills vary in their religious enthusiasm. Many are less fulsome than the ones cited, which are striking examples of how Catholic piety continued up to the very moment when the tidal wave of change overtook it — not just in 'benighted' Yorkshire and the rest of the north, but in the Midlands, Westminster and the City of London. The examples are not unique, however. On the contrary: it is

---

[12] M. McGregor (ed.), *Bedfordshire Wills proved in the Prerogative Court of Canterbury, 1383–1548*, Beds. Hist. Rec. Soc., 58 (1979), 165–9.

the will that makes no religious bequests that is unusual.

Alas, because such terms used to describe testators as 'labourer', 'husbandman', or 'yeoman' are imprecise, it is impossible to plot any relation between socio-economic condition and religious bequests, even if there were one to be discerned. The impression is that on the whole bene-factions were proportionate to wealth. Perhaps a more important fact is that wills were made by quite humble men and women. So, as has been said, to turn from the pre-rogative courts of Canterbury or York, which handled the wills of the wealthier sort, to wills proved at diocesan or archdeaconry level, is to come into contact with people who left behind no other remains — and hence to glimpse the spiritual and material worlds of men and women who would otherwise, often enough, not even be names to us. The experience can be very moving. On the other hand, it poses problems. Wills require careful interpretation.

Two major questions about them have to be tackled. The first is obvious enough. It is: when one reads a will, whose voice is being heard — that of the testator or that of the scribe presiding at the deathbed (or at least a sickbed), usually the parish priest? The answer is probably as follows. The preamble and perhaps some of the initial, routine pay-ments, like the regular donations of a few pence to the 'mother' church (i.e. the cathedral church of the diocese), were probably included on the nod and were the scribe's doing. Since he was often the local parson, he would pre-sumably have been keen to jog the testator's conscience into making the familiar last-minute payment of sometimes quite large sums for 'tithes forgotten' or 'tithes omitted'. But it is difficult to see why the local priest should have encouraged bequests to (often) six, eight, ten or more parish churches besides his own. It is difficult to believe that a secular cleric would have encouraged donations to the regular clergy. Above all, it is difficult to believe that an earl of Shrewsbury, a Robert Burgoyne or any lay person of substance would have allowed any mere parson to tell him what to do with his or her money. Besides, bequests are often so detailed, so full of provisos and contingency plans about, for example, who would get what if the testator's widow remarried or if the child then being carried by a son's wife were a boy — in other words, they are so clearly personal and dependent on an intimate knowledge of the testator's resources and family, that they could not have been devised by an outsider. Hence, as far as the great majority of religious bequests are concerned, we are indeed hearing the testator speak and are not being deceived by clerical ventriloquism.

The second question is much larger: what conclusions can be drawn concerning the quality of the testator's religious commitment from donations made, as they usually were, on or fairly near the deathbed?

Obviously, a pious will is not necessarily proof of a pious life. Quite the contrary may often have been the case. Many gifts to parish churches may have been made precisely because attendance there had been intermittent or worse. Many bequests for requiem masses, dirges, funeral tapers and mourners may have been wordly displays of conspicuous consumption as well as, so to speak, overdue 'fire insurance' payment, made with more than half an eye on a hereafter which had not previously received much of the testator's attention. The pattern of giving would have been to some extent a cultural matter and in that sense conventional. Deathbed generosity to the Church is quite compatible with previous anticlericalism and scepticism. With his face about to turn to the wall and no more chance of enjoying his wordly possessions, a testator had nothing to lose and perhaps something to gain from an attempt to propitiate his Maker with a last-minute flurry of offerings. On the other hand, many of the bequests may have sprung from genuine piety and a habit of generosity. To take a completely cynical view of things is as illicit as interpreting deathbed piety as proof of a lifetime of Christian zeal.

The answer to this second question, in fact, is that we cannot know. We cannot know because we cannot know the whole truth about anyone's motives at any time.

So then one must ask: does it matter that we cannot know? The answer is — happily — 'no'.

It does not matter because, even though we cannot test motives, these wills still allow us to draw some conclusions. First, when it came to the crunch, the overwhelming majority of people who made wills showed that they still gave some kind of acceptance to the world-view which the medieval

Church had taught them. They still believed, or thought it worth believing, in Heaven, Hell and Purgatory, the communion of saints, the need for expiation and the possibility of it. They accepted the efficacy of the mass, prayer for the dead, the usefulness of veneration of saints and the numerous other ways of intercession and expiation which bequests to altars, lights, organs, church-building and so on afforded. To describe this as conventional is to go a long way towards accepting the very case I am trying to argue. The old order was still part of the fabric of society, still part of the air people breathed, still as much a part of the accepted scheme of things as the sun and the moon.

Secondly, many folk, well-to-do ones in the know as well as the humbler sort, were endowing many of the old structures right up to the moment when they were abolished. Since people tend not to invest in things which are thought to be threatened with imminent liquidation, we must presume that there was little apprehension that these institutions were about to collapse and little sense that the old ways would not continue as they had for generations and until the end of time.

At this point, I must emphasise what I am *not* saying. I am not saying that all was well. I am not claiming that pre-Reformation England was a land of zealous, God-fearing Christians (though I suspect that there were many more of them than some recent historians would admit). I *am* saying that, however imperfect the old order, and however imperfect the Christianity of the average man or woman in the street, there is no evidence of loss of confidence in the old ways, no mass disenchantment.

Such a claim is vulnerable to the riposte that it is easier for a will to show support *for* something than opposition or disengagement. More evidence is needed if the case is to be clinched.

We can turn first to a phenomenon that is easy to grasp and familiar to many: the enormous amount of church-building in the fifteenth and early sixteenth centuries. There were new starts or major rebuilds all over the country that produced spectacular results — incomparable St Mary Redcliffe in Bristol, for instance; the parish churches in Bodmin, Chipping Campden, Cirencester, Coventry (St Michael's), Dedham,

Grantham, Halifax, Newark, Rotherham, Saffron Walden and Wakefield, not to mention 'wool' churches of East Anglia or what are today the cathedrals of Manchester and Sheffield, and so on. A complete list would be enormous. Then there was a vast amount of adding to and enlarging existing churches — above all with western towers (or sometimes their spires) and extended naves, to which were added clerestories and new, flatter ceilings and roofs. There were new aisles and lengthened old ones, and plenty of porches.

Medieval parish churches are one of the glories of England. No other country is more richly endowed. In the hundred and fifty years or so before the Reformation, the high noon of the perpendicular style, an average of two out of every three underwent at least one major building programme of this kind — whether they were humble village churches or grand fanes of town and city.[13] Those who believe in the decline of the late-medieval Church have to explain this widespread and enthusiastic building.

It continued well into the sixteenth century. Whole new churches were built or rebuilt between 1500 and the 1540s, such as St Michael-le-Belfry in York, and churches in Launceston, Great Panton (Lincolnshire) and Barton-under-Nedwood in Staffordshire. Louth's steeple, the towers of Derby and St Neots, the town aisles and chancel chapels of Walthamstow — to pick just a few examples — belong to

---

[13] This statistic is based on analysis of *Buildings of England* (ed. N. Pevsner), particularly the volumes for Cornwall, Derbyshire, Essex and Warwickshire. The picture seems fairly uniform across the country. On average, about 75 per cent of churches are noted as having major perpendicular features. The perpendicular style began to appear in the 1330s. Assuming that it took some time to reach parish level (especially in remoter counties) and that the years immediately after the Black Death were not propitious for church building, it seems reasonable to suggest that over 60% of churches had major additions or rebuilds in the perpendicular style in the 150 years from *c.*1380. My count excludes minor works and such furnishings as fonts, chancel screens, choir stalls, etc. I should add that my argument was anticipated decades ago by the remarkable Charles Cox who, in his *Architectural Styles in the English Parish Church* (n.d.), p. 198, pointed out that the evidence of wills and churchwardens' accounts was in 'flat contradiction' to the idea of a late-medieval decline in church-building, etc. Others have reiterated this view, pointing to 'wool' churches and the like. My point is that there is much more to it than that. The stunning churches of prosperous Cotswolds and East Anglia are but the more spectacular examples of a nationwide flowering.

these decades. Money was left in 1542 for the massive west tower of Ormskirk parish church; Solihull's major works began less than ten years before. And so on. Once more, a complete list would be enormous. And, incidentally, there had been similar large-scale, self-confident building right up to the last minute in quite a few monasteries (for example, at Colchester, Evesham, Fountains, Rochester, Waltham, Whalley — not to mention Bath and Bolton, where the dissolution halted major building in midstream). The evidence of stone and timber (and brick) is striking. So, too, is the fact that in the middle of the sixteenth century church building suddenly came to a virtual halt and was to remain for roughly the next fifty years at its lowest level for centuries before and since.

A crucial question is: who paid for all the towers and clerestories and the like which many parish churches were acquiring in the later Middle Ages? Sometimes it was a single wealthy benefactor; but most commonly it was the parishioners themselves. The donations came in bequests, as has been said, in cash and in kind. The living also contributed. Money was raised at churchales, a forerunner of today's church fête or bazaar, but usually much more rumbustuous and alcoholic than its decorous descendant (it could last for days, there was morris-dancing and wrestling, entertainment by strolling players, etc.). Then there were local subscriptions and donations of materials and labour. For example, when Solihull set about major work on its nave in 1533/4, the leading citizens supplied timber (one man gave three whole trees) and seventeen people are recorded in the churchwardens' accounts as having donated carriage for the materials.[14] When Bodmin began to rebuild its church several decades earlier, 460 parishioners subscribed and so did local confraternities — to the tune of £268. Much of the building material was donated, much of labour voluntary. The vicar presented a whole year's salary.[15]

---

[14] Warwick CRO, DRB 64/63, fos. 14–15. Similar stories come from (e.g.) Romsey and Wymondham. Cf. R. Morris, *Cathedrals and Abbeys of England and Wales. The building Church, 600–1540* (1979), p. 227. He emphasizes the fact that the later Middle Ages saw greater building activity at parish rather than, say, cathedral level.

[15] N. Pevsner (ed.), *Buildings of England. Cornwall* (1951), pp. 252–3.

One of the main reasons for raising the central nave walls and then piercing them with clerestories was to let in more light into the middle areas of the churches concerned. And one of the main reasons why more light was needed was probably the fact that many aisles were being shut off by parclose screens of stone or wood, with the result that naves were increasingly starved of light. The aisles were being filled with chantry and, often enough, confraternity chapels.

The confraternities are important enough to be the subject of the next chapter. For the moment it suffices to say that they were so numerous and, it seems, popular that they must have been a major feature on pre-Reformation England's religious landscape, and that they illustrate the theme of this chapter, namely the apparent stability of and lay accord with the old ecclesiastical order.

To reiterate: it is not (of course) that all was so well that no complaints could be made against the old order or that pre-Reformation England was a model Christian society. The historian cannot judge the quality of a society's religious life or understanding. He or she measures quantity more easily than quality, and it is quantity which has been reported here.

There may be several reasons for putting up a church tower, enlarging a nave or adding a porch, other than for the glory of God. Not all the reasons for joining a confraternity were religious. The point, however, is that much building was going on in churches and many people belonged to confraternities. Many people were extremely generous to churches and clergy on their deathbeds (and, as the sparse evidence suggests, in their lifetimes, too). All this meant involvement and investment by the laity in the life of the old Church.

There is more to be said in defence of the claim that the English Reformation came primarily from 'above', that is, from monarch, ministers and some leading ecclesiastics, rather than from a groundswell of popular discontent and resentment towards the old religion. There is the striking fact, for example, that, up to the very moment of the Reformation, the bulk of the numerous religious works produced by the printing press (in England as elsewhere), presumably to satisfy public tastes, consisted of wholly traditional works of piety and devotion — and lives of saints.[16] There is the fact that there was no shortage of candidates for the priesthood and that recruitment was apparently plentiful in pre-Reformation decades.[17] Some monasteries were thriving: Glastonbury, for instance, seems to have had more inmates in the 1530s than it had known for years.

Once again we must be cautious, however. Facts such as these are not proof of spiritual well-being; they are not in themselves proof that all was objectively well. Many will argue (as Protestants were soon to do) that the pre-Reformation diet of hagiography and often conventional piety was an impoverished and impoverishing one, and a poor substitute indeed for the immeasurable riches of the Scriptures, which were not available in the vernacular. The healthy recruitment to the ranks of the clergy may have partly reflected the fact that the population had probably climbed back to its previous, early-fourteenth-century peak, and was rising steadily beyond it.

Much, but not all, of late-medieval Catholicism may have been mechanical and ill-formed. Beneath the official life and teaching of the institutional Church there may have lain much popular religion that was shot through with semi-pagan survivals, sub-Christian folklore and magic. As events were to prove, pre-Reformation Catholicism was vulnerable. But there is little sign of growing popular hostility towards it. And this in turn helps to explain another fact: the more

[16] This was pointed out half a century ago by P. Janelle in his *L'Angleterre Catholique à la veille du schisme* (Paris, 1935) — as by F. A. Gasquet in *The Eve of the Reformation* (1919 edn), esp. pp. 285f. — and has been noted often since by such historians of early English printing as H. S. Bennett. See Crofts, 'Books, Reform and the Reformation', for telling evidence from Germany in the 1510s. Janelle also made extensive use of wills for assessing religious life on the eve of the Reformation (*L'Angleterre*, pp. 28–32). He and the others were making an important point: to my mind, however, what was wrong with their case was the claim that the will and the contemporary religious literature, etc., were proof of the health and genuine vitality of pre-Reformation Catholicism.

[17] M. L. Zell, 'Economic Problems of the Parochial Clergy', in R. O'Day and F. Heal (eds), *Princes and Paupers in the English Church, 1500–1800* (Leicester, 1981), pp. 20ff., and the authorities cited there. Cf. Bowker, *Henrician Reformation*, pp. 38ff. Lincoln and London dioceses show a decline in ordinations around the mid-1520s. They recovered somewhat later in the decade only to fall away sharply in several dioceses after 1536. Cf. Bowker, 'The Henrician Reformation and the parish clergy', *Bull. Inst. Hist. Res.*, 50 (1977), 34.

we know about the spead of Protestantism in England, the more obvious it is that the process was, on the whole, slow, piecemeal and painful. Of course, it spread faster in some places than others — usually thanks to the accident of proximity to Protestant influence or the efforts of a zealous bishop, preacher or lay patron (male or female). But even in those areas where the new creed prospered most and fastest, the 'Protestantisation' of English men and women was an uphill task and never perfectly achieved.[18]

We will return to these themes in later chapters. To end this one perhaps particularities (drawn from wills, once more) may be apposite.

First, Etheldreda Swan, a woman of very modest means who lived in a village near Cambridge: she left a shilling apiece to the high altar, the bells and torches of her parish church, 20*d.* to church repairs, her best coverlet and a sheet to one of the chapels in that church, and 6*s.*8*d.* to another church nearby. She gave 13*s.*4*d.* to 'Our Lady's light', and a mere 7*d.* for her funeral (including 2*d.* for the bellringers). She donated a platter to one confraternity in her home parish and a brass pot, silver spoon and some pewter dishes to another.[19]

In July 1532 in the western extremity of Somerset an

[18] See esp. Bowker, *Henrician Reformation*; D. M. Palliser, 'Popular Reactions to the Reformation during the years of Uncertainty, 1530—70' in F. Heal and R. O'Day (eds), *Church and Society in England: Henry VIII to James I* (1977), pp. 35—56; A. L. Rowse, *Tudor Cornwall* (1941), pp. 312—14; R. B. Manning, *Religion and Society in Elizabethan Sussex* (Leicester, 1961), esp. pp. 256—60; Haigh, 'Some Aspects', and other authorities cited there. As Haigh points out (p. 105), even in those areas and towns where the Reformation spread quickly (London, Bristol, parts of Kent, etc.) it was 'not a walkover for the Protestants, it was a real contest'. There was nothing inevitable about 'the final Protestant victory'. Obviously Protestantism spread at different speeds in different places — thanks, among other things, to proximity to foreign influence, the accident of local patronage by bishop or influential lay people. P. Clark, *English Provincial Society from the Reformation to the Revolution: religion, politics and society in Kent, 1500—1640* (Hassocks, Sussex, 1977) shows why and how the new creed took root in the south-east. Cf. (for Bristol) the work of K. G. Powell, esp. his 'The Beginnings of Protestantism in Gloucestershire', *Trans. Bristol and Glos. Arch. Soc.*, 90 (1971).

[19] BL, Add. MS 5861 (Ely wills), fo. 70.

affluent gentleman called James Hadley left one shilling to every church in four of the county's hundreds and one shilling to every parish priest. He left a shilling to every unbeneficed cleric in the diocese of Bath and Wells, and £1 to every religious house — except Glastonbury, which was to have £2. He left 5s. to the high altars of six named churches and a shilling to every other altar (i.e. the side altars) in those churches, to have his name entered on their beadrolls (the lists of deceased folk to be remembered at mass). He left £2 for the repair of a reliquary in his parish church, and money for thousands of masses. He bestowed fourpence on every householder in eight towns and gifts of money for his tenants, for prisoners in Wells and Bristol, for a bridge, some hospitals and a lazar house. Furthermore, 'forasmuch as I have been negligent to visit holy places and going on pilgrimage', he left gifts of money to twelve shrines, including Walsingham, Canterbury, Hailes abbey, Henry VI's tomb and pilgrimage centres nearer home. He gave £5 for building a chapel in honour of the Visitation and St Christopher.[20]

Perhaps he had much to atone for. Perhaps Etheldreda Swan did, too. But how many men and women of commensurate status today shower their wealth so generously on good causes, religious or 'secular'? These wills, like those already quoted, are typical of their times. It is unjust to describe as merely 'conventional' or 'conformist' such personal, carefully thought-out munificence; and to describe the piety that prompted it as the fruit of folk religion or rural superstition is insensitive and condescending. A religion that can elicit such deathbed generosity is not to be so lightly dismissed.

---

[20] F. W. Weaver (ed.), *Somerset Medieval Wills, 3rd series, 1531–58*, Som. Rec. Soc., xxi (1904), 13–14.

2

The Importance of the Lay
Fraternities

Religious fraternities (or confraternities, brotherhoods, religious guilds — the terms are interchangeable) had a conspicuous role in the religious life of pre-Reformation England, so much so that their suppression, a result partly of the so-called Chantries Act of 1547 and partly of royal injunctions of that same year which outlawed their basic activities, while certainly not as momentous in respect of lands and buildings as the dissolution of the monasteries or the chantries, may have had as deep an effect on many layfolk as did either of those events.[1] And if the absence in post-Reformation England of the multiplicity of orders of monks, canons, friars, clerks regular and numerous kinds of nuns which had emerged in the Middle Ages and the sixteenth and seventeenth centuries would have been one very obvious contrast between this country and Catholic Europe, so also would have been the lack in England of the lay fraternities and sodalities which proliferated during the Counter-Reformation.

First, a definition. What was a fraternity? It was an association of layfolk who, under the patronage of a particular saint, the Trinity, Blessed Virgin Mary, Corpus Christi or

---

[1] The standard work on these guilds is still H. F. Westlake, *Parish Gilds of Medieval England* (1919). Cf. L. Toulmin Smith (ed.), *English Gilds*, Early Eng. Text Soc. (1870). D. M. Owen, *Church and Society in Medieval Lincolnshire* (Lincoln, 1971), pp. 127–31, is a good local study.

similar, undertook to provide the individual member of the brotherhood with a good funeral — as solemn and well-attended a 'send-off' as possible — together with regular prayer and mass-saying thereafter for the repose of the dead person's soul.

Living members were required to come together on the patronal feastday for a special mass for past and present brothers and sisters, at the altar or in the chapel (which might be a free-standing one) belonging to the fraternity, when candles galore might burn, the sacred plate and vestments of the guild be brought out and its livery (if it had risen to such heights) worn. After this solemn annual mass would come the annual general meeting: the presentation of accounts, the election of officers, the reading of the guild statutes, the collection of subscriptions (if any) from the members, and, if the guild had any real estate, decisions about sales, leases, building, repairs. The annual dinner would follow.

In their most modest form, therefore, fraternities were simply poor men's chantries. They were inseparably connected with the doctrine of Purgatory and the whole idea of satisfaction for sin, veneration of saints, the intercession of Mary and the rest of the heavenly host. These were their fundamental *raisons d'être*. That being so, it is right to distinguish them from craft or trade guilds which, though they also had religious functions, were primarily concerned with the mundane matters of regulating and protecting the economic interests of the group concerned. The spiritual well-being of their members and relatives was secondary — though it could often be conspicuous.

The humblest village fraternity might aspire to no more than the individual funeral mass for every deceased member, for which all the living members had to subscribe a 'mass penny', plus an annual mass and audit (with penalties, such as a fine of a penny or half a pound of wax, for non-attendance at either). Many guilds undertook to bring back for decent burial a brother's body from wherever he happened to die. Some required by statute that every brother should bequeath to the fraternity a certain amount of his worldly goods — one shilling for every pound's worth of chattels, up to 40s., in the case of the guild of St Mary and Holy Cross in

Chesterfield, for instance — as well as an annual levy for alms.

The richer guilds had this-worldly purposes also. They gave material help to younger members. They sometimes supplied food and shelter for old, sick and blind brethren. They could provide food and coal and even interest-free loans to widows and orphans, and dowries for daughters. They often guaranteed rescue for any brother who fell victim of flood, fire, theft, shipwreck or business disaster (provided these were not the fruit of gambling, laziness, lust or folly). They acted as executors for deceased members and distributed their estates.

Because it was a *fraternity*, a guild's statutes commonly contained pious exhortation to members to greet one another in brotherly fashion, banned back-biting, violence and swearing and forbade a brother to go to the law against another before arbitration by the guild master or warden had proved ineffectual. Any brother could seek the support of all the brethren in any suit against an outsider. Most statutes forbade admission to anyone guilty of adultery, conjuring (magic), blasphemy or uncouth behaviour, and prescribed expulsion for persistent sinners.

Many of the larger fraternities, like those in Abingdon, Aylesbury, Banbury, Chester, Chesterfield, Colchester, Derby, Henley-in-Arden, Hull (St Mary's and Trinity), Maidstone, Taunton, Newcastle, Stratford-on-Avon, Warwick and Worcester, ran schools and/or almshouses for their own members — and there is plenty of evidence that they provided a good deal of practical help for poverty-stricken colleagues and of education, right up to 1547. Most owned property, including a guildhall or guild house (often called 'the brotherhood house') and sometimes a free-standing chapel exclusively for their own use, as well as tenements which provided rent-free accommodation for a few members whom misfortune or old age had overtaken. Some provided that the guild priest should do some teaching, though nothing as ambitious as a school building had been acquired.

Many guilds looked after bridges and highways. Wisbech's guilds included in their duties the maintenance of seabanks and sluices, and played a major part in the town's long battle against the sea. Birmingham's Holy Cross fraternity maintained a chiming clock and paid for the local midwife. St Lawrence's guild in Ashburton in Dorset looked after the lead pipe which brought water into the town.[2] Guild money helped towers and spires (like Louth's) to be built, naves to be lifted, windows replaced, whole churches (like Bodmin's) rebuilt. Larger confraternities employed their own priests — and these could be a useful auxiliary clergy, to help out beneficed parish priests or look after chapels of ease. The guild of St Mary in West Tarring in Sussex was founded in 1528 with the express purpose, among others, of providing an assistant priest for the town.[3]

These larger fraternities were often so dominated by the local town oligarchies that they might well be described as the local corporations at prayer — or providing for their own obsequies. Indeed, there could be more to it than that, because for towns like Banbury and Henley-in-Arden, which had not yet achieved incorporation, guilds and guildhalls gave some corporate identity to the leading citizenry and prepared the way for full legal identity — by providing a centre of gravity over and against surviving manorial authority.

Then there was a top flight of fraternities which went beyond anything that Abingdon or Derby and the like had to offer, and provided proto-banking services to members, exercised considerable cultural and religious patronage, were major property-owners, recruited members from the highest echelons of society and from well beyond the boundaries of their towns or even beyond England's shores. They included St Anne's (the 'Great Guild') of Lincoln, the major guilds of York, St George's in Norwich, Ludlow's Palmer's guild, Holy Trinity in Coventry and Holy Trinity, Wisbech. One of the largest was St Mary's, Boston, which perhaps outshone Holy Trinity Coventry, even though the latter was itself an amalgam of no less than four separate confraternities.

All these would have been able to hold their heads high in the company of the best that continental Europe had to offer, including the rich confraternities of Florence or the *scuole grande* of Venice. Most had received full legal definition by royal grant of incorporation, which included the right to hold land in mortmain, and often handsome initial endowment by a wealthy benefactor. Some had papal privileges

---

2   *VCH, Cambs.*, iv, 255; *VCH, Warks.*, viii, 319; E301/15 no. 35.
3   *VCH, Sussex*, vi, pt i, 278.

as well, splendid guildhalls and formidable rent-rolls. Boston's St Mary's guild had an annual income of over £900 in the mid-1520s, derived from lands, tenements, mills, barns and so on, as well as members' subscriptions.[4] If Holy Trinity Coventry was not the biggest single landlord in that city, it must have been a close second. Its membership included people from all over the land — plus foreign dignitaries.[5] Palmer's guild in Ludlow was not nearly as rich: its income was probably around £250 a year. But its stewards were collecting annual payments in cash and kind from members as far away as Bristol and London.[6] Great institutions like these had aldermen and wardens, chamberlains to prepare the accounts, stewards to collect annual subscriptions from far-flung members, almoners to administer their charitable work, and cupbearers, keepers of jewels, macebearers, esquire bedells, etc. They might have their own choirs and organists. And, of course, they had an often formidable array of clergy to carry out the religious duties which, however weighty the social, economic and political functions, were still the heart of the matter. Coventry's Holy Trinity had thirteen full-time priests and owned the fine church of St John Bablake, and even a small guild, like Trinity and St John the Baptist in Shepton Mallet, with an income in 1547 of £15 13s. 6d., had two priests. A fraternity in nearby Corsecombe had four.[7]

For the great guilds the annual celebrations would last two or three days. There would be music, dance, mimes, pageants and performances of guild plays. There would be processions from chapel to guildhall and splendid displays of livery, solemn recital of the roll of the dead and living members, requiems and dirges, perhaps before a catafalque draped with a pall embroidered with jewels that sparkled in the dancing light of a palisade of plump candles. All this was

---

[4]   BL, Egerton MS 2886, fo. 294. This magnificent account book covers the years 1514 to 1525.
[5]   Its register and other documents have been edited for the Dugdale Society (vols. xiii and xix, for 1935 and 1944) by M. D. Harris and G. Templeman respectively.
[6]   *VCH, Salop*, ii, 134—7.
[7]   E. Green (ed.), *Somerset Chantries: survey and rental*, Soms. Rec. Soc., ii (1888), 133, 140.

a long way from the annual mass of the rural confraternity which boasted little more than a light before its patronal altar, presumably hired a cleric to do the necessary duties on feast and obit days and at funerals (perhaps the nearest unbeneficed cleric to hand), and concluded with an annual celebration as modest as the material succour it could offer to members buffeted by misfortune.

A number of interesting features of all fraternities are worth remarking.

First, they were lay controlled. They were run by layfolk elected by layfolk. There were often clergy among the members (at least of the larger guilds) — local parish priests as a matter of course, local monastic figures, often a bishop. But these almost never held office.[8]

As has been noted, the guild clergy were appointed and paid by their lay masters. So, for example, the accounts of the modest fraternity of Our Lady in Chard record that William Piers, clerk, received £7 a year 'for his wages by thandes of the wardens' — an entry which throws interesting light on the relations between laity and clergy in pre-Reformation England.[9] Interestingly, the number of clerical members of guilds seems to have increased in the first decades of the six-teenth, century. It is not clear why, because it is impossible to know who was doing whom a favour in such cases, i.e. who took the initiative. Were clergy wanting to be more at one with influential laymen, or were lay organisations wanting to woo the clergy? Or is it simply that guilds were feeling the pinch and were ready to take fees off anyone who came forward? Whatever the answer, there is no sign of mounting tension between lay and clerical estates here: rather, there is symbiosis.

---

8   York's Corpus Christi guild is a rare exception: its leading officers were clergy. Several guilds had been founded by clergy, however (e.g. Holy Trinity in Mancetter, founded by the abbot of Merevale in 1458, and Abingdon's Holy Cross guild, which had a bishop of Lincoln as co-founder). They were neverthe-less run by layfolk. It was probably common for a guild priest to act as clerk to the guild — but he would have been appointed by the lay officers. Cf. F. J. Furnivall (ed.), *The Gild of St Mary Lichfield*, Early Eng. Text Soc. (1920), p. 9.
9   Green, *Somerset Chantries*, p. 19.

Women could be full members of religious guilds in their own right and not just as wives. All the surviving guild registers, except that of St George's Norwich, include single women and widows in their lists. (Why Norwich should have been so chauvinist I do not know.)[10] Women could have special privileges: Ludlow's Palmer's guild, for instance, provided dowries for sisters on their marriage or entry into religion. Moreover — and this is an astonishing fact — women could be officers of a guild, though I admit that they seem rarely to have been, at least in the bigger ones. There was no other institution in late-medieval society in which lay women could stand on their own feet, be separately listed as autonomous human beings or (at least in theory) hold public office.

Not a few members of guilds were already dead when they were enrolled. Living members could bring into the confraternity dead parents and children, friends and even servants so that they, too, could benefit from the stream of intercession offered to Heaven by the guild's living members and clergy. At Stratford-on-Avon, dead members were enrolled at half-price.[11] Moreover, one could leave a lump sum in a will to meet several years' posthumous membership fees, perhaps even without having been a member while alive.[12]

Some fraternities had high entry fees and subscriptions, and had therefore become fairly exclusive, but others retained their open character. Rural guilds probably continued to charge a few pence a year plus a penny at any member's death. Stratford-on-Avon's Holy Cross lowered its once-for-all entry fee in the fifteenth century from £1 to 3s. 4d. for a single person and a noble (6s. 8d.) for a married couple. So, in a guild of that kind, rich and far-from-rich, male and female, layman and cleric could meet and rub shoulders as nowhere else. And when a guild had squeezed out the *hoi polloi* by putting up its fees (and imposing heavy charges for livery, annual feasts and so on), enterprising people could and did

---

[10] See M. Grace (ed.), *Records of the Gild of St George in Norwich, 1389–1547*, Norf. Rec. Soc. (1937).

[11] I.e. for 20d. See entries in J. Harvey Bloom (ed.), *The Gild Register: Stratford upon Avon, 1406 to 1535* (1907).

[12] Thus in 1530 a Londoner left money in his will to pay for twelve years' posthumous membership (at 6s. 8d. a year) to the guild of Our Lady in Grainthorpe (Lincs.).

form new guilds beneath the expensive ones — just as they formed lesser craft guilds beneath those of the urban elites.

The fraternities we are examining here merge imperceptibly at one edge into those genuine craft and merchant guilds which, as has been said, also had religious purposes even though they were primarily this-worldly.[13] To complicate matters, religious guilds could also be set up by or recruit from a particular craft or profession. Large cities might boast several religious guilds for particular tradesmen — weavers, hatters, shearmen, for instance. London even had a confraternity for parish clerks. Moreover, the somewhat hazy dividing line between the secular and the religious brotherhood could be crossed in either direction by a particular guild in the course of its history. Thus the sailors of Holy Trinity Guild in Hull, like the sailors of Bristol, had a well-organised religious confraternity (with an almshouse) by the mid-fifteenth century. But their work became so focused on piloting ships in and out of Hull and in training in nautical skills that a primarily religious guild evolved into a primarily craft one, and survives today as the Trinity House pilots.

At another shifting edge the religious guild was so like a common-or-garden chantry that the terms 'guild' and 'chantry' could be interchangeable.[14] Indeed, a guild could contain as well as grow out of a chantry and individuals could set up a quasi-chantry within a confraternity by endowing masses specifically for their family, as well as relying on the communal prayers and obsequies of the whole brotherhood. In that case the guild was effectively acting as trustee for individual members.

Another hazy edge remains. It is difficult to determine how many of those 'lights' which were frequently the object

---

[13] They, too, often had altars in parish churches and chaplains. The religious activities of London's liveried companies were often extensive. See below, pp. 123–4.
[14] Thus chantry certificates could speak of the chantry *or* guild at Thame (Oxon) and the service *or* guild in Topcliffe (Yorks). See E301/38 no. 8 and 63 no. 4. Of the fraternity in Sittingbourne in Kent, the commissioners said it was 'in controversye whether hit be a brotherhed or a spittle house'. St James's guild in Tong was also described as a fraternity *or* hospital. See E301/29, nos. 82 and 108. Such confusion indicates how variously guilds could operate — and perhaps also how their main functions could change over time.

of early Tudor legacies, were maintained by guilds. Some of the lights at high and side altars, by roods and Easter sepulchres were administered by the churchwardens and presumably did not belong to guilds. There was no brotherhood responsible for their upkeep and bequests went straight to the churchwardens. But some lights certainly were administered by, and were the focal point of, small religious confraternities. St Mary's church in Bridport in Dorset, for instance, had a confraternity of the Light before the Cross and a brotherhood of the Two Torches (the latter maintaining two lights which burnt on Corpus Christi, other feastdays and Sundays, and, from his death until burial, by the corpse of a deceased member). Guild lights and torches would burn on patronal feastdays, at wakes, month's minds and anniversaries, and so on.[15] As already remarked, bequests of wax for the candles were common; and so, it seems, were fines of a pound or half-pound of wax for non-attendance at funerals or a guild's annual solemnities. Maybe we should not distinguish completely between 'lights' administered by the churchwardens and a confraternity of this or that 'light': perhaps the former could grow into independent guilds.[16] Since the comparatively informal rural guilds inevitably had their ups and downs and could disappear and reappear as suddenly as they had appeared in the first place, perhaps churchwardens sometimes took over the lights of defunct brotherhoods. We shall never know. The obscurity is increased by the appearance of, for instance, a 'St Anne's light'

[15] Dorset CRO, B3/CD, 15 and 16, are some scanty survivors of their fifteenth-century records. There are some membership lists, accounts and ordinances for two other fraternities in the town (B3/CD, 22 and 56), plus the accounts for one year — 7 Edward IV — for a third (B3/CD, 32), which record that 59 people paid 4*d.* each that year. Cf. T. Wainwright (ed.), *Bridport Records and Ancient Manuscripts* (Bridport, n.d.). Some accounts and membership lists for the guild of St Mary Magdalene in Wolviston, Co. Durham, show that 4*d.* a year was the average fee for a small town guild at the other end of the country too. Durham Dean and Chapter Muniments, Misc. Charter 7233.

[16] Many other churches had brotherhoods of 'torches'. Thus in Culworth (Northants) there were 'torchmen' or 'lightwardens' who handed over 'old stocke' (profits?) to the churchwardens each year. Northampton CRO, 94P/21, pp. 21, 39. Elsewhere there were lights dedicated to saints which were maintained by fraternities — as well as Maiden's lights, Ploughmen's lights, 'cross beam' (roodscreen?) lights, etc. It is impossible to know exactly what these involved and how they were maintained.

in a Staffordshire church which a group of local weavers, apparently forming a craft guild, used part of their admission fees to maintain.[17] A secular brotherhood, then, had a light in the parish church: a not uncommon practice.

The next thing to say about religious guilds is that many people belonged to several — two, four, even six or more. And the last thing to say is that there were an astonishing number of them: hundreds.

Well over a hundred existed in Northamptonshire alone in the early sixteenth century, for instance, including perhaps fourteen in Northampton itself. St Mary's, Boston, has been mentioned: there were seven more in that town. There were five in both Stamford and Louth. In all, Lincolnshire boasted about 120. There were seven in Leicester. They were thick on the ground in Huntingdonshire — the town of Godmanchester near Huntingdon had six; the village of Yaxley seven (and a guildhall). There was quite a good sprinkling in Durham and Yorkshire (one East Riding village had three guilds on the eve of the Reformation and Hull may have had half a dozen). They become dense down the east coast and in East Anglia — as far as Essex. Sussex is disappointing, Devon better. Bedfordshire, Oxfordshire and Warwickshire perform well enough. Wiltshire and Herefordshire do not. Somerset has plenty, Shropshire a modest amount.[18]

One of the densest areas seems to be Cambridgeshire. In one hundred of that county (south of Cambridge itself and including Granchester) fifteen villages boasted twenty-five guilds. The four hundreds in the north-east of the county, running out to Wisbech, had about fifty, divided among some twenty-four parishes and with a big clutch in Ely. There may have been as many in March as in Ely. In 1542 there

---

[17] *VCH, Staffs.*, xvii, 204.

[18] The data in this paragraph come from *VCH* for the counties concerned; from wills (i.e. bequests to guilds); and from *CPR* for Edward VI and Elizabeth, recording crown sales of former guild lands, guildhalls, etc. Some of the smallest guilds are known by only a single mention in one of these sources. Since humbler guilds doubtless came and went fairly easily it is not certain that all of these survived until 1547, but all are noted as existing some time during the decades immediately preceding the Reformation. On Boston, Stamford and Louth, cf. Owen, *Church and Society*, pp. 127–9, and A. Rogers, *The Making of Stamford* (Leicester, 1965), p. 53. On the Huntingdonshire guilds see *VCH, Hunts.*, ii, 293n. 295, and iii, 247.

were ten in Whittlesey, including a guild of St Thomas Becket, imprudently not yet renamed. Whittlesey was then the second largest town in the Isle of Ely; but its population in 1563 was reckoned to be not more than about 1500 — and it had had ten guilds.[19]

It is impossible to give exact figures. Country guilds in particular (as has been said) came and went over the years, changed their names, amalgamated with others or sank without trace. The records of only a handful survive — and these are often mere scraps. We know about most of them from casual mention in wills and from sales of guildhalls and seized possessions after their suppression.

Most had neither royal foundation nor permanent landed endowment and so left no trace in official records. Simply because they were neither part of the official lay establishment nor 'religious' in the clerical sense, their records had no obvious protector when the deluge came. They were too religious (and papistical) for secular safe-keeping; too lay for clerical custody. Archivally, they were neither fish nor fowl. Hence even the biggest guilds are known to us today through a lamentably small and haphazard collection of registers and account books — a tiny fraction of what must once have been voluminous and (to judge by one or two splendid survivors) magnificent records.

Many questions that spring to mind cannot be answered. We cannot know exactly how many guilds there were. It is impossible to begin to assess how much they influenced lay conduct, how often (if ever) their sanctions were invoked against wayward sisters and unbrotherly brothers, how great was their contribution to the economic life of their communities, or how significant their cultural patronage.

We cannot know the total national membership of fraternities at any one time and hence what proportion of lay society would have been involved in their activities. It has been reckoned that York's biggest guild had 70,000 members in the course of its fairly long life.[20] Between 1505 and 1509 some 1,176 men and women joined Ludlow's big guild.[21] In

---

[19] *VCH, Cambs.*, iv, v, and vi *passim*. For Whittlesey, ibid., iv, 124, 133.
[20] Westlake, *Parish Gilds*, p. 54.
[21] *VCH, Salop*, ii, 138.

1533 Coventry's second largest guild, Corpus Christi, listed some 390 members.[22] Doubtless many others had long rolls of names. But these figures do not mean very much because of the common practice of belonging to several guilds at once. And they cannot answer another important question: was membership rising, falling or stable in the decades immediately preceding the Reformation?

There are occasional precious glimpses of fraternities' charitable work. In 1548 the guild of Salve Regina in St Magnus' church in London was paying 2s. a week to a brother in prison, 1s. 2d. a week to a blind brother (for life), 1s. to a sick sister and 10d. a week to three other members who had fallen on hard times. Over a third of the guild's income went on relief of its poor. Another London guild, Our Lady's in St Bride's in Fleet Street, was giving relief to five women and two men. Our Lady's guild in Uxbridge was providing rent-free accommodation for a blind man.[23] Then there were the almshouses. Most of the larger guilds had one. Some provided accommodation, food and clothing for as many as twenty-four poor brothers and sisters. The fact that many towns fought to ensure the survival of confraternity almshouses, and that many survive to this day, suggests that they were making a useful contribution.[24]

It is difficult to say anything very precise and impossible to give overall statistics. All one can say is that there were plenty of guilds, and that the evidence of wills and the few surviving registers of members suggests that they mattered to plenty of people.

If that is so, why have they received little attention from historians of the Reformation? (Those writing national accounts at any rate have largely ignored them; local historians have done better.) The answer is twofold. First, we have been so absorbed, until recently, by the dissolution of the monasteries that we have given little enough attention to even the chantries, let alone the guilds. The second reason is

---

[22] Coventry RO, MS A6, fos. 299ff.

[23] C. J. Kitching (ed.), *London and Middlesex Chantry Certificate, 1548*, LRS, xvi (1980), 16, 52 and 65.

[24] The guilds also ran schools. The chantry certificates of 1548 record over thirty schools run by religious fraternities — and probably additional, but less formal (and unendowed) teaching was being done by some guild priests as well.

the poverty of surviving records. Even the mightiest confraternities, as has been said, are now known to us by the sparsest records. From Boston's St Mary's one splendid volume of accounts survives, for the years 1514 to 1525. It was presumably one of a series. Bridport has a handful of touching fifteenth-century records of some of its guilds, all modest ones, which happened to get into the borough records and have survived. A few others still exist, but hundreds like them would have been simply thrown aside — and subsequently lost, burnt, consumed by damp, worms or mice, because there was no place for them to be kept and they were no longer of interest to anyone.

Furthermore, when the royal commissioners went out in 1546 and again in 1548 to survey the colleges, chantries, obit lands, guilds and fraternities which the crown was about to seize, they were interested in institutions with permanent endowments of land and property: that was what the government was after. Since most of the brotherhoods, particularly the numerous rural ones, had no such endowment but lived on annual subscriptions and *ad hoc* payments of mass-pennies or fines for absenteeism, the number of guilds returned on the so-called 'chantry' certificates was only a fraction of the total in existence. For example, only six guilds were returned for Bedfordshire: but we know there were about three times that number. The certificates for London and Middlesex list twenty-eight confraternities, but there were over fifty. The certificates for Lincolnshire mention twenty-four guilds, i.e. endowed ones. The total number for the county was, however, about five times as many.[25]

Thus, historians who have used only the official returns have been deceived.

---

[25] These higher totals result from adding to the returns by the chantry commissioners (who listed only the endowed guilds) all the lesser guilds whose existence is known from other sources, such as *VCH*, *CPR* and wills. The wills used are in A. F. Cirket (ed.), *English Wills, 1498–1526*, P. Bell (ed.), *Bedfordshire Wills, 1480–1519*, and M. McGregor (ed.), *Bedfordshire Wills proved in the PCC, 1383–1548*, Beds. Hist. Rec. Soc., 37, 45, 58 (1957, 1966, 1979); I. Darlington (ed.), *London Consistory Wills, 1492–1547*, LRS, 3 (1967); Kitching, *London and Middlesex*; and C. W. Foster (ed.), *Lincoln Wills, 1505–1530* (2 vols.), and *Lincoln Wills III, 1530–32*, Lincs. Rec. Soc., 5, 10, 24 (1914, 1918, 1930).

How can one meet the suggestion that guilds were important and popular before the Reformation precisely because and insofar as they had evolved beyond their original religious purposes and provided layfolk with increasingly numerous worldly advantages, such as loans, social advance, a camaraderie full of opportunities for talking shop and doing business, not to mention perhaps access to urban properties at favourable rents, and so on?

That could not have been true of many rural guilds, for they had nothing like the temporal advantages to offer their members which the leading guilds in larger towns could provide; and they were the great majority. Bequests show them receiving steady support from members who, since they were making bequests, evidently expected returns after they died; in other words, they still valued the guilds' religious role. Benefactors' generosity could be remarkable. Take the village of Morebath in Somerset, for example, where in 1529 one man left 20*d.* apiece to five parish organisations and another man left a swarm of bees to two (plus 14*s.* for vestments). A woman bequeathed a silver cross and her wedding ring to two more; a second woman gave 5*s.*[26] Such were the bequests in one small village in one year. To take another typical example: John Gonne of Eastbourne in March 1528 left £5 to the Jesus guild in his town to pray for his own soul, his grandmother's, his parents' and those of all Christian men.[27] In September 1534 a London vintner thought fit to include in his will that, on his death, his wife should make sure that all the fraternities to which he and she belonged should 'be warnyd to be at my buriall'.[28] Maybe he feared that she might not have been much ruffled when he went to

---

[26] E. Hobhouse (ed.), *Churchwardens' Accounts of Croscombe, Pilton, Milton, etc.*, Som. Rec. Soc., iv (1890), 213–14. The bequests were made to the 'stores' (of St George, Jesus, Our Lady, Young Men, Maidens, etc.), which I take to mean the possessions of the guilds concerned. No less than eight 'stores' are listed. Some may have been very humble affairs boasting only a 'light' or a statue (the wedding ring referred to in the text above 'dyd hylppe make Sent Sydwyll ys scowys', i.e. was used to provide the shoes on the statue of the patron, St Sidwell). All the 'stores' had wardens and a variety of possessions, including sheep, and presumably a membership.

[27] W. H. Godfrey (ed.), *Transcripts of Sussex Wills...up to the year 1560*, ii, Sussex Rec. Soc., 42 (1938), 113.

[28] PCC, 26 Hogen, fo. 182v.

his reward. Maybe she was forgetful.
important to him that he should have
his last rite of passage. The guilds' pro
matter of importance still.

If guilds had been reducing the nun
shifting income from religious activities
poor or nascent capitalist ventures (proper
members, etc.), such a verdict would have
However, such reallocation of resources do
have taken place (as far as very sparse sur...ng records
allow us to judge). Corpus Christi guild in Coventy had
reduced the number of its clergy from five to four by 1531
and then to three in the early 1540s.[29] But that decline kept
in step with the decline in the total income of the guild,
especially of rents, which itself was a symptom of the grie-
vous economic condition of the whole city and cannot be
used as evidence of a loss of confidence in clergy or their
role. The guild of St George in Norwich, on the other hand,
increased the annual stipend of its priest by 6s. 8d. in 1533
to help him meet the recent royal tax on the clergy. He was
given another increment in 1535. So Norwich was paying
more for its spiritual services in the 1530s — inflation-
proofing, allowing what today is elegantly called 'incremental
creep' — while Coventry was cutting back.[30] The two exam-
ples cancel each other out.

There is another criterion. If it could be shown that the
enrolment of new members who were already dead had
declined, that would be sure proof that the original and
fundamental religious function of the guild had been over-
taken by other considerations.

Alas, the registers which both distinguish between living
and dead recruits and go well into the sixteenth century are
few and far between. Ludlow's guild shows a decline in
posthumous enrolment between the later fifteenth centuries
and the early sixteenth.[31] But Stratford's Holy Cross points
in the opposite direction. Its surviving register runs from
1406 to 1535. In the year 1529/30 twenty-seven new living

29 Coventry RO, MS A6, fos. 289, 344v.
30 Grace, *Records of the Gild*, pp. 134, 137.
31 *VCH, Salop*, ii, 138.

were enrolled, including a chief justice of the
Bench, several local couples, an abbot and nearby
ate, one single male and one widow. There were, however,
no less than fifty-three payments for dead relatives, friends
and dependants. They included six deceased children of one
man, several wives, a priest, servants, a local wheelwright, a
capper and a glover. That was the highest number ever
recorded![32] So that guild was still being used as a public
chantry by folk in and around Stratford. Its basic religious
purpose was as conspicuous as ever: more so, in fact.

Which was the more typical, Ludlow or Stratford? We
cannot know. But if truth, obedient to British rules, lies
somewhere between Ludlow's decline and Stratford's 'high',
the verdict would be that on average the decades before
the Reformation saw things carrying on much as they always
had. And perhaps the evidence already cited from wills tends
to support that conclusion.

The social and economic roles of the great urban guilds
were probably paramount. But these were a small fraction
of the whole — and even they indulged in lavish and expensive religious ceremonial. In England, as on the Continent,
Purgatory was both big business and a matter of intense
concern for ordinary men and women. Confraternities in
England, as in much of Western Europe, had become a
conspicuous part of lay religious life.

That being so, the largest question of all looms. If they
were so important and entwined in the daily lives of many
folk, the grand, the middling and the humble, why did they
disappear? How was it possible to destroy them? To some
extent that question is part of a larger one awaiting at least
an attempt at an answer in the next chapters. But some
things can be said now in order to set the scene.

First, though guilds seem to have been numerous and
healthy on the eve of the Reformation (by which is meant
the decades before the early 1530s), there is scattered but
persistent evidence that thereafter there were difficulties.
One of Boston's lesser guilds, Corpus Christi (a poor cousin
to the great St Mary's but important because its register is

---

[32] Harvey Bloom, *The Gild Register*, pp. 234—6. Stratford's guild (like the town
itself) was obviously flourishing.

one of the few which has survived for the period) was recruiting about ten new members a year in the 1520s, including a fair proportion of clergy. There were only four new names in 1533, three in 1536 (two of them clerics) and only a trickle during the rest of the decade. There was none for 1540, 1541 or 1542. The registers peter out sadly in 1543, when one cleric was admitted — though the remaining pages have been carefully ruled and marked out.[33]

A similar impression — of a once-vigorous institution wasting away — is given by the account book of one of Coventry's lesser guilds. Small by Holy Trinity Coventry standards, huge by those of many other towns, Corpus Christi guild's subscriptions were falling by the late 1520s, and lists of members cease after 1535. To take another example: Sleaford's Holy Trinity confraternity had boomed in the 1520s but slumped badly after 1536, and was but a shadow of its former self when its only surviving account book comes to a scrappy end in 1545.[34]

It must be said again that there is so pitifully little evidence that generalisations are dangerous. But what evidence there is points one way. In part the decline may have reflected the religious and political uncertainties of the times, as we shall see. But we must remember that many of the old towns were also, for a wide variety of reasons, suffering severe economic hardships. Coventry was in the depth of recession, a fact which shows itself clearly in the decline in rented income of Corpus Christi guild: tenements could not find tenants. Boston was on hard times. If other urban guilds, like York's, were also in difficulty (and I do not know that they were), the acute problems which they, like York, were facing would go a long way to explain the malaise.

So it is likely that, even if they still had a good deal of fat on them, some of the great guilds were in no condition to fight for their lives when the time of testing came in 1547. There is no evidence that rural guilds were in decline, but who would have been ready and able to fight for them? They had no clout. If rich urban fraternities fell, village brotherhoods were doomed.

---

[33] BL, Harleian MS 4795, fos. 60ff.
[34] BL, Add. MS 28, 533.

Finally, it was probably important that, though London had plenty of guilds (over forty), none of them was big. The richest had an income of £49 a year; the majority of the endowed ones recorded on the chantry certificates were in the £10—20 income bracket.[35] Compare that with the giants of Boston, Coventry or York. The reason for the contrast is that Londoners had cast most of their bread on the waters of the big livery companies (which themselves had religious functions, of course), and these had quite overtaken the confraternities. So Londoners would not have had the same incentive to fight for their guilds as did the burgesses of, say, Coventry. Moreover, what emerged as the Chantries Act of 1547 was decisively different from the original bill. The latter would have handed to the crown the possessions of *all* guilds, including the secular ones. London's livery companies were in jeopardy, therefore. However, for tactical reasons, because it was forced to, or because it had never intended such drastic action, the government climbed down. A new bill was introduced which encompassed only the religious foundations and spared the liveried companies (or at least their purely secular activities).[36] Some lambs had been lost but the oxen were safe. No doubt London's MPs, like those of other major towns, could feel grateful that things were not as bad as they might have been and hence fought less keenly than they might have done. Intentionally or otherwise, they had been bought off.

Nonetheless there was a fierce fight in Parliament, as we shall see. The result was a close-run thing.

It is impossible to know what ordinary folk felt about the passing of the guilds or what social or spiritual vacuum their demise left in town and village. We cannot know how quickly those guilds which had no endowments (and hence were not within the compass of the act of 1547) disintegrated. Their death-knell was the condemnation of prayer for the dead and

---

[35] Figures taken from Kitching, *London and Middlesex*. Our Lady's guild in St Margaret's Westminster had an income of £55 (ibid., p. 65).
[36] A. Kreider, *English Chantries: the road to dissolution* (Cambridge, Mass., 1979), pp. 187—208, gives a full account.

the final repudiation of Purgatory in 1547.[37] Of course, neither act nor royal injunctions forbade the social and convivial sides of guild life. Hence St George's in Norwich, for instance, survived in much reduced form as a social adjunct to the town corporation. Strenuous efforts were made by some towns to recover guildhalls and guild lands for secular, 'non-superstitious' purposes. But whether rural guilds had much to offer once their central *raison d'être* of intercession for dead members and lighting lights had been swept away is doubtful.

Guilds began to reappear in Mary's reign, when the old religion was reinstated. Basingstoke, for example, successfully petitioned to recover the former possessions of its Holy Ghost guild and the full restoration of the confraternity.[38] A guild was restored in Calais.[39] In July 1556 the famous London guild which had had its chapel in the crypt of St Paul's, called Jesus 'of the Crowds' (or 'shrouds', i.e. crypt), was restored after a local parish had bought the lease of the chapel in order to prevent it being turned into a wine cellar by the man who had previously leased it from the crown — an interesting example of layfolk taking steps to prevent sacrilege by layfolk. But this seems to have been more than an exact restoration. The crown gave it an elaborate constitution of president, vice-president, rector, masters and wardens, and named the first office-holders. They were predominantly clergy. The president, for instance, was to be David Poole (soon bishop of Peterborough), the vice-president a man called Thomas Derbyshire. He was the nephew and vicar-general of Bishop Bonner of London. Later on, in Elizabeth's reign, he attended the Council of Trent and ended his life as a Jesuit. We are witnessing here, perhaps, the foundation of a Counter-Reformation fraternity, rather than the restoration of a medieval one.[40]

Only a handful, therefore, of restorations took place. Perhaps this indicates that guilds had previously been less

---

[37] I.e. by the Chantries Act and the Injunctions of 1547. The latter also finally forbade 'superstitious' veneration of statues and images, use of candles and tapers, pilgrimages and many ceremonies.
[38] *CPR, Philip and Mary*, iii, 262—3.
[39] Ibid., 389—90.
[40] Ibid., 274—5.

important than we have supposed. Perhaps it indicates the advance of Protestantism. More probably it reflects lay nervousness about re-endowing any religious foundation in those uncertain times. Finally, it probably owes a good deal to the fact that, despite what has been said about the re-foundation of the Jesus fraternity in St Paul's, Mary's policy was to restore, not to innovate. But recovery of the physical possessions of former guilds — guildhalls, lands and so on — had already become very difficult and was largely a matter of luck.

Presumably the Marian refoundations perished with the queen — and thus finally ended a story which, at its best, had not been without real achievement, some grandeur and idealism. Confraternities had raised fine buildings, enhanced civic pride, patronised arts and crafts, nourished prayer and loyalty, and given humble folk some sense of security against the hazards of this world and the next. Most of their charitable and educational foundations survived — under new management. But only a harsh person would assume that nothing worthwhile was lost with their extinction.

One question remains: since these religious guilds seem to have been most numerous in eastern, lowland England and since they gave special opportunities for lay initiative, must there not have been some connection between them and the spread of English Protestantism?

The answer is probably 'no'. In the first place, the geographical coincidence is more apparent than real. Guilds were popular in, for example, Lincolnshire and Cambridgeshire, neither of which was conspicuously Protestant (the former, indeed, was the site of a conservative rebellion in 1536); they were not particularly prominent in areas like Essex or Kent (or London and Bristol) where heresy took root fastest; they played their part in much of Yorkshire, where recusancy was later to prosper.

Next, there is no evidence that pre-Reformation heresy and anticlericalism found fraternities to be natural seedbeds (as they could be on the Continent). Of course there is so little evidence to go on that that assertion is not a weighty one. One incident, however, is worth relating: in 1536

William Clopton of Stratford upon Avon, scion of a major local family (they gave the town its grand bridge across the river) rallied the burgesses in the chapel of Holy Cross guild in order to mobilise support against the vicar of a nearby village, Hampton Lucy, who had been preaching against the old religion.[41] So we have at least one guild which, far from being a breeding-ground of heterodoxy, was a bastion of lay conservatism against clerical innovation.

The truth is, of course, that the theology on which the religious guild rested and which was its *raison d'être* (belief in Purgatory, the sacrificial efficacy of the mass, veneration of saints) was the very antithesis of Protestantism. Moreover, though the new creed denied the priestly (i.e. sacrificial) role of the cleric, much of his sacramental function and his 'apartness', the Reformation did not bring universal liberation to the laity. Far from it. It will be argued here that, for most lay people, the establishment of Protestantism caused a marked shift in the balance of power in favour of the clergy.[42] After all, the confraternities disappeared. So did the army of unbeneficed clergy who before were largely under lay control. The new Protestant minister, if he was a zealous servant of the Gospel, was a disciplining, preaching authority-figure. He may not have had the sacramental powers of the old priest, but he expected rank-and-file lay people to be more passive, more attentive and more regular church-goers. The 'lay religion' of the fraternities did not find its fulfilment in the new Established Church — did not and could not. Perhaps what had animated the smaller, rural guilds, i.e. those with solely religious functions, found an outlet in the sects. There was little place for it in the 'official' magisterial Reformation.

41 *LP*, xii, ii, 302–3.
42 See below, pp. 164–70.

3

Criticism of the Old Order

A twentieth-century English Catholic looking back on his pre-Reformation forebears may find plenty to criticise. First and foremost, late-medieval spirituality was focused on Calvary rather than the Resurrection, on Christ as Suffering Servant rather than Risen Lord, on his self-humbling and self-sacrifice rather than his victory, on Good Friday rather than Easter Sunday. Not that the victory was denied; it was that the main emphasis was placed elsewhere. There was little sense of the new order inaugurated, of living in the 'last' days. The Second Coming was not denied; but concern with it and the Kingdom was often associated with, and had indeed produced, dangerous millenarianism.

This impoverishment of understanding of the mystery and meaning of Redemption owed a good deal to, and was made worse by, the lack of a historical sense and hence a devaluation of the Holy Spirit. The Church was scarcely 'in time'. It was no 'Pilgrim Church'. The idea of development was foreign to a theological outlook which was basically static and platonic. 'Quod semper, quod ubique, quod ab omnibus' [what has been believed always, everywhere and by all] was the presumed norm for all Christian teaching and practice, a view of things which proved vulnerable to humanist and Protestant appeals to Scripture, the Fathers and early Christian history.

To descend to a lower level: that episcopacy is, and should be seen to be, eucharistic was a truth largely ignored. Bishops exercised their canonical jurisdiction, they administered, appointed, judged, excommunicated, visited, ordained, confirmed and (some of them) preached. They did not see themselves as, supremely, the eucharistic ministers of their local churches, i.e. their dioceses.

We now appreciate that much of late-medieval scholasticism, particularly its philosophy and natural science, was alive and fruitful. But there was little good theology and probably too much canon law — too much of the latter, perhaps, simply because so much theology was repetitive and strait-jacketed, preoccupied with peripheral issues and too inclined to take the easy way out by using existing practice as the norm to be defended.

Much preaching was more concerned with moral uplift than doctrinal instruction and was commonly the victim of astonishingly ingenious, but ultimately sterile, allegorising, or naive accounts of miracles and lives of saints. And there was doubtless some truth in the reformers' central charge that pre-Reformation Catholicism was shot through with semi-Pelagian ideas on merit and the efficacy of human works, as well as with superstition and near-idolatrous devotion to saints. Certainly the multiplication of masses, especially 'private' ones, and the preoccupation with externals and numerous special devotions and observances seemed to support the complaint.

Then, of course, there were those familiar shortcomings of the clergy (especially the rank and file) for whom, despite much effort, the medieval Church could never provide adequate spiritual and intellectual formation: the problems of pluralism and its bedfellow, non-residence; careerism and a false attitude to benefice, namely, seeing it as a bundle of rights to be exploited rather than a 'cure'; sexual scandals and so on. We need not prolong the agony.

A major reason why we need not go into detail about those abuses is that, for most people, these were not occasions of serious disquiet. To put the same thing another way: the past ills that we confidently diagnose today were then either not perceived or, in the main, were accepted as part and parcel of the workaday world. Indeed, some of the things which we today regard as weaknesses, such as an unhistorical view of the Church and its unchangeability, were then regarded as strengths.[1]

On the whole, the laity had a Church which they wanted and found congenial — reasonably tolerant and easy-going, but neither complacent nor unable to make useful contributions to society.

It did not intrude excessively into the average layman's life. Its correctional work was, by and large, welcome. It provided many opportunities for social integration and neighbourly cooperation in the form of processions, festivals and pilgrimages. By tolerating (if not promoting) churchales, maypoles and wakes, it retained a human face. By blessing shrines, relics, holy wells and so on — even if some were of dubious authenticity — it nourished local pride and loyalties, as well as piety. By encouraging or at least allowing lords and abbeys of 'misrule', boy-bishops and 'masters of merry disports', as well as numerous forms of charivari or licensed 'topsy-turvydom' at Shrovetide, Hocktide and major feasts, all of which temporarily inverted social norms with parody and burlesque, it allowed communities to let off steam, settle scores, cut the bumptious or aggressive down to size and indulge in a good deal of innocent ribaldry and 'knocking' the Establishment. All this released social tensions, broke down barriers, and helped communities to cohere.[2]

The protection given by church bells, holy water, blessings,

[1] A comprehensive bibliography for the foregoing would exceed the limits of these pages. Some of the points, however, are pursued in H. W. Blench, *Preaching in England in the late Fifteenth and Sixteenth Centuries* (Oxford, 1964), a worthy successor to the works of the celebrated late G. R. Owst; P. Heath, *The English Parish Clergy on the Eve of the Reformation* (1969); and H. Oberman, *The Harvest of Medieval Theology* (1963). John Fisher's voluminous writings show many of the traits noted above, as do many contemporaries and later recusant authors. Their unhistorical and Calvary-centred theologies were largely endorsed at Trent. As Newman and, indeed, the Second Vatican Council, demonstrated, they survived well beyond the sixteenth century. The reaffirmation of the eucharistic nature of episcopacy is a recent achievement.

[2] A particularly telling contribution to this fashionable theme is C. Phythian-Adams, 'Ceremony and the citizen: the communal year at Coventry, 1450—1550', in P. Clark and P. Slack (eds), *Crisis and order in English towns, 1500—1700* (1972), pp. 57—85. Cf. I. Luxton, 'The Reformation and popular culture', in F. Heal and R. O'Day (eds), *Church and Soceity in England* (1977), pp. 57—77.

relics and exorcism mattered — even if, as the sceptic will say, they gave security and comfort only because they were believed to give them. We now know that the church courts, whose jurisdiction covered much of lay life (including sexual offences, matrimonial causes and wills) were more popular and useful than the textbooks have had us believe, and could provide swifter, more flexible and accessible justice than the king's courts (with the exception of Star Chamber and Chancery in which clerics, particularly one cleric — Wolsey — were conspicuous).[3]

Many well-to-do laymen owned advowsons, that is, the right to nominate incumbents to clerical livings. Such clergy were then appointed (instituted) by the local ordinary, i.e. bishop. But more striking is the fact that many clergy were directly employed by layfolk, without reference to any local ordinary, to act as chaplains to religious and craft guilds and as 'service' priests; and though episcopal approval was required for appointments of chaplains to fully endowed ('perpetual') chantries, this was probably only a formality. So there was a whole regiment of clerics to a large extent hired and (presumably) 'fired' by layfolk, and at the beck and call, full-time or on an *ad hoc* basis, of employers who were their social equals or perhaps even their inferiors.[4]

The pre-Reformation Church did not allow the laity an active part in its public worship, especially the mass. They went to mass to watch what little could be seen through the chancel screen and to hear what little could be heard (and understood) from the nave. Above all, they went to adore the consecrated species at the elevation. That was the climax of their worship. They did not participate in the 'ascending', sacrificial action of the mass. That was 'done' for them. They communicated rarely. If they prayed, they prayed *at* mass, not *the* mass. Otherwise their attention was to be focused on

---

[3] For important reappraisal of the place of the ecclesiastical courts in pre-Reformation society, see R. Houlbrooke, *Church Courts and the People during the English Reformation* (1979); S. Lander, 'Church Courts and the Reformation in the Diocese of Chichester, 1500–58', in O'Day and Heal (eds), *Continuity and Change*, pp. 215–37; and M. Bowker, 'The Commons Supplication against the Ordinaries in the light of some Archidiaconal *Acta*', *TRHS*, 5th ser., 21 (1971), 61–77.

[4] See below, p. 167.

the crucifixion scene that surmounted the chancel screen:
Christ hanging on the cross, with Mary and John standing on
either side, and a Last Judgement on the wall behind.

But it would be wrong to conclude that a layman therefore
felt excluded from the Church's liturgical life and had been
reduced to passivity, or that individualism had triumphed.
In the first place, thanks to the increase in the number of
votive masses for all manner of intentions (for recovery
from sickness, a good harvest, safe return from a journey,
good weather), as well as the enormous number of requiem
masses (for the dead), most masses were in fact offered for
the welfare of lay people in this world or the next. Mass was
not simply worship of God on behalf of the community by
a priestly caste set apart from the laity by ordination, vows,
celibacy, a cultic language, dress and ceremonial. It was also
for the laity. Secondly, the communitarian nature of the
mass had not been entirely obscured. At the 'Pax' the congregation made visible its unity in reconciliation by passing
around the veneration (i.e. kissing) a holy picture or tablet
inscribed with the sacred monogram IHS and perhaps mounted in silver. Again, and perhaps more importantly, at the
end of mass it was common for blessed bread (often called
'holy' or 'singing' bread) to be distributed and consumed,
so that, although holy communion was infrequent, the
symbolism of actively sharing bread and being made one
thereby was affirmed: a poor substitute for the eucharist,
later generations may think, but a custom that mattered.[5]

Most parish clergy were probably locally born and, once
appointed, remained in post until death. Though a surprising
number of them (and of guild, chantry and service priests)
were university-trained, clerical culture was not separated
from lay as it was later to be by the seminary and its distinc-
tive training. Most clergy were 'of' the people in a deep sense.
So were the churches. The parish church was the largest
building in a village and many a town. It provided social
space. For many people it would have given the first and
even only experience of painting, formal music, sculpture,

[5] Cf. J. Bossy, 'Essai de sociographie de la messe, 1200–1700', *Annales*, 36
(1981), 44–70. He stresses the importance of the 'Pax' but not of holy bread,
which I think was more significant.

architecture. Its tower was an arsenal; it displayed the village clock, perhaps the only timepiece. Its bells summoned, warned, and told the time, gave dreadful majesty to death and celebrated marriage joy, at the same time proclaiming the social status of the departed or the bride and groom; and they warded off evil spirits, thunder and lightning. The bells also provided churchwardens with incessant business — taking them down, repairing and putting them back, mending cracked clappers, regreasing and renewing ropes, bawdrigs and shafts.

The parish church was a political centre, in the largest sense of the word, where churchwardens, constables, and many other local officers, such as dog-muzzlers and mole-catchers, were elected, the church rate or tax (if there was one) agreed and the upkeep of church fabric and church-yards, the repair, leasing and sale of church houses and tenements in the village discussed. The church employed glaziers, plumbers, masons, carpenters, tilers. Larger churches had a paid staff — presumably mostly part-time — of sexton, bell-ringer, organ blower, grave-digger, etc.

The church would have been the object of local pride and a symbol of a community's integrity, continuity and wealth. Layfolk, living and dead, had paid for it, built some of it with their own hands, given the timber and stone, endowed altars, presented torches, statues, lights and so on. If their active involvement in public worship was slight, the church was nonetheless 'theirs', just as a great deal of what went on there was also 'theirs'. The parish clergy could call the chancel and pulpit their own; the laity could do the same for the rest of the church.

So it is wrong to say that the pre-Reformation layman was second-class and put upon. There was a partnership between layman and cleric — or, to use a word that has appeared before, a symbiosis. It is not claimed that there was no anticlericalism. There was (and presumably there will always be in even healthy Christian societies). There were rubs and rows. We have recently been reminded, for instance, of the way tithes could easily get Londoners into a fury.[6]

---

[6] S. Brigden, 'Tithe controversy in Reformation London', *Journ. Eccles. Hist.*, 32 (1981), 44—70.

Individual clergy could be very unpopular. Old Bishop Nix of Norwich is a good example of one, and like many another peppery prelate he assumed that it was the laity who were being awkward. No doubt there were plenty of occasions for that form of anticlericalism which is really disappointment at clergy who have failed to live up to their ideals and exasperation with authorities who tolerate endemic mediocrity. But this is fundamentally aimed at the individual, not the office.

There may have been a substantial part of English society, in Weald and Chilterns, remote dale and border country, for instance (as also among urban 'proletariats'), which had scarcely been Christianised at all, and where folk religion and semi-paganism still thrived under a veneer of official Christianity. Here lay people would have had little time for Catholic clergy and the Catholic Church, and anticlericalism of that deeper and more serious kind which generates bitterness and bloodshed could have festered. We cannot know how much sub-Christian paganism was present in pre-Reformation England, but we can know something about it. It seems to have been docile, non-violent. There had been no crusade against it, no Albigensian bloodbath to leave bitter memories and hatred. It had not so much rejected Christianity as failed so far to accept and be absorbed by it.

Much the same can be said about Lollardy — not that that simple non-sacerdotal, non-sacramental protest can be fully distinguished from pre-Christian survivals. It scarcely threatened the old order. It had little social or political 'clout'. Though the Christian Brethren, the organised wing of the movement, raised cash, produced books and provided impressive leadership, on the whole Lollardy remained a disparate, dispersed, undangerous movement. Only occasionally — as, for example, in the diocese of London in the later 1520s — do the authorities seem to have been seriously alarmed.[7]

It is difficult to assess the influence of Erasmus and his merciless satirising of clerical inadequacies, lay superstition and gullibility, official obscurantism, intolerance and so on.

---

[7] The best introduction to the highly complex subject of Lollardy (and to its considerable literature) is in A. G. Dickens, *The English Reformation* (1964), ch. 2. Cf. the interesting article by J. Davis, 'Joan of Kent, Lollardy and the English Reformation', in *Journ. Eccles. Hist.*, 33 (1982), 225–33.

In the first place, we have no way of knowing how many read him or heard his message at secondhand. It is likely that his writings and those of fellow-humanists, and even the splenetic outpourings of a Simon Fish, were familiar to the clerical intelligentsia and perhaps the more sophisticated lay town-dweller and professional, but passed over the heads of the great mass of English men and women. Erasmus, like Marsilius of Padua or William of Ockham, has received more attention from historians than he did from his contemporaries. Furthermore, it is not as though he was cold-shouldered by the authorities and turned into an angry dissident. His best friends in England in 1529 were the archbishop of Canterbury (former lord chancellor), the bishop of Rochester, the bishop of London (lord privy seal) and Thomas More (lord chancellor). That was scarcely ostracism. And these friends not only agreed with much that he said: they were trying to do something about it. The only humanist and Erasmian aspiration which the authorities positively refused to consider was an English Bible. But how many shared Erasmus's and Thomas More's urgent desire in this matter we cannot know. Probably not many.

Then there is the larger question of what Erasmianism did to people anyway. Of the four just named, two died as martyrs for the old Church, Archbishop Warham of Canterbury nearly did so and Cuthbert Tunstall, translated from London to Durham in 1530, was a staunch conservative who went to prison under Edward VI, was restored by Mary and finally dispossessed by Elizabeth. Erasmianism did not necessarily radicalise, though it undoubtedly helped to undermine the old order nonetheless.

The affair of Richard Hunne, a London merchant found hanged in the bishop of London's prison while awaiting trial for heresy, was a *cause célèbre* in its day and has attracted much attention since. But perhaps a striking fact about it is that it was the only really serious case of its kind that the anticlerical lobby of the time could produce and which modern historians have been able to cite. The awesome statute, *De heretico comburendo*, was still in force, of course: persistent heresy was punished by death by burning. Though no one was martyred by Wolsey, Lollards were burnt earlier in the century and by other bishops of his day. Immediately after the cardinal's fall his successor, Thomas More, personally unleashed a new wave of persecution against leading Protestant dissidents. But how much this shocked people and to what extent the activities of the layman Thomas More brought odium on the clergy is difficult to say. England had no tradition of torture conducted by clerical inquisitors. Before the late 1520s most of the heretics seem to have done no more than express often bizarre views against veneration of saints or rail against the sacrament of the altar in a way that suggests ignorance more than malice. And in the great majority of cases their punishment was public penance on several Sundays in the form of carrying faggots to the parish church and wearing penitential dress. There was no mass execution. England produced no Torquemada — and, for that matter, no Tetzel or indulgence scandal.

England could not match the bitter and violent anticlericalism that was to be found on the Continent — in much of Germany for instance — on the eve of the Reformation.[8] Perhaps one reason for this is that late-medieval England was a fairly prosperous place and did not suffer from the oppressive landlordism, clerical and lay, which was to drive German peasants to desperate action.[9] Another reason for the muffled anticlericalism was the comparative lack of clericalism — by which, in this context, is meant abuse by and for clerics of ecclesiastical wealth and privilege.

Episcopal pluralism was commonplace on the Continent. There, papal, royal and ducal nephews and dependants could

---

[8] Certainly the first session of the Reformation Parliament in 1529 seemed to unleash such anticlerical passion that, in John Fisher's famous words, the Commons had but one cry: 'down with the Church'. But how far was this typical and spontaneous? There is a strong sense of careful stage-management here, and the remark of the imperial ambassador, Chapuys, shortly before that 'nearly all the people here hate priests' must be treated with equal caution. Was Chapuys in a position to know what 'the people' really thought? Was he not simply reporting the official line to his master, and perhaps doing exactly what was intended, i.e. warning the emperor that Henry's affairs were not to be dismissed lightly.

[9] See H. J. Cohn, 'Anticlericalism in the German Peasants' War, 1525', *Past and Present*, 83 (1979), 3–31. Many German peasants had to face no less than three kinds of seigneurial authority and imposts. Their plight was markedly worse (and often declining fast) than that of the average English copyholder.

amass several archbishoprics, bishoprics and abbacies apiece. It is a striking fact that Wolsey was the first English bishop ever to hold more than one English see at a time (he also held an abbey, that of St Albans). But both before and after the Reformation a Valois, Wittelsbach or similar younger son could have had sees and abbacies heaped on him even before he was ordained. England could produce nothing as scandalous. John Fisher was ordained five years below the canonical age of twenty-six, with a papal dispensation, and became bishop when he was a mere thirty-five. None of his fellow-bishops had been promoted so young. And anyway, no one could suggest that his advancement was an abuse of the system.

On the Continent, *commendams*, that is, the temporary grant of jurisdiction and incomes of (usually) major clerical offices to absentees, lay like the blight on much of monasticism, especially among the Cistercians. Abbacies and other plums were snapped up by careerist cardinals and bishops, even by laymen. In England, the bishop of the poor see of Bangor retained the Cistercian abbacy of Beaulieu *in commendam* when he was raised to the bench: otherwise (and apart from Wolsey's acquisition of St Albans) the country was spared this abuse, just as it suffered from little of that domination by wealthy families of cathedral chapters which was also a conspicuous feature in, say, Germany.

Careerism, pluralism and non-residence did exist, of course, but there was little of the cynical exploitation of the richest ecclesiastical offices by princes and aristocracies to be found elsewhere.[10] And, though widespread appropriation of livings (the division of tithes due to a parish church between the rector, usually a monastery, and the vicar who carried out the spiritual duties) was part and parcel of that larger tendency to treat benefices as sources of income for sinecurists who then paid deputies and hirelings to perform

[10] England was not completely immune, of course — as the case of the earl of Dorset's brother (below, pp. 58—9) illustrates. But such abuse was not common. Similarly, episcopal nepotism was never as scandalous as at the papal court or, say, in many German states. Anyway, since a John Fisher could employ a brother as steward and a Protestant like Nicholas Ridley shower his family with favours, 'nepotism' is not always easy to judge: it was not necessarily bad nor a Catholic monopoly.

the official duties, that income at least remained within the
Church and did not end up in lay purses.

Tithes and glebes (the land with which parsonages were
endowed) were often leased to layfolk. But that was different.
They still generated an income for clergy and they were still
clerical property.

There was not the clerical indiscipline which could be
found in say, Ireland, where bishops, abbots and clergy not
only sired sons in plenty but sought and received papal
dispensations for offspring to hold benefices in their father's
churches, and where *commendams* were like a cancer. Ireland
produced stories of simony, violence and even arson by high
ecclesiastics, clerical murder and thuggery and so on on a
scale which England could not match.

Careers in the English Church were indeed open to those
with talents (and the right patronage). On the eve of the
Reformation none of the bishops was the son of a nobleman;
most were of modest origin. The Church in England had not
been 'aristocraticised' as had much of it in Europe. Some of
the bishops were undistinguished, but none (except Wolsey)
is known to have broken his vow of celibacy. One, Fisher,
was a model pastoral bishop. Fox of Winchester, West of Ely
and Tunstall enjoyed his high esteem, which he did not
bestow lightly. Longland of Lincoln was a decent man
honestly trying to do his duty and making a real mark on
his over-large, unmanageable diocese.[11] And so on. The
overall impression is of a well-trained, fairly conscientious if
uninspired group of men — a typical hierarchy, perhaps.

Late-medieval archbishops, bishops and abbots were no
less concerned to provide themselves with comely residences,
tombs and chantry chapels than their lay peers. But they
were no less public-spirited and made a respectable showing
in the upsurge of new schools founded in the two or three
generations before the Reformation, in their home towns
or the abbey precincts. Between them they made a notable
contribution to the two universities. The works of such
bishops as Alcock, Fisher, Fox and Cardinal Wolsey suggest
that, on the whole, the upper clergy were pulling their weight.

11 M. Bowker, *The Henrician Reformation.* On the lower clergy see also her *The
Secular Clergy in the Diocese of Lincoln, 1495—1520* (Cambridge, 1968), and
P. Heath, *English Parish Clergy.*

It is customary to sneer at doles and handouts at funerals, month's minds and obits, as well as at abbey gates, and to dismiss them as likely to have encouraged the very disease they were trying to cure. Without falling into an equal and opposite error of romanticising what may have been a very imperfect response to poverty and vagrancy and so on, it is worth acknowledging that a great deal of relief in the form of cash, food and clothing was distributed. Of the fourteen endowed obits in Walsall church, for instance, all but one provided for gifts to the poor on the obit days. About a third of the income of Berkshire's obits went to the poor.[12] Roger Waltham's chantry in St Paul's (and it was not uncommon for a chantry foundation to provide for a handout on the anniversary of the founder's death) had an income of £2 1s. 8d. earmarked to provide the poor each year with ten lots of a hundred starlings — surely one of the most unusual examples of outdoor relief. Alice Danby of Heston in Middlesex left land for her obit and to provide the poor with three bushels of wheat for bread, four bushels of malt for ale and one shilling's-worth of cheese.[13] They may not have been enough; but these innumerable gifts all over the country for the poor, the blind and the lame, for widows and orphans and the rest would have been better than nothing. The same must have been true of the relief provided by religious houses.

How much of monastic income was being devoted to the poor and hungry on the eve of the dissolution is a question which has been answered as definitively as it ever will be: a mere three per cent or thereabouts. But a more important question remains: would this have meant a little or a lot of relief of human suffering? Might it not have meant a lot, at least in some places and sometimes? Simple percentages of national totals can obscure much important detail.

Consider what two Cistercian houses in Warwickshire, chosen at random, had to offer. At Merevale the staggering total of 3,000 herrings, plus bread, beer and 5s. in cash were to be distributed on Maundy Thursday, together with a weekly dole during the rest of the year of bread and beer

---

[12] *VCH, Berks.*, ii, 29n.
[13] Kitching, *London and Middlesex*, pp. 56, 76.

to the value of £5 13s. 8d. The sum of £50 was also to be earmarked for the hospice, which provided hospitality to wayfarers and other visitors. Further south, in the centre of the county, Stoneleigh Abbey distributed £4 5s. 4d. worth of bread, beer and more herrings on Maundy Thursday, and bread and beer each week to the annual value of £5 7s. 8d. It also supported five corrodians and one annuitant, and had forty-three other dependants, including fifteen servants and twenty-one farmworkers. Each house, therefore, was distributing bread, beer and fish every year worth about twice as much as the annual pension which the average choir-monk could expect to receive from the crown when his house was suppressed. Neither house had a large local population. Stoneleigh village, indeed, could not have had more than a few score inhabitants, so, if the monks were really doing their duty, they would have been handing out enough to give every family a square meal at frequent intervals and enough beer to keep all the adults content.[14]

Those who dismiss all this may perhaps tend to forget two things. First, there is an important place in society for apparently 'indiscriminate' almsgiving without too many questions being asked or attempts made to reform those who, for various reasons, have taken to the road or to mendicancy. Besides, casual relief can be a life-saver for an individual in a sudden crisis who might well be ashamed to seek aid via a more orderly system and perhaps might not even qualify under it. Secondly, it is not immediately obvious why church-wardens, guild wardens and the like who were responsible for distributing relief to the needy should have been any less discriminating than later poor-law officers. They would have known the local scrounger and had a good idea of real local hardship. Places in local almshouses and rent-free accommodation would not have been distributed lightly, especially if there were pressure on them. Similarly, it is not clear why monks, who could be tough landlords and efficient administrators of their own houses, should be presumed to have distributed their bread and soup or whatever mindlessly.

In areas where resources were good and the pressures had not got out of control, the combination of what

14 *VCH, Warks.*, ii, 77, 81.

churchwardens and guilds on the one hand and the religious on the other could offer could probably have made a major contribution to the relief of indigence and suffering. As usual, the picture is complex. Its complexity is well matched by the story of the state of hospitals (a term used then for hostels, hospices, almshouses and hospitals in the modern sense). Many foundations bearing that name on the eve of the Reformation were but shadows of their original selves. Some, like many similar institutions, had completed a perhaps brief life-cycle and fallen into decrepitude. Others had been stranded by a shift of population or had decayed because the plague had slackened ('lazar houses' because leprosy was not so prevalent). Whatever the causes, the fact was that scores of 'hospitals' were little more than sinecures providing absentee masters with an income. Others simply sank without trace, were amalgamated with neighbours or refounded and given a new lease of life. There was nothing new about this, incidentally. Institutions like these had come and gone by the dozen during the Middle Ages.

At the other end of the scale there were hospitals like that of Newark, St Leonard's in York, or the Savoy in London which were very much alive and well, and boasted impressive facilities.

Whether or not these old resources could have coped with the strain of the sixteenth-century population explosion and large-scale population movement is an open question. They may already have proved inadequate in those towns where longstanding economic decline was made more cruel and dangerous by the influx of unemployed folk from the neighbouring countryside. On the other hand, there was a response — with almshouses and the beginnings of specialised provision for the insane and orphans, for example (not all of which, it should be noted, survived the Reformation). And perhaps that was an accelerating response. The old order was neither insensitive to need nor incapable of adapting to it. The Savoy Hospital pointed an important way forward. England could later have had its fair share of those religious men and women dedicated to relief of the poor, sick, lame and hungry which the Catholic Reform, particularly in Italy and then France, was to produce in plenty, not to mention such institutions as the *misericordia* and *monte di pietà*.[15]

To some extent the ability of the old order to cope with new needs would have depended, of course, on its readiness to reallocate resources, deliberately and on a large scale, and not just as a result of local initiative or accident. That being so, it is worth pointing to the significance of what John Fisher, instructed and abetted by the remarkable Lady Margaret Beaufort, achieved for Cambridge.[16] Using the wealth of decayed religious houses for founding colleges was not a new idea. But this was more ambitious than any previous redisposal of ex-monastic wealth; it came from the 'top' (it effectively had royal impetus), and it paved the way for Wolsey's even more ambitious foundations of the 1520s, when, with papal approval, twenty-nine decayed monastic houses were dissolved to provide the wherewithal for his school in Ipswich and his massive college in Oxford. Layfolk were apparently still prepared to endow local religious houses, provided they were tolerably fervent and useful. Doubtless there was much discontent with the corrupt and parasitic; but Wolsey — and Fisher before him, among others — had been trying to pull out the worst of the weeds. What had been thus begun could have been brought to a conclusion; and no one would have objected if it had.

In 1529 there were few Protestants in England. What is more important, English men and women, by and large, were profoundly addicted to the old ways.

Their zest for venerating saints and relics is indisputable. Their continuing dedication of churches, guilds, 'services', chantries and lights to Our Lady is eloquent testimony to their esteem for her, as are the large number of her pre-Reformation English shrines and pilgrimage-centres. Later devotions, like that of Corpus Christi, flourished. And so on.

It is difficult to know how much pilgrimage-going survived until the end. One catches occasional, but striking mention

---

[15] I.e. a fraternity which provided corporal works of mercy (and hospitals) for the community at large and not just its own members, and the formal provision of low-interest loans (often secured by pawning) for the poor.

[16] Not to mention what she did elsewhere, e.g. Wimborne, whose college, school and almshouses turned the town into almost a 'model' community.

of Englishmen on expeditions abroad: for instance, Sir Robert Throckmorton, father of the great Warwickshire dynast, MP and thorn in Henry VIII's side, Sir George, died in Italy on his way to the Holy Land; and in 1533 Sir John Gifford, friend and fellow-MP of that same Sir George was granted royal permission to go on pilgrimage with a large entourage to Amiens.[17] Certainly Walsingham continued to attract pilgrims until the end, and Reformers' complaints about the English appetite for 'running' from shrine to shrine as well as their delight in exposing such alleged frauds as the Blood of Hailes suggest that the taste for pilgrimage was still strong, even if less strong than in earlier times.[18]

There can be no doubt about English preoccupation with Purgatory, the mass as propitiatory sacrifice available for the living and the dead and for temporal as well as spiritual aid, and the whole idea of expiation for sin (plus the accompanying belief that the punishment due for sin in the next world could be commuted into reparation in this).

A former caveat must be repeated. It is not claimed that all this shows how healthy late-medieval English Catholicism was. Of course, Protestants argued that the obsession with prayers and masses for the dead, expiation and Purgatory, were very unchristian, that belief in Mary and the saints as intercessors was virtually polytheism, and preoccupation with lights, shrines and pilgrimages and so on semi-pagan or worse. The important thing here is that, whatever else they were, these things were emphatically not Protestant. They pointed in exactly the opposite direction to the Reformation.

What fired Protestant zeal was not any sign that English men and women were outgrowing their 'childish' past or beginning to see through what Reformers regarded as Catholic idolatry, monkish conjuring tricks, empty rituals and semi-magical incantations, and a Pelagian reliance on 'works' and externalism. Rather, it was that their fellow-countrymen

---

[17] *LP*, vi, 737 (4).

[18] Cf. Knowles, *The Religious Orders in England, III. The Tudor Age* (Cambridge, 1959), 249 & n. But pilgrimages could still matter to testators (see above, p. 18) and even vicarious pilgrimage-going was possible. In 1525 Joan Francis left money in her will for her executors 'to hire one to go for me' on pilgrimage to Canterbury. BL, Add. MS 5861, fo. 94.

remained 'hooked' on these things, duped. The old order was not withering away. It seemed as strong as ever, though the stirring events in Germany and Switzerland obviously gave new grounds for hope. Converts to Protestantism, however, reported how their individual conversion had not been preceded by slow disenchantment with old ways or after a long period in a spiritual wilderness. It came as a sudden release from an elaborate way of life which, up to the moment when scales fell from eyes, had enjoyed their wholehearted commitment.

The English Protestant divine, Thomas Becon, is one who recounted his spiritual Aeneid, in Luther-like terms. He conveys to us the same sense of deliverance from what, for him, had been a servitude and of gratitude for the way in which all had been simplified. He wrote indignantly of his former life:

> How ran we from post to pillar, from stock to stone, from idol to idol, from place to place...How gilded we images, painted their tabernacles and set up candles before them...What confidence we had to be delivered out of the pope's pinfold [i.e. Purgatory] after our departure, though we lived never so ungodly, through the popish prattling of monstrous monks and the mumbling masses of those lazy soul-carriers...What affiance did we put in auricular confession and in the whispering absolution of the papists...How believed we to please God highly if at the pope's commandment certain days we abstained from a piece of gross smoky bacon or salt-withered beef and pampered our bellies with all kinds of dainty fish and other delicate fare.[19]

People who had sat in darkness had indeed seen a great light. But the Protestantisation of England, insofar as it was ever accomplished, was really a consequence, not a cause, of the Reformation. And it is only when we appreciate how deeply the old ways had penetrated the warp and weft of English life that we can understand why the spread of Protestantism in England was a slow and painful process.

Finally, it is difficult to find much anti-papal feeling in

19 Becon, *Jewel of Joy* (addressed to Elizabeth I) in *Works*, PS 13 (1844), 413–14.

England on the eve of the breach with Rome. Papal authority intruded little into daily English life, and then usually at the request and to the benefit of English men and women. Bishops were appointed by Rome and, together with a handful of abbots, paid 'services' (taxes which by this time were commonly called annates) for their bulls; but they were royal nominees. Rome never refused the crown. Two English sees, Salisbury and Worcester, had for decades been held *in commendam* by absentee Italians. This was manifest abuse, but the English crown wanted it. It was useful to have a small lobby at the papal curia and to pay the cardinal-protector of England (the man responsible for looking after English affairs at Rome) in this way. So when Cardinal Campeggio, England's 'protector', received Salisbury in 1523 he had been enthusiastically nominated to the see by the king himself.[20]

Clerics and layfolk sought all manner of ecclesiastical dispensations, licences, privileges and indults from Rome. Again, these were never refused, as far as one can see. Often enough, especially in matrimonial cases, Rome would concede the dispensation and then hand back to local judges delegate responsibility for implementing the decision in detail. Since the papal collector in England and then Cardinal Wolsey were given powers to grant dispensations (for example, for marriage within some of the forbidden degrees), any sense of being subject to 'foreign' jurisdiction would have been attenuated and Rome's *plenitudo potestatis* made less oppressive than ever.

Of course, everything had to be paid for, like the bishops' bulls of appointment. And the English still showed their special loyalty to Rome by the annual donation called Peter's Pence. But the volume of cash going to Rome was by this time only a trickle (though large enough for indignation, real or contrived, to be expressed in Parliament in 1532 at the drain of English treasure).

The English were keen on indulgences, i.e. on saying prayers and doing good deeds which, by virtue of papal authority, were believed to secure whole or partial remission of the punishment in Purgatory for sin committed on earth,

[20] Roman Transcripts (PRO 31/9) vol. 3, p. 36.

and available for both the living and the already-dead. Religious houses, cathedrals and shrines offered indulgences to visitors and benefactors. Indulgences served good causes: they could be earned by contributing to such things as the upkeep of bridges and churchbuilding. Popes often took their share of the offerings (that was part of the deal) and suspended the grants of indulgences to major pilgrimage centres during a Holy Year (1525, for example) so as to attract more visitors to Rome. In 1496 Alexander VI granted plenary indulgences to all who made donations during Holy Week to the Augustinian friars in London, Oxford, Cambridge, Ely and Lincoln, as these houses were allegedly in bad repair. He required a one-third cut.[21] There were certainly occasions when Rome took the initiative, that is, when popes offered indulgences for their own purposes, such as raising money for defence of the papal states, or for ransoming captives in Turkish hands. But in most cases Rome was responding to English requests. Even when this was not the case, the papal thirst for cash could be tempered by English self-interest. A very good example of this is provided by the fateful indulgences proclaimed in 1508 when the rebuilding of St Peter's had just started. Julius II wanted England to contribute. He even (it seems) tried to withdraw indulgences conceded to places like Westminster Abbey, as though it was a jubilee year. But he had to climb down in the face of protests from Henry VII, the archbishop of Canterbury and others. Westminster retained its privileges; and one-quarter of the proceeds was clawed back for Henry to use for 'pious causes and other meritorious works', a good example of how a tough prince could shield his country from papal fiscalism.[22]

For the rest, as has been said, it was much more a question of Rome acceding to suits from England, granting the English clerics and layfolk their indulgences, dispensations and privileges, however egregious, whether for an 'unprecedented' royal plan to assign a quarter of the income of the bishopric of Durham to repair damage to the walls, houses, castle, etc. of Durham inflicted by the Scots, for blatant pluralism by careerist clerics (even for a twelve-year-old brother of the

21 Ibid., vol. 61, pp. 150–2.
22 Ibid., vol. 1, pp. 99–101.

marquis of Dorset to hold three incompatible benefices)[23] and most obviously for ever more extensive and 'unprecedented' grants of legatine authority to Wolsey. So it was not surprising that Henry VIII should have been taken aback when the otherwise compliant Rome demurred at finding his marriage invalid. There had been little sign previously of a tender conscience.

The primacy of Rome and the special authority of its bishop as successor to Peter, focal point of unity and vicar of Christ on earth were an accepted part of the scheme of things. Acknowledgement of papal authority came so easily off lips and pen, whenever it was appropriate, that it was clearly a commonplace. But it was not of much relevance or urgency. The average lay man or woman was scarcely more concerned to think about or defend the papal primacy than he or she was aware of or dismayed by the inadequacies and corruption of Renaissance Rome. These things were not denied, nor, when they were thought about, were they dismissed as unimportant; but religious interest lay elsewhere. It was focused mainly on other things — Purgatory, for example, and veneration of Mary and the saints — perhaps not least because Rome was distant (and, as has been argued, unobtrusive) and because pre-Reformation England apparently had no interest in anti-papal conciliarist ideas.

Like Protestantism, anti-papalism was more a consequence than a cause of the Reformation. 'No Popery' became deeply ingrained in the English character and as important to the Englishman's religious psychology as papalism had been unimportant to his ancestors. Like the 'Black Legend' and anti-Spanish sentiment it was partly the baleful result of events of the later sixteenth and seventeenth centuries, and partly the creation of assiduous and skilfully orchestrated propaganda.

The two or three generations before the onset of the Reformation was a period of unusual calm in the life of the Western Church, like the half-century before the Second Vatican Council, despite the gravity of events without. The

[23] Ibid., vol. 62, pp. 73–4, 105–9, 218–22.

storms of the conciliar movement had dispersed, though, on the Continent, conciliarism was scotched rather than dead. The tumults released by Wyclif and Hus had been contained. Remarkably, no new heresy stirred. No great causes were in debate.

England basked in this calm, this equilibrium, more than did most countries. The Church in England had its defects, moral and structural, but there were plenty of green shoots on the vine. And, above all, there was little sign of lay disenchantment with the ecclesiastical *ancien régime*, no angry alienation, no seething discontent, little expectation that the old order would not, could not and should not endure until the end of time.

Events were to show, of course, how vulnerable that old order was. But the vulnerability probably owed more to precisely that habitual acceptance of the old ways and unthinking presumption that they would continue until Kingdom come than to any large-scale hostility towards them. Indifference was probably more dangerous than anticlericalism. Few people (probably) felt real animosity towards the religious; but probably not many had a very profound appreciation of the religious life. Papal authority in England was at risk not so much because it was vexatious or offensive to national pride or whatever, as because it did not matter very much in daily life.

4

The Old Order Disintegrated

My argument is that the religious changes of the sixteenth century were acquiesced in and accepted by the English laity rather than initiated or promoted by them. Of course these changes could not have been carried through without some cooperation from 'below'. But the drive, timing and organisation came primarily from above.

The thunderbolts arrived suddenly and out of a fairly clear sky. That was the first reason for their success. Another was that, though they came thick and fast in the 1530s and then in Edward VI's reign, they picked off targets one by one and piecemeal. 'Absolute restraint' of annates in 1534 was preceded by an act of 1532 which had been 'conditional', i.e. had merely threatened to halt these payments to Rome (and face the consequences if Rome retaliated). The act of 1539 ratifying the dissolution of the larger monasteries had been preceded three years before by a statute which dissolved the smaller ones, and even that act had been tempered by frequent royal exemptions for houses which put up a fight. The final achievement of the royal supremacy in 1534 was the climax of five years of thrusting and manipulation, punctuated by several false starts, retreats and changes of tack. Above all, it was the peculiar character of the English Reformation that its first victories, the royal supremacy and the destruction of the religious orders, officially owed nothing and in practice little to Protestantism. Though the Ten Articles of 1536, the first statement of the supreme head of the faith of that new institution, the Church of England, had an alarmingly Lutheran ring to it, and eventually English monks and nuns were being required to repudiate the religious life on the Protestant grounds that it was vain and impious, these were but premonitions of things to come and at odds with the rest of royal policies. To the astonishment and disappointment of continental Protestants, England failed to declare for their cause during Henry VIII's reign, even though he had apparently taken the first strides towards it and logically could not stop there. But England did, more or less; and Henry indulged in negotiations with hopeful Protestants in Germany only when it served his political ends.

After the last of the monasteries went down there was a lull of seven years before the attack on chantries and guilds effectively began. There was a fifteen-year gap between the assertion of the royal supremacy and the repudiation of the mass. Shrines went in the later 1530s. But it was ten years later that the intercession of saints was finally forbidden. Some official hesitation was expressed in 1536 and 1538 about Purgatory, but it was not denied until Edward VI's reign. Had Rome, the mass, monasticism, chantries and guilds, saints and Purgatory (not to mention pilgrimages and paxes, indulgences and holy days, and so on) been put down together, in one fell swoop, what might the popular reaction have been?

There was plenty of bullying. Churchmen were bullied, collectively (as in the hectic days leading up to the first, and crucial, royal victory over the clerical estate in May 1532), and then individually.[1] The penalty for obstinacy, we must never forget, was imprisonment in local gaol or the Tower, and eventually a horrendous death. Fear was one of the king's best friends.

Of course, the Reformation was accomplished by statute. The claim that it sprang primarily from 'above', therefore, runs up against the fact that it was implemented through and with the consent of Parliament. Sadly, it is impossible to know much about what went on in the two houses in Henry VIII's reign and scarcely easier to know what happened in his son's, because of the lamentable dearth of surviving records. But perhaps the following things can be usefully said.

[1] Cf. M. J. Kelly, 'The Submission of the Clergy', *TRHS*, 5th ser., 15 (1965), 97–119; J. J. Scarisbrick, *Henry VIII* (1968), pp. 273–81, 329–31.

The image of Parliament as the arena in which the monarch and representatives of the political nation, by a process of give and take, worked out policies to their mutual satisfaction and profit, can make things too bland and amiable. We know there was opposition. We can catch glimpses of conflict – followed by royal retribution. We know, by chance, of a group of knights of the shire, led by Sir George Throckmorton of Warwickshire, who used to meet secretly at the Queen's Head in Fleet Street to discuss parliamentary tactics: an opposition group of five named men of considerable substance 'and others', who were in close touch with leading dissidents like More and Fisher. Sir George ended up in the Tower.[2]

Later, a Richard Fermor went to Marshalsea, convicted of misprision of treason and stripped of his worldly possessions. The ostensible reason for this was his support of a very papistical cleric in his native Northamptonshire who had stoutly maintained the pope's authority in public, had shouted down a neighbouring vicar when the latter was preaching against it, and had merely waxed over the word 'papa' in his service books, instead of erasing it completely. But the French ambassador thought that Fermor was being punished for opposition to the king's policies in Parliament.[3] We know that Throckmorton spoke out against the Act in Conditional Restraint of Annates in 1532 and that the major act of 1533, halting appeals from England to the Roman curia, also met some opposition. We are told that two MPs fled the country in 1540.[4]

Most members of the Reformation Parliament were townsmen representing their boroughs. It is likely that their major concern was with the particular interests of the communities they represented, with local rather than national issues. What would most of them have known or understood about such 'mysteries of state' as Henry's tussle with the hierarchy, his assault on the legislative independence of Convocation, his

[2] *LP*, xii, ii, 952. This important sidelight on the Reformation Parliament was first brought to our attention by G. R. Elton in 'Thomas More and the opposition to Henry VIII', *Bull. Inst. Hist. Res.*, xlvi (1968), 19–34.
[3] *LP*, xv, 697. The story of Fermor's misdeeds is given in KB 9/544 (rex), ro. 12.
[4] *LP*, xv, 697.

challenge to the pope's jurisdiction in England? What might many country gentlemen have known about these things? Annates and appeals to Rome would have been of little direct interest to them. What would they have made of the furious personal contretemps between their monarch and a pope they had neither seen nor heard? Is it surprising that such lay opposition as there was seems to have been centred on men like Sir George Throckmorton and fellow knights of the shire, like Sir William Essex, Sir Thomas Gifford and Sir Marmaduke Constable, men whose education and social rank would have supplied a wider knowledge of the world and some awareness of what was afoot at Westminster? And if an MP had agreed to that first step in 1532 (which, after all, was merely 'conditional', a suspended threat to be used as a bargaining weapon), it would have been difficult to jib at the second in 1533 and the third, fourth and so on thereafter. It would have been too late to turn back. Anyway, who were they — the mere burgesses — to gainsay a prince, especially one who was also 'Defender of the Faith'?

The crown apparently made little or no attempt to pack the Reformation Parliament by directly interfering in elections, but there was certainly subsequent pressure on members of both houses — fighters like John Fisher or George Throckmorton — to stay away from particular sessions. Others removed themselves out of fear. Hence the crown's most dangerous opponents were absent during crucial days in 1534, and most of the abbots and leading conservative peers were not in the upper house in 1536 when the first attack on the monasteries was launched.[5]

Henry probably expected Parliament to be as dutiful as his judges usually were whenever the outcome mattered, and hence to do what he wanted. His awesome presence brooded over it. We cannot know exactly how much he intervened, nor how much the presence of his ministers in both houses

---

[5]   See S. E. Lehmberg, *The Reformation Parliament, 1529–1536* (Cambridge, 1970), esp. pp. 253–4. I take a less rosy view of royal dealings with Parliament than does the author of this admirable book. In his *The Later Parliaments of the Reign of Henry VIII, 1536–1547* (Cambridge, 1977), pp. 3–10 and 41–46, he allows that there was some government influence on subsequent elections (though the evidence is difficult to interpret), particularly for the Parliament of 1539.

affected proceedings (because they could control much of the business, dominate debates and committees, etc.). Again, we can catch glimpses. We know how completely (and skilfully) the complicated episode which culminated in the first decisive capitulation of Convocation in 1532 was manipulated by the king and Thomas Cromwell; from the time when a revised version of what was originally a genuine (?) commons' complaint was reintroduced into the lower house as the 'Supplication against the Ordinaries', to the final submission of a brow-beaten 'rump' Convocation in May 1532.[6] Meanwhile, Henry had won the major victory in Parliament, too: the first inroad into England's allegiance to Rome, namely, the Annates Act of 1532, was a personal triumph. He came to Parliament and forced the first recorded division in parliamentary history — in effect inviting those who opposed him to stand up and make public defiance.[7] He was active in Parliament in 1536 and even more so in 1539, when he played a large part in pushing through the Act of Six Articles (as it happened, a conservative measure).

In short, there is repeated and widespread evidence of manipulation and bullying. And the initiative for the Reformation statutes almost always came from above. Perhaps the most striking confrontation, however, occurred in 1547, when the old king was dead and power lay in the hands of Protector Somerset.

An act for the dissolution of chantries, guilds and the like had been passed in 1545. Typically, it had not made a head-on assault on these institutions; that (presumably) would have been too provocative. Rather, it disarmingly empowered the king to dissolve only such chantries and the rest which had been victims of recent embezzlement or already wound up by private initiative. In accordance with the previous policy of gradualism, the crown was to acquire the possessions of only such chantries, etc., which had already had

---

[6]   G. R. Elton, 'The Commons' Supplication of 1532: Parliamentary Manoeuvres in the Reign of Henry VIII', *Eng. Hist. Rev.*, lxvi (1951), 507–34; Kelly, 'Submission of the Clergy'.

[7]   Lehmberg, *Reformation Parliament*, pp. 137–8. He had made three appearances in the Lords as well. He intervened vigorously in 1531 and again in 1533 to speed the Act of Appeals on its way. Scarisbrick, *Henry VIII*, p. 329n.

sentence of death passed on them by individual subjects.[8]

As we shall see, the mere fact that the crown was likely to be on the prowl again had frightened founders into themselves making off with what they could. The act itself, moreover, encouraged the very 'abuse' to which it purported to be a response. Doubtless this was foreseen. We are dealing here with a version of the self-fulfilling prophecy. However, it could still seem that nothing very radical or ungodly was intended. Furthermore, the crown was forced to accept an important limitation to the act: it would lapse with the king's death. Since Henry was obviously bloated with ill-health there was a good chance that the measure would never be implemented. In fact, he died before commissioners sent out to prospect and report back had been able to complete their work. The act therefore lapsed.

However, eleven months later, in December 1547, a new bill was introduced. This made a direct attack on institutions whose joints and foundations had already been loosened. It provided for the expropriation of all chantries, all guilds and fraternities (including 'secular' ones) and all surviving colleges of secular clergy. It also handed over to the crown all other endowments for obits and prayers for the dead.

This was a much more drastic measure than its cautious precursor, even though it did not include hospitals in its purview, as had the act of 1545. It struck at ordinary layfolk as no previous Reformation statute had done. It was precisely the sort of measure which burgesses would recognise as of direct consequence for their own communities and to which they would react. Not surprisingly, it provoked one of the most furious rows in Tudor parliamentary history.

Opposition to the bill was immediate. It was led by the burgesses of Coventry and Lynn. Their explicit concern was the defence of their guilds against the crown, not of chantries. But the representatives of these two towns evidently managed to rally such support that there was imminent danger not

---

[8] Even so, it encountered such opposition in the lower house (not, apparently, in the Lords) that the king's secretary, William Petre, reported that 'it escaped narrowly and was driven even to the last hour and yet then only passed by a division of this house.' *LP*, xx, ii, 1030 (2). We are not told on what ground the Commons resisted so furiously that a division, still an unusual procedure, was necessary.

only that the government's designs on the guild lands would be 'dashed' but that the whole bill would be thrown out. There was an alternative danger that, inspired by the men of Coventry and Lynn, others might have added so many last-minute provisos to the bill that what reached the statute book would scarcely have been worth having. And if London MPs had also joined in and added their leadership to the revolt the confrontation would have been complete.

Swift action was required. First, the bill was withdrawn and a new draft substituted which spared the ordinary craft and mercantile guilds (and hence the big livery companies of London — except so far as their overtly religious functions were concerned). That would have begun to defuse the situation. Next, important provisos were allowed to the new text, including one which exempted any institution whose possessions had been confirmed by the present monarch, Edward VI, or his father. That would have reassured quite a few. Then, Edward's mentor Protector Somerset (the person in charge of the whole business, of course), took the men of Coventry and Lynn aside and quietly promised them that, if they desisted from 'further speaking or labouring against the said article', their towns would be given back their guild lands once the act was passed. In other words, the leaders of the opposition were bought off.[9]

The tactics worked. The bill was passed by the commons on 21 December 1547. It was read three times on the same afternoon, doubtless by members eager to get home for Christmas. To use modern parlance, it was rail-roaded through after the lower house had been nobbled.

And after it had been bamboozled. A year after this bargain was struck with the government, Coventry had recovered the church of St John Bablake, the chapel of Holy Trinity guild, but no more. The promise to restore the rest of the lands and numerous town properties of that fraternity and the others had not been honoured. Angry and disillusioned, the city petitioned for what had been denied it. Eventually, in September 1552, it was granted a large collection of former chantry, obit *and* guild lands

[9] *Acts of the Privy Council, 1547–50*, pp. 193–5. Cf. Kreider, *English Chantries*, pp. 187–208.

within its boundaries, to the value of £169. The understanding of 1547 had been that these would be returned as a gift. In the event, however, the city had to pay over £1,300 to recover what it had been solemnly promised nearly five years previously; and the recovered lands also carried a rent to the crown of £90 a year.[10] Coventry had been duped.

Any attempt to understand how the English Reformation 'happened' must turn most attention to the dissolution of the monasteries, for this was the capital event. It affected daily life more deeply and widely than did the breach with Rome and was more difficult to repair. England had been a land of fair abbeys, had poured much wealth and many skills into building them; and it owed much to them. If they could be struck down there was nothing that was safe or sacrosanct. England without monks, friars and nuns was an England that had indeed turned its back on the past. Yet English monasticism was destroyed, and in under four years.

It is an arresting fact, however, that little responsibility for this can be laid at Parliament's door, even though it passed two acts of dissolution of monasteries. The first, of 1536, affected only smaller houses, those with an annual income of less than £200.[11] Since its preamble claimed that these houses were being put down only because they were dens of vice, since it thanked Almighty God that in larger houses — to which inmates of smaller ones could transfer — the religious life was 'right well and truly kept', and since it empowered the king to exempt from its operation those smaller houses which were found to be in decent condition after all, some could have supposed that the act was intended to improve English monastic life, not to prepare the way for its obliteration. A naive person (and perhaps the many who trusted the king) could have been lulled into thinking that the act was a piece of genuine reform of the sort that, say, even a Thomas More or John Fisher would have approved, and marked the conclusion of the purge of hopelessly decrepit houses that

[10] *CPR, Edward VI*, iv, 337–8.
[11] Text in *Statutes of the Realm*, iii, 575ff. It is important to note that the act carefully protected rights of 'founders', leaseholders, annuitants and all other lay interests, etc., a fact which surely eased its passage.

had been taking place on and off for decades, especially in the previous decade under Thomas Wolsey. Moreover, after the act was passed a considerable number of houses were indeed granted (i.e. sold) exemption; *and* there were official denials that any further dissolution was intended.[12]

So this first, crucial act could have been easily misinterpreted by the unwary, and even by wordly-wise knights of the shire, let alone more innocent burgesses. Furthermore, the bill's passage had been carefully stage-managed. As it was introduced, the Commons were given a resumé of the highly coloured reports of royal visitors who had been touring monasteries at great speed in previous months and collecting 'evidence'. The stories of vice and decay apparently so shocked the members that there were (spontaneous?) shouts for action. To complete the scenario, Henry himself (probably, at any rate) appeared in the house to commend the bill in person.[13]

Three years later the second act was passed, which dealt with the remaining houses. But this was largely retrospective in effect, because many of the survivors, the larger houses, had been dissolving themselves in the meantime. They had been surrendering individually to the royal agents. So had the friars. The act of 1539, though it did indeed authorise further surrenders by the remnant which still stood, was more important for its confirmation of the royal title to those houses which monks, nuns and friars had already made over to the crown. It gave statutory legitimation to what was already, in large measure, a *fait accompli*.

Certainly there had been many critics of monks and friars and much grumbling about 'abbey lubbers' and so on. Monasticism may no longer have enjoyed as honoured and conspicuous a place in English life as it had once done; but that is a long way from saying that it had been repudiated. It was not an 'avenging' laity which precipitated its downfall.

[12] Thus in January 1538, Richard Layton (one of the royal visitors) told Cromwell how he had denounced as 'vain babbling' and slander of their 'natural sovereign' rumours in Cambridge that all houses would fall. *LP*, xiii, i, 102. An official account of events a year later repeated the assurance that total expropriation was not intended. *LP*, xiv, i, 402. Much wool was pulled over many eyes.

[13] Cf. Lehmberg, *Reformation Parliament*, pp. 225—7. The story was told (some years after the event) by Hugh Latimer (*Sermons*, PS, 19 (1844), i, 123).

Critics had always been noisy. But another kind of layman's attitude to the religious is well illustrated by one Michael Sherbrook, a minister of the Established Church, who, in the latter part of Elizabeth's reign, wrote a book about the dissolution. The story that follows is a familiar one;[14] nonetheless it bears retelling.

For Sherbrook the whole thing had been a disaster: moral, social and economic. Such pungent and, one would have thought, imprudent views need not detain us. One of his asides may, when he tells how he had asked his father, who had joined in the final despoiling of the local abbey of Roche in Yorkshire, about what had gone on in his mind when he was taking part in the pillage. Michael put two questions. The first was whether his father, up to that time, had thought well of the religious and of 'religion then used'. His father said, 'yea'; he had thought well of them. Then, asked the son, 'how came it to pass that you were so ready to distroy and spoil the thing that you thought well of?' To this excellent question the father made a celebrated reply. He had done what he did because everybody else was doing it. 'What should I do?', he protested. 'Might I not as well as others have some profit of the spoil of the abbey? For I did see all would away; and therefore I did as others did.'

Those who have told this story before have usually underlined the last part of the story ('I did as others did'). But perhaps the more telling piece is that clear statement that the father had previously had no animus against monks and monasteries. He had thought well of them; but once his local house had been condemned, its inmates paid off by the royal commissioners and the building gutted, he joined in the mass scramble for loot. This is a precious insight, and it helps us to read with fresh eyes some of those begging letters which came upon Henry and Cromwell thick and fast when the monasteries began to fall.

Take the one from Thomas Lord Audley, written in September 1538.[15] It began with a plea that the two large houses in his county of Essex, namely, Colchester and

---

[14] It is to be found in A. G. Dickens (ed.), *Tudor Treatises*, Yorks. Arch. Soc., 125 (1959), 125.

[15] *LP*, xiii, ii, 306.

St Osyth's, should be allowed to stand, not as Benedictine houses but as colleges of secular priests. Like more than one correspondent, Audley was apparently innocent enough to believe that Henry was hostile simply to monks and monasticism and not bent on seizing their possessions.[16] So he pleaded that the houses should continue, under new management, since Colchester gave daily relief to 'many pour people', both houses gave needed hospitality to their end of the shire and both were crucial to the well-being of their surrounding communities. Moreover, while making the 'translation', the king could cream off £2,000 income from the two houses and would have all the appointments to the new colleges in his gift!

Audley insisted that their survival could bring no material advantage to himself. As he explained, he had already been allowed to exchange lands and 'thynges' with them. He declared himself satisfied. Even though his request, pressed hard more than once, was accompanied by the offer to Cromwell of a large douceur of £200, it is difficult to see that it was completely insincere. As we shall see, the idea of converting abbeys into 'colleges' was put about by the king for probably discreditable purposes: Audley apparently welcomed it because it would protect that part of the realm for which he had some responsibility for 'good lordship' from what could be the serious consequences of complete suppression of the former houses. If he had all along been set on gaining these prizes for himself his best bet would have been to have denounced them as dens of vice and parasites on the community, which he did not.

Nonetheless Audley did later ask for St Osyth's for himself. Four months after writing the letter just quoted, he was begging Cromwell for a grant of the very house which he had several times also begged should stand (albeit as a secular college).[17] Like Michael Sherbrook's father, Audley had no animus against these houses; on the contrary, he insisted that both played an important role in their localities. But (and this is the point) if they were doomed he could not stand aside and let others overtake him. As letters from

[16] See below, pp. 77–9.
[17] *LP*, xiv, ii, 775.

others confirm, what occasioned the scramble, the 'gold-rush' fever, was not just greed. Without sounding too perverse, it is even possible to suggest that some may have been reluctant (at least initially) to join in the bonanza, because of the disruption involved and because the necessary capital could perhaps have been raised only by selling off bits and pieces here and there or by incurring expensive debts. But family honour and the rights of 'founders' (i.e. their descendants) were often at stake. The inescapable claims of clients pressed, and the local balance of power, the 'pecking order', was at stake. Only Audley should have St Osyth's, if St Osyth's must fall. Or, as Sir Richard Grenville explained, though a suitor like him might have taken no part in putting down the houses, he subsequently clamoured for his share of the spoils above all because of that social imperative, the need to be in the same 'case' as other men — and, he might have added, not to be outshone by inferiors.[18]

There are no examples in England of the dissolution unleashing pent-up violence against monks and nuns or of mobs ransacking religious houses as they were vacated, as was to happen elsewhere. On the contrary, what little violence there was came from supporters of the old religion. There were the women in Exeter who fell upon the royal commissioners preparing for the dissolution of the local houses and locked them inside a church.[19] There was the abbot of Norton in Cheshire, who attacked the royal agents as they were packing up the abbey's jewels and plate with 200 men and forced them to barricade themselves in the tower. When the sheriff turned up with a posse to rescue the king's men he found the abbot and companions roasting a celebratory ox in the abbey precincts.[20] Some violence was used against monks during the rebellions of 1536; but this was the reaction of rebels angered by the refusal of monks to give support — money, food and so on — to a rebellion mounted not least to defend them against royal

---

[18] Printed in J. Youings, *The Dissolution of the Monasteries* (1971), p. 229.

[19] See ibid., pp. 164—5. The women attacked the commisioners with shovels and pikes, 'minding to stop the suppressing of that house', St Nicholas's priory. Subsequent efforts to explain away the incident as merely an attempt to stop two Bretons pulling down a crucifix in the church do not ring true.

[20] *LP*, xi, 681, 787.

depredation. An abbey which closed its gates could understandably be in trouble: it was a traitor to the cause.[21]

An impressive number of layfolk wrote letters begging for houses to be spared — or, if that were unacceptable to the king, that they should continue in some new form and their resources, in whole or part, be retained for such good purposes as providing preachers, educating local youth, or providing additional chapels of ease. It was not just local people who made these proposals. Dr London, one of the leading royal commissioners, often pleaded what may be called the 'commonwealth' cause and begged on behalf of towns like Northampton and Coventry that the king's appetite should be restrained.[22] Most interesting of all are the letters of the second set of commissioners, mainly local gentlemen, appointed in 1536 to follow up the work of the notorious royal visitors who had carried out the first whirlwind enquiry into the religious some months before. Their verdict on the state of the houses concerned was almost always at odds with what the earlier visitation had reported (and far less damning).[23] They often made urgent pleas for houses to be spared. Two of the commissioners, George Gifford, who wrote on behalf of houses in Northampton, and Sir Thomas Arundel, who implored mercy for a house in Cornwall, knew that they would be accused by the king of having been bribed by the monks and nuns concerned.[24] They had a strong reason, therefore, for not writing as they did. Like Dr London later, they were putting their careers at risk. Hence their testimony must carry some weight.

Monasticism had not been repudiated by the laity. Of course it is naive to suppose that the reasons for protecting religious houses were all 'religious' in the loftiest sense of

[21] It is wrong to think that monks joined the Pilgrimage of Grace (if at all) only reluctantly. The abbot of the Cistercian house of Holmcultram (Cumbs) urged his tenants join the insurrection, held processions in church for their success and went in person to Carlisle to urge its surrender, seeing all this as a way to save his abbey. *VCH, Cumbs.*, ii, 170–1.

[22] E.g. *LP*, xiii, ii, 367; xiv, i, 3(5), 42.

[23] Knowles, *Religious Orders*, iii, 298–302, 480–2.

[24] *LP*, x, 916–17; xii, 4. When Gifford, with others, including Robert Burgoyne, had written begging that two other houses in Northants be spared (*LP*, x, 858), Henry said they must have been bribed. So when he wrote on behalf of another house, Gifford (like Arundel) knew what he was risking. Cf. *LP*, x, 551, 787.

that word. As well as being centres of prayer (and perhaps hallowed burial places of ancestors), they were centres of employment and consumption, they were havens — or repositories — for younger brothers, 'surplus' sons and unmarried daughters. They were trustees for corrodies (annuities) for aged dependants and pious bequests; they often supplied 'hospitality', served travellers and attracted pilgrims; they were familiar objects on the skyline, reassuring and often beautiful. A dozen and one considerations could have led to defending them, and an equal number of anxieties and fears: fear of what might happen to stranded ex-religious who were also daughters, sons or cousins, and so on; fears of what an abbey's demise might do to local balance of interest and power; fear lest outsiders, London money-lenders or courtiers might intrude; fear that the pattern and fabric of local life might be so badly torn that nothing would be the same again. Fear, in other words, that a Pandora's box was being opened.

Tudor England had its fair share of men and women who would despoil the sacred and beautiful without too many qualms. It had its mockers and scoffers, as well as its vandals — but it had only its fair share. This was not a time of especial depravity, boorishness or greed. True enough, layfolk were to fall upon the monastic spoils with uncommon speed and few blushes, once those spoils were on display. There is no sign of predatory designs before then. The opportunity created the appetite, the supply the demand.

It is wrong to see the religious houses going down like a house of cards at the puff of a king. Some eighty of the smaller houses which came within the compass of the act of 1536 fought successfully, and at no small expense, to be exempted. Others tried and failed.

The Observant Franciscans and the Carthusians had already been severely mauled before that act was passed.[25] Ten houses were forcibly suppressed after the Pilgrimage of Grace, when, with dubious legality, houses were declared

---

[25] And hence potentially dangerous centres of opposition had been dealt with beforehand.

forfeit to the crown by reason of the attainder of their governors. Big houses like Woburn and Lenton fell only after their abbots and some of the monks had been put to death. The abbots of Glastonbury, Colchester and Reading were hanged at their abbeys.

The larger houses were picked off individually from late 1537 to early 1540. Some undoubtedly fell because, following the death or deposition of a former abbot and a (rigged?) election, a pliable successor was installed. Evesham and Welbeck, to pick out two random examples, were badly weakened by the appointment of royal nominees. The collapse of some other houses came easily probably not least because of the generous pensions which were awarded to their governors. Elsewhere intense pressure could be applied, with the royal visitors sometimes virtually laying siege to a house, interrogating the inmates in order to rake up scandal or set community against abbot, making threats and giving bribes. Isolated from the outside world, knowing little about how brethren in the rest of the order were faring and unable to make common cause with neighbouring houses, they had little chance of surviving long. Even so, some fought hard. In September 1538, for example, Cromwell was told by his agent how he had laboured unsuccessfully for three months to get the abbot of Darley in Derbyshire to submit. The abbot of Cerne Abbas in December 1538, brushing aside pressures, offered Henry 500 marks and Thomas Cromwell £100 for his monastery to be allowed to survive.[26] The abbot of Combermere in Cheshire was actually summoned to London to surrender his house, but arrived asking that he and his brethren be allowed to continue in their monastery.[27]

Perhaps the most interesting incident of all occurred in June 1537 when the small nunnery of Wallingwells, near Worksop in Nottinghamshire, which had already paid heavily for exemption from suppression under the act of 1536, concluded an agreement with a Yorkshire gentleman called Oglethorpe whereby they would lease to him their entire possessions for twenty-one years and in return he would

[26] *LP*, xiii, ii, 408; *ibid.*, 1092.
[27] *LP*, xiii, i, 969, 1087.

allow them to continue to use the convent buildings. He was also to provide them with a chaplain, a prioress's maid, another maid for the nuns, a cook and a butler, and a weekly allowance of bread and corn. He was to supply four fat swine, six calves, twenty sheep and six stone of cheese a year, plus adequate salt and 40s. for purchase of fish. The prioress was to receive one load of coal, ten of wood and twelve pounds of candles: her sisters twelve loads of coal, twenty of wood and candles. Finally, the convent was to have four cows.[28]

The nuns, having previously purchased a stay of execution from the crown, were clearly trying to avoid extinction by making this detailed arrangement with a sympathetic layman. Presumably the lease to Oglethorpe was implicit recognition that they had no right in canon or common law to alienate permanently the convent and its possessions; and twenty-one years could have seemed long enough to see them through the storms that raged. The manoeuvre did not work, the convent fell.[29] But perhaps the most striking thing is that it should ever have been tried, let alone by a small community of women.

The incident gives sudden new insight into the capitulation of the religious and causes one to think again about those other conveyances of monastic property which had taken place on the eve of the act of 1536 and which that act declared null and void. It has often been assumed that these were last-minute favours to friends and relatives by prudent monks who were thinking of their own futures *after* they had been expelled from the comfort of monastic life. In the same way the clandestine sales of monastic plate, the sudden felling of trees and so on were presumably carried out with one eye on rainy days ahead (and perhaps to spite the king). However, this may not be the whole story. The act talks about 'feoffments, estates, grants and leases' having been 'fraudulently and craftily' made by religious not so much to cushion themselves after closure of their houses but 'for the

---

[28] W. Dugdale (ed.), *Monasticon Anglicanum* (1718), iv, 298–9. Remarkably, Knowles failed to note this story, though it is given in *VCH, Notts.*, ii, 90.
[29] Though not until December 1539 — very late. Margaret Goldsmith, the prioress, had put up £66 13s.4d., more than a whole year's income, to secure exemption from the act of 1536. *LP*, xiii, ii, 457, i (3).

maintenance of their detestable lives', which seems to mean that, 'dreading the suppressing' of their monasteries, they had taken all manner of evasive action in order to continue in existence. If those 'feoffments' included feoffments to use, that is, transfer of legal title to trustees (feoffees) while allowing continued use by the grantors (the monks), the religious would have been employing a familiar legal device in order to frustrate the crown. We may never know whether this was happening in the months before the act was passed and, if so, on what scale; but it must be likely that other communities had tried vainly to do what Wallingwells later attempted, and, in order to stay together, colluded with layfolk to alienate or lease possessions to them in return for continued use of monastic buildings and a supply of food and other necessities. The statutes of 1536 and 1539 did not outlaw monasticism (i.e. the religious life) itself; they took away the lands of monks and nuns. If there were monks and nuns who could show that they had no legal title to any earthly goods they would have been free to continue to live in their cloisters.

Three further points must be made about the demise of the monasteries. First, as has been mentioned, it was still being officially denied, months after the final attack on the remaining monasteries had begun, that total suppression was intended: an assurance (apparently fortified by the fact that there had indeed been a trickle of royal refoundations in the interim) which doubtless caused some to drop their guard. Secondly, in its dealing with the religious, the government often seemed to have the best interests of monasticism at heart. For instance, the royal visitation of 1535 had been accompanied by 'injunctions' concerning monastic life and observance which were apparently intended to reform and purify.[30] Even as late as 1538 a royal visitor could seem to have come in order to mend rather than destroy.[31] Thirdly, the crown put it about that, when it turned its attention to the larger monasteries, it had high-minded plans for turning them into 'colleges' where preachers would be maintained and youth educated, etc. This was a widespread expectation.

[30] Printed in Youings, *Dissolution*, pp. 149–52. See Knowles, *Religious Orders*, pp. 275–9 for comments.
[31] *LP*, xii, ii, 56.

A house near Pontefract, for instance, quickly volunteered for this metamorphosis. Cambridge university made a strong bid for endowments. Bishop Latimer of Worcester, excited by the idea (as a Protestant would be, of course) of providing for preachers, urged that the Benedictine house at Great Malvern be converted to these new uses. Similar ideas came forward from Coventry.[32] The abbot and convent of Evesham formally petitioned that their fine establishment should follow suit.[33] And, as has already been noted, Lord Audley pleaded that the two large houses of Colchester and St Osyth's should be allowed to survive as colleges. This is what at least some people thought the king intended.[34] In other words, when the attack on the remaining houses, the larger ones, began, it could have seemed that full-scale destruction and secularisation were not intended, so much as conversion to new, and primarily religious, ends. Since there were also plans for converting some of the larger monastic churches into cathedrals, many of these other houses may have been lulled into surrendering in the belief that they were to be reconstituted, rather than destroyed. Moreover, many monks would have found it harder to stand firm when faced with proposals which were apparently enlightened and likely to benefit religion. They may honestly have believed that they were not handing over their houses to profane lay use. When the act of 1539 went through Parliament (easily, it seems), was it important that there should have been rushed through at the same time another act indeed converting some former monastic churches into secular cathedrals? This measure, its preamble written by Henry himself and promising even better things to come — endowment of preachers, schools, Greek and Hebrew studies, poor relief, highways, etc. — could have given a quite false impression of royal intentions and greatly reassured waverers. As actually executed, the dissolution was not what many folk had expected or what perhaps most MPs (i.e. those looking

---

[32] *LP*, xiii, ii, 285, 593 and 677, 1036; xiv, i, 183.

[33] *LP*, xiv, i, 1191 (repeating *LP*, xiii, i, 866).

[34] The petition from Evesham explicitly says that the writers understand that it is the king's intention to convert monasteries for these new uses. Cambridge University thought so, too, and told Cromwell that his own words had encouraged them in this hope (*LP*, xiii, ii, 677).

for foundation of colleges and so on) had thought they were voting for.[35]

Henry was later to explain to Scotland's rulers how they should set about the extinction of religious life in their land. He stressed the need to keep intentions 'very close and secret', else the clergy would use all kinds of tactics to thwart their opponent. Next, faithful commissioners should be sent round the monasteries 'as it were [i.e. seemingly] to put a good order in the same', but really to 'get knowledge of all their abominations'. After that the prince, 'with the chief of the noble men', should agree to share the lands of the abbeys among them, 'to their great profit and honour', and also win over the bishops with promise of 'some augmentation' of their resources. Finally, the religious themselves should be offered 'reasonable' financial recompense for quitting.[36]

Thus, to a striking extent, was the suppression made 'the more easy and facile' (to use Henry's words) in England also. But if we remember how skilfully the operation was directed, if to all those houses which bought or tried to buy exemption from the acts of 1536 we add those put down by violence, those brought down by bullying and manipulation (especially by introducing pliant new heads of houses) and those which strove to survive, and if we then recall the generous pensions for the co-operative and the penalty (death by hanging, even on the abbey gate) for the obstinate, the story of the demise of the religious orders in England perhaps has a different look to it.

It is still true, of course, that many monks and nuns and friars walked out of their houses apparently without batting an eyelid. Some had probably gone in involuntarily in the first place in obedience to parental command and social habit, and had had little or no vocation to the religious life. Conversely many who were reluctant to quit may have been

---

[35] In the autumn of 1539 there was still talk of new bishoprics *and colleges* to be erected by the king. *LP*, xiv, ii, 429/30 lists some candidates for collegiate status, so perhaps there were genuine plans for this conversion of at least some larger religious houses. Cf. the French ambassador Marillac's report in May 1539 (when the act for dissolution of larger houses was before Parliament) that members wanted 'certain abbeys' to be converted to serve as schools and hospitals (*LP*, xiv, i, 988).

[36] *LP*, xv, 136; xviii, i, 364.

held back by fear of the outside world (this could obviously have been true of women with nowhere to go and the vow of celibacy still binding them), by attachment to a comfortable routine and by many other considerations which could not be described as 'religious' in any worthwhile sense. Yet others may not have thought very much at all about what was happening. They may have been caught in a whirlwind — simply swept out of the cloister into the profane world — or, to change the metaphor, stampeded into quitting because everyone else was. We must always remember how fast it all happened — a mere three and a half years. We must make the effort of imagination to visualise a society innocent of modern communications and media, and therefore unable quickly to know much about what was happening nationally, unable to consult, to plan collectively, to call up distant help, and so on. In such situations purposeful governments served by fast-moving and well-briefed agents have a clear advantage over their subjects. What was previously unthinkable or, if thought, impossible can be accomplished almost before most people have realised it has begun.

The dynamics of change are often unpredictable and inexplicable. We can remark, for instance, some of the things that overtook the Roman Catholic community in the decade or so following the Second Vatican Council — the buffeting of many of the religious orders, the decimation of seminaries, the departure from the ministry of secular priests by the hundred. These were not only unintended by the Council but could never have been predicted when it began. Indeed, it was those religious orders, male and female, that seemed most serene and were most prestigious, and it was precisely those parts of the Church where morale was the highest that suffered the most severe ravages. How far and why the Council occasioned all this is not our concern, so much as the fact that it played a crucial role and that a unique convergence of ideas, aspirations, discontents and euphoria, an unplanned conjunction of currents and tensions, caused sudden changes which no one had envisaged and which left many bewildered. For some, something similar was happening in the 1530s. The influence of events on the Continent where the Reformation gathered momentum, the toll of Erasmian humanist criticism, the confrontation between king and pope, king and Church, the executions, the political uncertainties, the first attack on monasticism and so on, unsteadied and undermined.[37] By the late 1530s men and women were walking out of a past not because they had been pining to do so for years but because it had suddenly become mentally and psychologically possible to do so. A world and way of life therein, which could have sailed on with commendable success and to the unquestioning satisfaction of most of those involved, suddenly fell apart.

To accept all this is to allow to the Tudor state perhaps more power to shape and coerce than is fashionable today. In fact, it is to recognise that Tudor government, though almost laughably ineffectual and sketchy from some points of view (and, of course, by modern standards) could also often be astonishingly efficient and formidable, particularly when directed by a Thomas Cromwell.

Most lay people acquiesced in the Reformation because they hardly knew what was going on, were understandably reluctant to jeopardise life or limb, a career or the family's good name. Some probably would not have cared even if they had known. Many would have presumed that everything would 'blow over' and eventually things revert to age-old normality. They felt, no doubt, a basic loyalty to the monarch (though not many had ever seen him or had any personal feelings towards him); they were more or less abandoned by a pope about whom they knew even less.

The upheavals were not the result of some long-term and growing discontent which, containable no more, eventually heaved over the old order. Pre-Reformation English society, as its history abundantly shows, was certainly not a static one. But like many other traditional, pre-industrial societies before and since it was one which found the idea of change very difficult to fit into the scheme of things: alien, dangerous. In the 1530s such a society was required to cope with change

---

[37] And so, of course, would the sincere expectation of some that the ex-monastic wealth would be put to such admirable and urgent ends as provision of schools galore, relief of poverty, hospitals, etc., which all the talk about conversion of abbeys into 'colleges', already discussed, would have kept alive. Cf. Scarisbrick, *Henry VIII*, pp. 511–26.

on a scale and of an intensity which it had never before encountered. The topsy-turveydom continued in the late 1540s, 1550s and beyond.

In 1536 the largest rebellion in English history took place. The Pilgrimage of Grace was above all a protest against change, a conservative rebellion, a desperate attempt to restore what had been pulled down and protect what still stood. It was 'religious' in the widest sense of the word, that is, it was a protest on behalf of the old religion (above all in defence of the monasteries), though the reasons for clinging to the old ways may well have ranged from the highest and most unwordly to the most profane. And religion held it together, giving a multi-class rebellion what little unity and coherence it had — though that is not to deny that inevitably all manner of secular and local issues were caught up in it and criss-crossed the larger purposes.[38]

It could have toppled the regime had it moved southwards. East Anglia might have joined; Wales was far from secure. A butcher in Windsor was hanged in front of the castle for showing sympathy for the Pilgrims.[39] In Cornwall a priest was reported to have had a banner painted showing the Five Wounds: the Pilgrims' banner.[40] The failure of the Pilgrimage of Grace was perhaps more decisive than we can ever know, just as its occurrence showed how deeply a society could be attached to old ways and how resentful of outside threats to them.

The same fact was demonstrated in 1549 — and to say that is to step into no less of a minefield. The rebellions of that year certainly consisted in part, in East Anglia, in a rising that was economic in purpose and, if anything, had Protestant overtones. The rest were of a different hue, though exactly what that was is almost as difficult as determining the full geography of events.

[38] I stand by a previous view of the Pilgrimage, therefore, and am not convinced by a recent (and ingenious) reinterpretation of its genesis (as a last-fling protest from the north of a disaffected 'Aragonese' faction, led by Lord Darcy, which had failed to unseat Cromwell, etc., at the centre and thus resorted to provincial rebellion). So G. R. Elton has argued in 'Politics and the Pilgrimage of Grace', in B. Malament (ed.), *After the Reformation* (Manchester, 1980), pp. 25–56.

[39] *VCH, Berks.*, iii, 13.

[40] *LP*, xii, 1001. Apparently some people might have risen to 'have their holy-days' i.e. to restore holy days threatened by royal injunctions.

The Western Rebellion of 1549 was much more than a protest against a Prayer Book in English which Cornishmen could not understand. The rebels asked that all decrees of General Councils, all 'holy decrees of our forefathers' should be observed and restored. They asked for the mass in Latin, for prayers for the souls in Purgatory as of yore, for half the abbey and chantry lands to be recovered and two abbeys to be set up once more in every county in those places where once major houses stood. They wanted the blessed sacrament to hang over the high altar as of old 'and there to be worshipped'. They wanted their holy bread and holy water once more, their palms and ashes, their old statues and 'all other ancient old ceremonies used heretofore by our holy mother Church'.[41]

Their conservatism went to lengths which will offend modern liberals: they did not want the laity to communicate at the restored mass and they wanted only the celebrant to communicate normally at mass. The laity were to receive only at Easter and then only in one kind. The vernacular Bible was to be taken away, otherwise heretics would 'not of long time' be confounded.

The rising spread to the Midlands — Berkshire, Buckinghamshire, Oxford and into Northamptonshire. It is impossible to know how many were involved, or exactly where or why.[42] But the Privy Council was obviously intensely nervous and rightly fearful lest the rebels in the south-west should join forces with those of the Midlands. After order was restored the ringleaders were ordered to be executed: Oxford's

[41] Cranmer, *Works*, ii, PS 24 (1846), 163ff. Cf. J. Cornwall, *The Revolt of the Peasantry, 1549* (1977), for a recent account.

[42] Certainly economic grievances played a major part. No gentlemen joined (as in 1536); the ringleaders were humble folk. But the fact that four clergy were among the fourteen executed in Oxfordshire makes it likely that religious issues were involved. Obscure (and wild) plans were uncovered in August 1549 for a rising around Winchester which, having been joined by men from Sussex, would strike westwards and join up somehow with the Western rising. For this there was apparently clerical backing, *and* a banner prepared with the five wounds of Christ, a chalice and host, 'and a prest knelyng to yt upon the same banner'. SP 10/8, no. 41. So 'religion', in perhaps its widest sense, was involved here. And there was a protest in East Yorkshire against the suppression of chantries. Thus, difficult though the whole story is to interpret, it seems just to argue that religious conservatism animated, in varying degrees, many of the 'stirs' of 1549.

in Banbury, Bicester, Bloxham, Islip, Chipping Norton, Deddington, Thame, Watlington and Oxford itself. They included Henry Matthews, parson of Deddington, the vicars of Duns Tew and Chipping Norton, and John Wade, parson of Bloxham. The last two were to be hanged from the steeples of their churches.[43]

There was a third rising, in 1569: a third rebellion on behalf of the old order.[44] Like the others, it is difficult to interpret; like them (and particularly the second), often underestimated by historians; like them, testimony to the fact that, though England eventually acquiesced in the new ways, it did so only after not a few had put up a spirited resistance.

[43] SP 10/8, no. 32.
[44] See below, pp. 145–7, for further discussion.

5

The Spoliation

Between 1536 and 1553 there was destruction and plunder in England of beautiful, sacred and irreplaceable things on a scale probably not witnessed before or since. First, those hundreds of often massive and glorious buildings which had housed monks and nuns for centuries were razed, gutted or left without windows, roofs and stairs, for the elements to claim or new lay owner or local folk to despoil at their leisure; the inmates gone, the landed possessions seized by the crown, the lead and bells stripped, the cattle and household goods like beds, tables, kitchenware and everyday linen auctioned on site, the more valuable vestments, altar frontals, mitres and staffs, the plate, jewels and *objets d'art* sent off to London. Next, the shrines of Becket, Cuthbert, Edward, Richard, William and all the others, as well as the shrines of Our Lady, went down. From Canterbury alone came pearls, diamonds and emeralds galore, nine rings and a 'fair comb of gold' set with stones, plus Becket's 'staff' (set with pearls and stones), not to mention copes and other vestments. These were delivered into Henry's own hands by the treasurer of the Court of Augmentations, together with two altar frontals of cloth of gold (with gold embroidered lions and fleurs de lis), a canopy of cloth of gold, five bejewelled copes and their sets of mass vestments, fifteen other copes of cloth of gold or similar and an agate dish garnished with gold and precious stones from Westminster Abbey.[1]

Then came the attack on, and partial disendowment of,

[1] E116/10, no. 31.

the secular colleges like Beverley, Warwick, St Stephen's in Westminster, concluded and finally ratified by the act of 1547 which, of course, brought about the dissolution of guilds, surviving colleges, free chapels and chantries and placed them — and endowments of obits and 'services' (for requiem masses) — in the crown's hands. Their lands and halls were forfeit, as well as the lead, bells and stone of their chapels. Their less valuable possessions, furniture and live-stock, were sold off on the spot; their plate, richer vestments and ready cash following the path to the Jewel House or Court of Augmentation in Westminster which the possessions of monasteries and shrines had previously taken. The dissolu-tion of guilds and chantries, in that most were located inside parish churches (only the largest had their own buildings), prepared the way for the next phase, namely, the purging of parish churches of their Catholic furnishings, their high altars and remaining side altars, their statues, wall-paintings, holy-water stoups, and so on. These were dismantled, smashed or defaced. Down came roods and the statues of Mary and John on either side of the Crucifixion; the 'doom' (a picture of the Last Judgement) behind was whitewashed or removed; missals, graduals and antiphonaries were put away, their jewels, gold-leaf illumination and silver clasps and hinges cut off.

Finally, when Protestantism had been officially erected and the old liturgy expunged, the government embarked on the last act of spoliation and began to strip the parish churches of their remaining treasure, which they had cer-tainly had their eye on for some years. Early in 1553 the signal went out to royal commissioners in all the counties to seize for the king surviving mass vestments, sacred vessels, ornaments and so on of the parish churches, leaving every church with the bare minimum of plate for the new, simple communion service and a sufficient number of surplices and other cloth. As the young Edward VI lay dying in July 1553, there were trundling down the roads towards London, presumably under escort, cartloads of chalices, pyxes and paxes, silver sensers and incense boats, candlesticks, cruets and processional crosses, and wagon-loads of chasubles and copes of cloth of gold and silver (many richly embroidered with previous stones), bejewelled altar frontals, palls and reliquaries, or simply the precious thread and stones ripped off them — the wealth of medieval piety and, many of these objects, the finest work of generations of craftsmen and needlewomen.

A few random statistics will give some idea of the scale of those operations. The five great abbeys of Bury St Edmunds, Ely, Ramsey, Peterborough and Crowland between them yielded two-thirds of a ton of silver. Bury also produced 1,553 ounces of gold.[2] The 'shrine plate' of St Albans weighed 2,165 ounces, and the abbey also yielded a further 3,327 ounces of silver gilt, as well as plenty of rich vestments.[3] The fraternities, chantries, chapels and colleges in the West Riding of Yorkshire suppressed under the act of 1547 yielded 1,611 ounces of plate to the Jewel House and 29 fodders of lead, of which eight were given to the earl of Shrewsbury and the rest sold off at £4 each. Ten guilds in Durham produced 24 silver chalices. From London's guilds and chantries and the rest the Jewel House received over a hundredweight of plate and the Court of Augmentations £279 from the sale of ornaments on site. When it was the turn of London's parish churches to be purged (in 1553) the royal commissioners made off with 162 lbs of plate. About a fifth as much came from Wiltshire's churches. Devon's shed 288 chalices, 47 crosses, 154 pyxes, 34 incense boats and 56 sets of vestments, besides £468-worth of vestments and metal sold on site.[4] The meticulous and often beautifully wrought accounts of the plunder make dismal reading.

By the end, thousands of altars had gone, countless stained glass windows, statues and wall-paintings had disappeared, numerous libraries and choirs had been dispersed. Thousands of chalices, pyxes, crosses and the like had been sold or 'defaced' (smashed, presumably for easier transport) and melted down, and an untold number of previous vestments either stripped or seized.

To capture the full intensity and impact of this plunder we must remember two further things. First, monks, parish churches and chantries were not the only ones to suffer. At the same time as their possessions were being stripped away,

2 *LP*, xiv, ii, 777.
3 E117/11, no. 58.
4 E117/13, no. 64; 11, no. 19; 13, nos. 31 and 66; 13, no. 73; 2/7, fos. 6ff.

bishops were suffering often merciless depredation. They were forced into 'exchanges' of lands which often cost them their choicer manors; there was concerted pilfering of their London houses.[5] In part this was initiated by and for the crown; in part it was the crown's response to bids from courtiers and clients. Secondly, as people like them also besieged the Court of Augmentations to buy or lease the former lands and buildings of the religious houses, guilds, chantries, etc., much humbler folk joined in the scramble and, by fair means and foul, acquired plate and household chattels from religious houses, and candlesticks, vestments and altar cloths and so on from parish churches. Royal commissioners sold off large quantities of furnishings and stock on site. They gave away the last bits and pieces that remained unsold. But a great deal had disappeared before they began their work; and, after they had left, all and sundry fell upon the abandoned monastery or chapel to tear off doors, pull away remaining ironwork and to pick the bones clean of any tit-bits that the crown's agents had overlooked.

Even the universities trembled for their survival. The dissolution of the monasteries had resulted in the closure of dependent houses — Durham College, Canterbury College — in Oxford and Cambridge. Wolsey's foundation in Oxford apparently only just survived, thanks not least to a change of name from Cardinal's to King's College. Incredible though it may seem now, both universities braced themselves for a struggle to survive at least severe mauling by the crown.

Yet one can still maintain that there was little disenchantment with or active hostility towards any of these institutions up to the moment when they were despoiled: hence the telling fact that, though there was plenty of looting after the event, these decades showed little sign of spontaneous popular iconoclasm. There was a little in Edward's reign and some at the end of Mary's. The tabernacles of the parish church of Ashburton in Devon were solemnly burnt. The dean of Durham himself joined in eagerly when the shrine of

---

5 See F. Heal, *Of Prelates and Princes. A study in the economic and social position of the Tudor episcopate* (Cambridge, 1980), esp. ch. 5. Between 1529 and 1547 Canterbury parted with 46 manors, York with 74, and Norwich with 31 (ibid., pp. 115 and 123).

Cuthbert was torn down; and elsewhere the odd roodscreen was violently taken down.[6] Interestingly enough, perhaps the fiercest display of belligerence came from religious conservatives, not from innovators. It occurred in that same Durham over thirty years after Cuthbert's shrine was destroyed, during the Northern Rising of 1569, when the old religion was briefly restored and the altars which had been taken down in Edward's reign, put back in Mary's, and taken down again at the beginning of Elizabeth's were set up once more. The return of the mass was accompanied by an outburst of anti-Protestant fury. Bonfires were made of the heretics' books, women bringing straw and wood to start fires, while a large crowd of young people stood watching. One man in Bishop Auckland was seen tearing up the offending works with his hands and teeth. At least one communion table was smashed.[7] For the rest, however, there was little sign of violence or of rampaging mobs.

The impression derived from churchwardens' accounts is that altars, roods and rood lofts, statues and holy-water stoups and so on were taken down in Edward's reign, put back in Mary's and taken down again after Elizabeth's accession without great drama or disorder. The accounts that survive, a fairly random scattering of parishes across the country, show that men had to be paid to do this work. In Ludlow, for instance, two men received 26s. 8d. for whitewashing the rood loft, painting over the Last Judgement, and 6s. 8d. for taking down the rood and statues. Two men were paid 7d. a day each for seven days' work in pulling down the altars; it took four labourers eighteen days (at 6d. a day) to shift the rubbish out of the church.[8] At Halesowen in Worcestershire two men were paid 14d. for 'polyng downe ye hye alter and sent mare [St Mary's] alter' and taking out the stones. In Ramsey in Huntingdonshire 12d. was paid for

---

[6] J. T. Fowler (ed.), *The Rites of Durham*, Surtees Soc., cvii (1902), p. 69. There was a little popular iconoclasm in London and perhaps in one or two other towns. The story told by Thomas Hancock, vicar of Poole, of his doings reminds us that hot-gospelling clerics often led the way (J. G. Nichols (ed.), *Narratives of the Reformation*, Camden Soc., 1st ser., 77 (1860), 71–84).

[7] J. Raine (ed.) *Depositions etc. from the courts of Durham*, Surtees Soc., v (1845), pp. 175ff.

[8] T. Wright (ed.), *Churchwardens' Accounts of the town of Ludlow*, Camden Soc., cii (1869), pp. 33, 46.

'hewynge away ye carvyd work' on the rood loft, and in a parish not far away a mere 6*d.* for taking down the high altar and 10*d.* for 'whiting ye walles'.[9] There were frequent payments for putting back the altars, statues, rood and holy-water stoups in Mary's reign and restoring the 'dooms'; and yet more payments after Elizabeth's accession to undo what had but recently been restored, make good the walls and pillars from which altars and statues had been torn and finally cover up the papistical murals. And each time that altars and statues came down and the mass was outlawed, local folk gathered round to buy up stone, timber and iron, what sacred vessels, statues, altar frontals and vestments were on offer, surplus altar cloths, towels and all the rest of the remnants of the Catholic liturgy.

There was a frenzy of getting, grabbing, buying, begging without equal in English experience, and which, it is argued, would have seemed impossible until it began to happen. As has been suggested, the opportunity generated the appetite. What was happening (most of it) was legal. Everyone was doing it, from the king, Defender of the Faith (but not, apparently, of its material appurtenances), down to local squire and neighbour. All that would have sedated consciences, legitimised plunder. But — and to reiterate an important point — however eager the spoliation, England never produced the scenes of mob violence and iconoclasm witnessed in much of Reformation Germany, France, the Low Countries.[10]

Protestant zealots were as loud in denouncing the sacrilege as any Catholic would be. Things given to God, it was pointed out, were profaned as much by being seized by layfolk as by

---

9 M. O'Brien (ed.), *Halesowen Churchwardens' Accounts (1487—1582)*, Worcs. Hist. Soc. (1957), p. 97; Huntingdon CRO, MS 2449/25 for 1549 (no pagination) and 2280/28, fo. 5v. Cf. J. E. Oxley, *The Reformation in Essex to the death of Mary* (Manchester, 1965), pp. 164, 177, 188—91.

10 There was certainly violent desecration when altars, etc., were finally taken down at the beginning of Elizabeth's reign. See E. Peacock, *English Church Furniture etc. at the period of the Reformation* (1866), which lists church goods in Lincolnshire discovered by royal commissioners in 1566. There are frequent mentions of missals having been torn up (and in one place then 'sold to pedlers to lay spice in'), screens burnt, altars and chrismatories smashed, etc. Even a holy bread 'skeppe' could be sold for use as a 'baskette to carrie ffishe in' (ibid., p. 86).

dedication to popish idolatry. An alternative to a wrong was
not necessarily a right. Spoliation was addictive. Indeed, as
was claimed by John Whitgift, archbishop of Canterbury in
Elizabeth's middle years and a cleric with no illusions about
the world, Puritan zeal for doing down bishops was simply
the last manifestation of lay greed for clerical possessions.
Those keenest to despoil the monasteries had quickly abandoned the Gospel, and even turned to persecuting the
brethren, after they had got what they wanted. If authority
would stand up to these new would-be despoilers their
'wayward and contentious zeal' would blow itself out and
they would be seen for what they were, men with 'no sparkle
of godliness'.[11]

Whitgift warned, as many did, of the curse that fell on
those who helped Caesar and his friends to render unto themselves the things that were God's. Addressing Elizabeth, he
prayed, 'God prevent your majesty from being liable to that
curse which will cleave unto Church lands, as leprosy to the
Jews.' 'These curses', he warned, 'have and will cleave to
the very stone of these buildings that have been consecrated
to God; and the father's sin of sacrilege hath and will prove
to be entailed on his son and family....Church-land added to
an ancient and just inheritance hath proved like a moth
fretting a garment, and secretly consumed both.' As for
Elizabeth's father, 'God did so far deny him his restraining
grace, that as King Saul after he was forsaken of God fell
from one sin to another, so he, till at last he fell into greater
sins than I am willing to mention.'[12] Another English divine
explained how to 'scrape from the church is a pastime among
all others to laugh at and thought best gotten', and how a
minister of the Gospel is 'thought meeter to be spoiled by

But, though some of this occurred promptly in 1 Elizabeth I, much took place
several years later: one suspects on the eve of episcopal or royal visitation. Thus
the rood, the 'marie and Johnn and all other imagie of papistrie', and the rood
loft of Woolsthorpe were not burnt until 1564 (ibid., p. 169). Many other altars,
vestments, paxes, etc., survived several years. At Gunby, interestingly, the rood
and all the 'imagies' were burnt promptly in 2 Elizabeth I, but 'in the house of
Agnes Shawe, widdowe', not in public (ibid., p. 93). Perhaps such increased
violence reflects the growth of Protestantism; but it still lacks the character of
wholesale mob iconoclasm.

[11] J. Whitgift, *Works*, iii, PS, 50 (1853), 581.
[12] Ibid., pp. xiii—xv.

these cut-purses than Joseph thought meet to do to those idolatrous priests'.[13]

A treatise written in Edward VI's reign pointed out that the mass alienation of the Church's possessions had been sanctioned by no holy man and took from Christ himself what had been given to him and his Church in good faith, even if for superstitious purposes. It also played right into the hands of the papists, since even the most abandoned princes who 'adore the Roman Antichrist' nevertheless did not seize the possessions of antichristian monks and priests, even under the severest pressure. If it is wrong to covet a neighbour's goods or his wife, it must be wrong to despoil the Church. Such things strengthened papists in their obstinacy and impeded the Gospel. The emperor Justinian had declared gifts to the Church to be inviolable. The Fathers had justified worldly possessions on the ground that they made possible donations to the poor, to widows and to hospitals. Bucer, a Protestant hero, concurred in all this enthusiastically.[14]

Elizabeth's first bishop of Salisbury and scourge of papists, John Jewel — like others before him — hung his head in shame that the English Reformation, unlike the German, should have resulted in little former ecclesiastical wealth being redirected to schools, universities and the poor. Things had gone badly wrong. The Reformation had unleashed such greed, usury, rack-renting and callous unconcern for the poor and weak that, as the so-called 'Commonwealth' men had warned in the 1540s and 1550s, many looked back nostalgically to 'papistical times', when folk 'were wont to live of their lands, to keep good hospitality, to maintain schools and houses of alms', and so on.[15]

Much of this lament is today dismissed as uninformed romanticising of the past or unrealistic moralising about the present, quite rightly. On the other hand, perhaps there was a grain of truth in what Latimer, Crowley, Hutchinson and the others were essentially saying, namely, that what had taken place had corrupted. It had turned the English into a

[13] J. Pilkington, *Works*, PS, 3 (1842), p. 466.
[14] SP 10/15, no. 77.
[15] Jewel, *Works*, ii, PS, 26 (1847), 1011; Hutchinson, *Works*, PS, 4 (1842), 4 and 203.

nation of looters (though some of them may have been easy converts). Mammon had never had it better.

Latimer and the others, however, could not have understood how complicated the story was, especially as regards the fate of parish churches.

In the first place, of course, the crown was at work stripping out chantries and guilds, taking their lands, bells, plate, vestments and so on. This was more or less done by 1549. But since 1547 the crown had also been expressing concern for the rest of the churches' possessions, those belonging to the parishes themselves. The official ground for this apparently disinterested anxiety was that embezzlement was so rife that the supreme head, the king, could not overlook it. Accordingly, first the bishops and then, in 1549, lay commissioners (sheriffs and justices of the peace) were ordered to make inventories of the goods belonging to all parish churches and to check them annually. The real motive for all this, of course, was not to protect churches against local pilfering but to prepare the way for their gutting by the crown. In March 1551 the privy council decided that this could be delayed no longer, but for reasons unknown held their hand. Through 1552 further preparations were made, including a new 'view' of church goods and final checking of inventories against holdings. In January 1553 the decision was taken to strike. The trawl was only half accomplished when Edward VI died in the following summer.

During these years (and before) many individuals had certainly been making off with whatever they could. They stole; they embezzled. Churchwardens were particularly well placed to help themselves in this way, and the stern rules which the parishioners of St Nicholas's parish in Warwick, for example, drew up in Mary's reign for the guidance of their churchwardens are clear indication that there could be serious misconduct.[16] Naturally, churchwardens in turn accused others. In 1552 it was said that the dead vicar of Addington in Surrey had made off with vestments, altar cloths, candlesticks, a canopy and other items.[17] Maybe he

16 Warwick CRO, DRB 87/1 for 1556.
17 E117/9/4, fo. 4.

had. Maybe others did likewise; and maybe the considerable numbers of other thefts which churchwardens reported to the royal commissioners during Edward's reign were the work not of common-or-garden thieves but of people on the 'inside'.[18]

Something else was also happening. All over the country churchwardens were selling to local purchasers and London goldsmiths and the like plate and other church goods with 'the whole consent' (whatever that might mean) of their parishioners and not for private gain. On the contrary, the sales were often for unimpeachable causes: to pay for repairs to churches, whitewashing papistical wall-paintings, glazing church windows, setting up new pulpits, buying the new Book of Common Prayer or the Paraphrases of Erasmus. Many claimed to have sold chalices, candlesticks and vestments to relieve the poor or to pay for and equip men to fight the king's wars, be it against the Scots, Norfolk's rebels under Ket, or the conservative protestors of Devon and Cornwall.[19]

Prices were rising; perhaps incomes were falling (if layfolk were becoming wary, as well they might, of donations to religious causes). But perhaps some of this was deliberate policy to forestall the crown. For example, when a Norfolk village sold £30-worth of plate in order to buy houses and tenements as a permanent endowment of the church it was surely converting assets as a hedge against hard times and perhaps to put them out of royal reach. A nearby town realised no less than £102 from its plate, which it used to repair the church, grammar school and almshouses, and to repair the bridge. The rest went to the local poor. There may have been particular difficulties (the churchwardens tried to convince the royal commissioners that the fault lay with 'owttownesmen' who owned the best properties but inexplicably allowed them to decay and failed to contribute to the town's needs), but it also looks as though the town had been on a spending spree.[20] In Chester bells, a cross and a senser

[18] There are a suspiciously large number of thefts reported from Surrey, for instance, e.g. Barnes, Clapham, Camberwell, Streatham, Wimbledon (E117/8/8, fos. 1–12).

[19] See the commissioners' returns in (esp.) E117/2 and 3, and E315/495–515.

[20] E315/500. The places concerned were Brisley (between Fakenham and East Dereham) and Aylesham.

were sold by the dean and chapter to improve their houses and stipends. In Ely the dean and prebendaries sold a monstrance weighing 122 ounces, a chalice weighing 85 ounces, crosses, candlesticks and a holy-water bucket and sprinkler to pay for repairs and glazing, for building a new library and the purchase of books. Nuneaton parishioners sold two copes, a set of vestments, a cross and two candlesticks to pay for repairs of highways and alterations to the church, and to defray the costs of wringing from the crown a licence to refound their former chantry school as a free school.[21]

Of course, the religious changes of Edward VI's reign meant that these copes, mass vestments, crosses and so on were now, as they said, 'owte of use', so selling them would have made sense. But the sales began in Henry VIII's reign, well before any liturgical changes had been introduced. As early as September 1536 a sailor from Hull was boasting that his town had taken the precaution of selling church plate in order that the king should not acquire it. Next year a man in Thame was reported as saying that he feared the king would have the crosses and jewels of the church and it would be better for the parishioners to sell them off first.[22] This was certainly soon to happen elsewhere, if not in Thame itself. An Essex village sold £20-worth of plate in 1538, for instance. Ten years of steady sales of the possessions of Devizes church began in 1544, when there was 'consultacione' among the parishioners resulting in the decision to sell a chalice, two sensers and 'one powder boxe off sylver'. Churches on the Isle of Wight began to part with possessions in that same year. Louth had shed no less than 705 ounces of plate by April 1547 — i.e. before the new Prayer Book appeared —

---

21 E117/1, no. 47; E315/495, no. 31; E315/513, fo. 17. But out of 186 parishes of Warwickshire listed in the inventory for 6 Edward VI, 137 had sold nothing; ten had lost possessions through robbery since the previous inventory (see E315/513). Perhaps the most unusual entry came from a Norfolk village which had sold off plate, etc. to buy an organ and a clock, to 'whyght owre churche', find harness for the king during Ket's rebellion and milk and bread for the poor. They then wanted to sell more to clean up a 'noisum drove way' which was killing their cattle.

22 *LP*, xii, i, 481; xii, ii, 518. In 1552 Thame's churchwardens were accused of having sold off over £300-worth of chalices, crosses, etc., and dividing the cash among themselves and friends, so the Thame man's words were apparently listened to (*VCH, Oxon.*, ii, 34).

and may well have begun the sales several years earlier.[23] And
so on. A vast quantity of church goods — some of them, no
doubt, surplus items — had gone before the crown finally
pounced. Responsibility for trying to staunch the haemor-
rhage had been transferred to lay commissioners in 1549,
who were to call on churchwardens to show each year that
nothing had been purloined in the previous twelve months.
Eventually parishes were required to make good (in cash)
any losses which had occurred in the years immediately preceding the final dénouement; and no wonder, for the spoil
had been vanishing before the crown's very eyes.

Long before then, only the naive or those who had forgotten how the dissolution of monasteries, colleges, guilds,
and chantries had proceeded piecemeal and been accompanied by official claims that the crown was stepping in
only to halt private looting, could have failed to perceive
what was afoot. Inventories were ominous. So royal policies,
past and present, and royal pronouncements were precipi-
tating the very thing that those pronouncements deplored
and pretended was the sole occasion of their utterance. In
other words, the man of Thame was speaking for many when
he said it would be better if parishioners took the initiative
and forestalled the noble prince.

Inventories also whetted appetites. How could a government desperate for war finance have failed to be moved by
the news contained in inventories dutifully returned to
Westminster that, for instance, in Berkshire alone there were
262 chalices of precious metal and 544 bells, in Lincoln
(excluding the wapentake of Holland) 638 chalices and
1,753 great bells, in Devon no less than 788 chalices and
1,608 bells, or that the single college of St Stephen's Westminster possessed 98 copes and a huge collection of other
vestments and plate?[24] Religious scruples? A prince could
not afford them. That is probably what a growing number of
subjects suspected.

[23] E117/2, no. 25, fo. 1; E117/13 no. 98, fo. 2 (cf. *VCH, Wilts.*, x, 292); E117/2,
no. 68, fo. 3; E117/3, no. 55, fo. 1. Louth's plate was sold in London to purchase
lands 'for the rylyfe of the poore people' and other necessary causes.
[24] E117/1, no. 10; E117/3, no. 55; E117/11, nos. 17 (Devon) and 49 (St
Stephen's).

Dozens of chantries were dissolved by unauthorised private action before the Chantries Acts — thirteen in Somerset, for instance, four in Sussex, three wholly and four partially in Yorkshire. In most cases it was the patron or 'founder', i.e. the living representative of the family by and for whom the chantry had been erected, who carried out these clandestine suppressions. In Nuneaton the patron and parishioners acted together to convert a chantry into a school in 1542; in Monmouth a chantry endowment was converted to 'find' an organist; and so on.[25] Some of this may have been prompted by covetousness, some by official hesitation and doubts about Purgatory expressed as early as 1536 in the Ten Articles; some may have reflected the growing influence of Protestantism. But, as in the case of the widespread sales of church goods, some may also have been deliberately designed to foil the crown.

What was the meaning of a series of royal licences in the months preceding the Chantries Act of 1547 which allowed religious institutions to pass directly into the hands of laymen? In October of that year the chantry priest of Fladbury in Worcestershire was granted leave by letters patent to surrender his chantry to the 'founder', George Throckmorton.[26] Shortly before, the master and inmates of two hospitals and the priests of one college in the East Riding conveyed their houses to Sir Michael Stanhope, and the crown ratified the transaction. Two prebendaries of St John's Beverley did likewise. The rector, vicar and churchwardens of a London church were licensed to convey a chantry to one William Honning, clerk of the Privy Council in August 1547. At the same time Honning was confirmed in his possession of a hospital or free chapel in Bury St Edmunds which he had received from its master.[27] One's initial reaction is to assume that these were examples of courtiers and favourites (Stanhope was a partisan of Protector Somerset) being allowed to line their own pockets at the expense of the crown, which was at least assured of the annual payment by the new lay owners of the tenth due on all ex-ecclesiastical

[25] Kreider, *English Chantries*, pp. 155ff.
[26] *CPR, Edward VI*, i, 58.
[27] Ibid., 170, 182.

property. In other words, these were private suppressions of chosen institutions carried out with royal connivance. But there could be another explanation. The initiative could have come from the institutions themselves, particularly in the case of the two hospitals and the college, all of which were still going concerns. The masters, brethren and sisters, and the six chaplains of the college, might have turned to Stanhope precisely because he was a man of influence at Westminster and done a deal with him similar to the arrangement we know the nuns of Wallingwells had entered into with a Mr Oglethorpe in order to escape suppression,[28] i.e. they had resorted to the familiar device of the 'use', which set up Stanhope as feoffee of lands and buildings held by him to their use in the hope that this would shield them against any future statute which disendowed hospitals and colleges.

The former explanation remains the more likely. The latter is only worth suggesting because of the story of Wallingwells and because we know that there was a good deal of concealment of guild property, some of it perhaps inadvertent, some of it not, and that enfeoffment to use was a not uncommon way of trying to frustrate the crown. For example, all the possessions of Holy Trinity fraternity in Bedford had been given to the mayor and corporation of the town, to the use of the guild.[29] This was spotted by the royal commissioners and the lands confiscated by the crown. In nearby Huntingdon at least two villages concealed their guild possessions until the final round-up of missing lands by informers more than a decade after Elizabeth's accession. In one of these, Elton, the guild lands had been conveyed to feoffees in 1541 to the use of the poor and repair of roads, bridges and the church, and when the crown at last discovered and then sold them nearly thirty years later the feoffees fought back. They argued that the lands had not been given to superstitious uses and did not come within the compass of the act of 1547. They won their case, and Elton still possesses its 'town land', which yields an income for the upkeep of the church.[30] In St Neots things

---

28 See above, pp. 75–6.
29 E301/1, fo. 6. We are not told *when* this transaction occurred.
30 *VCH, Hunts.*, iii, 13, 166; *CPR, 1569–73*, pp. 40–1.

went the other way: an informer reported concealment and the land of the former Jesus Fraternity was seized.[31]

On the eve of the Chantries Act of 1547 the fraternity of Holy Trinity in St Botolph's without Aldersgate in London managed to procure a royal licence to alienate much of its property to a William Harvey, one of the heralds. But he was also a member of the fraternity. Two days after he had acquired the property he leased it back to the guild, which was thus able to survive the act of 1547 and emerge with its hall and some of its other property intact. These could no longer be put to 'superstitious' uses, but something had been saved.[32] Perhaps numerous such transactions were taking place, with varying degrees of success. This was just the sort of thing at which late-medieval English men and women had become extremely adept: enfeoffments, fictitious conveyances and concealments were meat and drink to them. And if all else failed, the crown could be outwitted by more straightforward means. The bailiffs of the town of Godmanchester simply ordered that all the deeds belonging to two of their guilds should be burnt and their possessions concealed from the royal commissioners.[33]

When we look closely at the story of the stripping of Catholic furniture and furnishings from the parish churches and the seizure of their plate and precious goods, a number of interesting features appear.

It is likely that leading families simply took possession ahead of the king's commissioners of sacred vessels and vestments which belonged to local churches. A nod would have been as good as a wink for them. To take three examples from Warwickshire: the churchwardens of Monk's Kirby reported that the local squire had taken into his custody a chalice, a missal, four burses, four sets of vestments and albs,

---

[31] *VCH, Hunts., ii*, 345.

[32] P. Basing (ed.), *Parish Fraternity Register*, LRS, 18 (1982), p. xxv. I am very grateful to Miss Basing for allowing me to read her work before it appeared in print.

[33] Kreider, *English Chantries*, p. 158. There had been six guilds there. Lands of two others were leased to members of the royal household — perhaps another way of trying to stave off closure? *VCH, Hunts.*, ii, 295.

a pair of candlesticks, two altar frontals, a pax and various other items. In another village one Sir Thomas Newnham, a major figure in the county, had custody of a set of requiem mass vestments in black velvet. In Polesworth a gown of velvet given by 'old' Lady Cockayne for a vestment was now back in, or had never left, her daughter's hands.[34] It is possible that all or most of these items had been donated by the families which now had custody of them. But the churchwardens who reported all this were careful to use the word 'custody' and, in the case of Sir Thomas Newnham, noted that what he held did still 'belong to the same churche'. The vestments and so on had not been sold or destroyed. They had apparently been handed over to the local gentlemen for safekeeping.

As has been said, when they concluded the suppression of a monastery chantry or guild, or finished gutting a parish church, the royal commissioners auctioned items which the crown would not want or simply gave them away. All manner of goods — vestments, altar cloths, stained glass, stalls and benches from monasteries — found their way into neighbouring parish churches. The few detailed accounts which survive of later on-site sales of church goods show how this process could continue. When the ornaments of St Mary's hospital in London were sold (the two pairs of organs for £3 6s. 8d., wainscoating, seats, the choir screen and steps before the high altar for £4, three statues of Our Lady for 6s. 8d., etc.) the parishioners of St Botolph's parish bought a silver lamp for 5s., presumably for their church.[35] On 18 March 1553 there was a big clearance sale in Canterbury at which the less valuable items from the city's churches came under the hammer. As usual, there were buyers from London with plenty of ready cash: one ironmonger, for instance, scooped £30-worth of vestments. But of the seventy-five lots, ten went to local clergy. For example, the parson of St Margaret's in Canterbury bought some cheap vestments; another cleric acquired one complete set of high mass vestments, three other chasubles and three copes for £1 6s. 8d.[36] So it was

[34] E315/513, fos. 18, 18v, 19.
[35] E117/11, no. 57.
[36] Ibid., no. 38.

not a question of absolute loss to the church so much as, to a small extent, a transfer of possessions from one part of it to another. One citizen bought some 'Lenten clothes painted' and other 'old stuff' for 6s. 8d. which were then given to the brothers and sisters of the nearby hospital of St John.

The sales of the trappings of Catholic piety to parishioners as recorded in surviving churchwardens' account of Edward VI's reign at first sight suggest that there was no shortage of local people who felt no scruples about buying up statues, altar cloths, gravestones, candlesticks and pots and so on previously belonging to their churches. William Smith of Ramsey paid 2s. 4d. for a vestment and an altar cloth; Nicholas Smyth 2s. 8d. for a 'towyl'. In Sherborne one man paid 5s. for the altar in the 'charnellhowse', another 2s. 8d. for five 'images', a third 4s. for a chasuble. In Melton Mowbray a Mr Adcock bought a chalice and William Green a tabernacle (for 12d.). In Ludlow one man paid 10d. for 'a Image of Jhesus', another 18d. for the statue of St George and a third (a celebrated entry, this) 7d. for 'the dragon that the image of saynt George stode upon'.[37] The lists sometimes go on for pages.

But some of the materials sold or transferred to local folk in Edward's reign turned up again, safe and sound, in Mary's. To take an example from Ludlow: Thomas Season, general factotum in the parish church, sold back to that church at the beginning of Mary's reign four copes, candlesticks and a statue which (presumably) he had acquired in Edward's.[38] In St Nicholas' parish in Warwick, a John Ray brought back a chalice, antiphonary, copes, a holy-water pot and a pyx, four years after acquiring them. The timber of the former rood loft was returned by the widow of one Master Brookes, who had bought it in 1550. Another came forward with the statues of Mary and John which had stood on either side of

[37] Huntingdon CRO, MS 2449 (for 1552); Dorset CRO, P155/CW 27; Leicester CRO, DG36/140, fo. 3; Wright (ed.), *Ludlow Churchwardens' Accounts*, p. 58.
[38] Wright (ed.), *Ludlow Churchwardens' Accounts*, p. 55. The statue was an 'ymage of the resurrexcon' (p. 91). He was paid for these items in instalments. I do not think he had originally bought them to give to the parish: a man of his modest means would scarcely have been able to bear the capital outlay. Rather, he was being paid in this way by an impoverished parish for goods which, as the accounts say, were thus '*restored* to the churche' (my italics), i.e. were recovered by the church.

the rood on that loft. A third man, Edmund Wright, sold back for 3s. 4d. the 'Easter sepulchre' used on Maundy Thursday as the altar of repose, which he had acquired, along with six 'banner cloths', for 5s. in 1550.[39] In a Worcester parish a Master Blunt in 1554 donated a number of items to the church, including a cross, sensers and a boat, cruets, a pyx, a chrismatory and a holy-water bucket. We are not told when or how he acquired them; but it is a reasonable guess that they had come from his church in the previous reign, as had two chasubles which former churchwardens sold back at the same time.[40] In a Somerset village a large quantity of mass vestments, copes and altar frontals had been distributed among five leading parishioners and were returned on Mary's accession.[41]

The explanation for this may partly be that consciences had been stirred, or perhaps some of the sales (but not all *were* sales) were prompted by a need for cash. A striking thing about these incidents is that the items concerned were still to hand and worth buying back. The copes and chasubles had not been turned into curtains and bedspreads, as often happened. Though it was three or four years since that rood loft had come down, the timber was apparently still intact and ready to be put back. So were the statues. The 'Easter sepulchre' which Edmund Wright of Warwick had bought in 1550 was worth recovering several years later presumably only because it was still in one piece and usable. In other words, what initially looks like unblushing spoliation by parishioners may sometimes have been nothing of the sort. Michael Sherbrook, already quoted in another context, explained later that 'some churchwardens, wiser than other some, sold many things to the use of the parish: yea, that thing for 1d. which cost xiid.'[42] Did he mean that they entrusted those goods to the safekeeping of parishioners, having formally transferred ownership by sale at nominal

---

[39] Warwick CRO, DRB 87/1 for 1—2 Philip and Mary.

[40] J. Amphlett (ed.), *Churchwardens' Account of St Michael's in Bedwardine*, Worcs. Hist. Soc. (1896), pp. 24, 30.

[41] Hobhouse (ed.), *Churchwardens' Accounts of Croscombe, Pilton, Milton, etc.*, p. 224.

[42] Sherbrook, 'The Fall of Religious Houses', in Dickens (ed.), *Tudor Treatises*, p. 139.

prices, in order that the parishes could continue to enjoy their use? If so, these sales remind one of what those enfeoffments of chantry and guild lands tried, with varying success, to do and of what those bright nuns of Wallingwells had attempted.

Unfortunately it is impossible to know how widespread this sort of thing was. In many parishes there may have been no qualms whatsoever about putting chalices, vestments and so on to profane use. In others, all manner of subterfuge may have been employed.

We can plot the spoliation of the superb ex-abbey church of Sherborne in Dorset step by step. In 1542 it possessed five chalices, sixteen copes, well over a dozen mass kits, fourteen albs and plenty of frontals, surplices, towels and so on. By 1549 it had lost one of its chalices (for reasons unknown). By 1551 disaster had struck. Three more of its chalices had gone and out of its rich inheritance of vestments there remained but seven copes, five sets of vestments and little else besides surplices and the like. Two years later it had only one out of its five chalices left and a pathetic collection of surplices and cloths. Then the tide turned: the Marian restoration of the old faith meant that by 1555 the parish could boast two chalices, two copes and two pairs of vestments, plus a senser and pyx and the like. By the end of Mary's reign there had been further improvement: the parish now owned three chalices, five copes, a reasonable amount of chasubles, a set of mass vestments in black velvet for requiems, and a decent supply of other equipment.[43] Catholic worship was back in something like its pre-Reformation style.

But the churchwardens had had to send to London for much of this (including a gradual for the huge sum of £10 6s. 8d. and an antiphonary for £4 6s. 8d., blue velvet vestments for 36s. 8d. and a cross for 13s. 4d.). They had also received local donations of two copes, the requiem mass vestments, a pair of candlesticks and such like. None of these donors (six men and one woman) was among the dozens who had joined in the buying spree when the spoliation was on some years before. Those who gave in Mary's reign were not those who had acquired vestments, albs, banners and altar

---

[43] Dorset CRO, P155/CW 20–31 (for 1542 to 1555).

cloths in Edward's. On the other hand, where did they get them from? Some of the vestments and hardware must have originated from parish churches (though maybe not this one) and have found their way to Sherborne by perhaps very devious routes. In some places the altars were put back quickly after Mary's accession. Indeed, it has been suggested that they were so soon in use again in Lancashire that they may never have been removed.[44] In Melton Mowbray the altar stones were back in place for mass to be said for Edward VI immediately after he died (and 8*d*. paid to 'the ryngers at the dyryge for the king' — all very Catholic and hardly what the dead prince would have approved).[45] The parish bought back £7-worth of ornaments and 'church goodes' at once and quickly recovered vestments. Elsewhere, of course, things went much more slowly, and we know that many parishes had not been able to restore even high altars by 1557 (let alone side altars), and were still short of vestments, bells and the like when the Marian restoration came to an abrupt end in November 1558.

There had been more resistance, concealment and evasion than has sometimes been supposed; more hesitation, more scruples about laying hands on sacred things. When the order finally went out in 1553 to gather up the possessions of parish churches the government was clearly nervous lest so provocative a step would lead to disturbances. Commissioners were told to act with great circumspection, and even some of them had qualms. The commissioners for Kent, for instance, were so loath to act that they had to be rebuked by the Privy Council before they would 'meddle' with the matter.[46] In Cambridgeshire, John Huddleston (true enough, a conspicuous

---

[44] C. Haigh, *Reformation and Resistance*, p. 144.
[45] Leicester CRO, DG36/140, no. 6, fo. 9.
[46] E117/13, no. 9 — an interesting account of what happened, although, since it was written in Mary's reign (1556), its protests of innocence should be taken with a pinch of salt. But it states openly that many parishes, 'percevvynge that the churche goodes should be taken from them', had sold plate and ornaments 'afore we sate in commyssion'. The commissioners had been bidden to use stealth (a 'discrete maner of proceding'), and 'wise persuasion', and to give as little occasion of alarm 'as may be'. Cf E117/1, no. 54.

conservative) simply refused to act on conscientious grounds.[47]

This part of the story of church possessions had a happier ending, from the point of view of churchmen, than the rest, because when Edward died in July 1553 not all the chalices and vestments and so on had yet been gathered up from the parishes. The new queen immediately ordered the commissioners to halt. No more church plate was to be seized; chalices and the like which had been seized but not defaced were to be handed back forthwith to the parishes whence they came. Moreover — and this is an astonishing example of royal largesse by any standards — parishes which had lost their goods would receive grants of cash with which to replace them (or to buy them back from parishioners who had acquired them?). The great spoliation had been halted and (temporarily) reversed.[48] A strong woman, the first of several in English history, had appeared on the scene.

After Elizabeth's accession the altars and statues and rood lofts came down again and the churches were finally purged of their Catholic past; as before, at varying speeds.[49] Once more huge quantities of plate, statues, vestments, cloths, banners and liturgical books were formally assigned to local people for safekeeping. Whether this was done in the expectation that they would one day be used again we cannot

[47] E117/14, no. 167. 'My conscyence was then well known to be agaynste the spoyle of the Churche', he said, and his refusal caused him to be 'not a lytell tawnted'. But he was also put out because he was named last in the commission, below other commissioners of 'thenferyor sorte'. So his scruples may not have been wholly spiritual.

[48] See, e.g., E117/11, nos. 27, 28, 60, 74, which show how much was saved for Hampshire (esp. Winchester) and Norwich; E117/13, nos. 30 (West Riding churches) and 104. In Somerset the despoiling of churches had hardly begun when Edward died, so plate was untouched except by embezzlement 'by private authoritie' (ibid., no. 172). This side of the Marian restoration is discussed by R. H. Pogson, 'Revival and reform in Mary Tudor's Church: a question of money', *Journ. Eccles. Hist.*, xxv (1974), 255—7. Striking light on what had happened is provided by the fact that Mary had to lend her new bishop of Norwich, John Hopton, a mitre and crozier because his diocese had none. Enough *episcopalia* had come into the crown's hands intact to enable this sixteenth-century 'Moss Bros' to be set up (Clay (ed.), *North Country Wills*, pp. 3—4).

[49] Some screens (i.e. the lofts thereof) were not removed for decades. Norton by Daventry, for example, kept its until 1579 (Northants. CRO, 243P/309, no pagination).

know, but that may well often have been the case. Certainly, a great deal was deliberately hidden, to be discovered decades, even centuries, later, or to be brought out when the Marian and later missionary priests started working clandestinely among the surviving Catholic community.

Yet despite this evidence, doubt may linger. Was the mass vandalism not so wanton and shocking that there must have been something badly amiss beforehand and something very profane and crude about a society responsible for it?

Certainly spoliation on this scale should make us wonder about what we are often told today concerning the deep superstition, with its attendant fear of curses, ghosts and divine retribution, which allegedly possessed sixteenth-century Englishmen. A man who turns a monastic church into his parlour, eats out of vessels formerly used at mass and off sometime altar cloths is clearly not too 'superstitious'. Churchmen like Whitgift could thunder, and a famous book later tried to show how families that acquired ex-monastic lands had come to a sticky end;[50] but all this did not deter or apparently cause many nightmares. We cannot have it both ways. Tudor society cannot have been both sunk in sub-Christian folk religion *and* massively indifferent to the hazards of sacrilege.

That is by the way. A more important point is that probably no other society faced with such sudden and unprecedented temptation (perhaps one should say 'opportunity') would have behaved better. What happened in Tudor England is what one would expect to happen anywhere once floodgates are opened. Subsequent desecration is quite compatible with previous benefaction; subsequent plunder is not proof of previous coveting or of growing irreligion. If indifference and scoffing were on the increase, this could have been a direct consequence rather than a cause of the looting. We today who have witnessed some heart-rending things done to the interiors of churches should know that one does not have to be irreligious to commit even the worst offences. Old,

---

[50] Sir Henry Spelman's *The History and Fate of Sacrilege*, written in 1632.

treasured and handsome things can be swept away by the most well-meaning and pious. Many of us, alas, have little eye or concern for the beautiful, and not much awe. We are also adept at overcoming scruples and, when put to the test, at succumbing to the lure of forbidden fruit.

The Reformation brought out the best and the worst in people. Much was destroyed and plundered. However, some things were rescued — not merely chalices and vestments but whole chapels of ease and even whole abbey churches, like those of Great Malvern and St Albans, which local inhabitants bought back from the crown. Elsewhere local action rescued merely a nave or transept.[51] Bath abbey church was bought by a local man who gave it to the town in 1560. This may not have been much. Today the sight of these few glories snatched from perdition, like the ruins of Tintern or Fountains, make the losses harder to bear; but they show the other face of Tudor society.

Humbler incidents reinforce this picture. For instance, when the rising of 1569 reached Durham and the old religion was briefly restored there, altar-slabs and holy-water stoups which had been taken down a second time at the beginning of Elizabeth's reign were soon back in position, and mass was said once more in Durham Cathedral and neighbouring churches. In Edward's reign the altar-stones of churches had commonly been set into chancel floors (possibly a gesture of reverence?); but some of Durham's had been hidden out of doors. People knew where they were, and when the signal was given they were unearthed. In Bishop Auckland thirty men with ropes hauled back one altar-slab into position. In one village two girls of eighteen and twenty, and three other women, brought in sand and lime to build the altar, and two women a barrowload of mortar.[52] A few weeks later the rebellion was over and the altars were taken down a third time. Once more they and the stoups were carefully hidden in gardens, under piles of rubbish in the chancel floor or church tower, waiting for another restoration.

[51] See below, p. 128, for more details of these extremely interesting transactions.

[52] Raine (ed.), *Depositions etc. from the courts of Durham*, pp. 179ff. There was also much concern (as elsewhere during Mary's reign) to restore holy water stoups.

And as one of the ringleaders was helping to hide a high altar-stone in a rubbish heap he was heard to say to it: 'dominus vobiscum [the Lord be with you]'.[53] No vandal he.

53 Ibid., p. 193.

6

Coming to Terms with the New Order

The Reformation occasioned an acute crisis of obedience for English men and women, because it required them, as never before, to face up to the disconcerting fact that monarchs, though they were hedged about by divinity and were even supreme head (or, in Elizabeth's case, supreme governor) of the Church, could nonetheless lie and dupe, rig trials, bend the law, be greedy and vengeful, show but moderate fear of the Lord, scant zeal for the Gospel and little disinterested concern for the poor or the higher things of life. This does not surprise or shock us. It may not have surprised or shocked the more hard-headed among those at the centre of Tudor political life, but for humbler subjects it would have been hard to bear. In the world-view of the day the Lord's Anointed did not have a dirty tricks department.

Henry VIII, for example, had violated shrines and fanes. He had lured the Pilgrims of 1536 into surrender. He broke his promise to hold a parliament in the north and took six years to honour his undertaking to visit his subjects there. Even as the attack on larger monasteries had begun, it was being officially denied that complete dissolution of religious houses (following the suppressions carried out under the act of 1536) was intended.[1] The list goes on.

He was a quintessential patriot king, and to that extent he was what the political nation wanted and admired. But

[1] See above, p. 69 and n.

his matrimonial career was as unedifying as his bloody assault on Carthusians, a man like Fisher or a former servant like Thomas Cromwell. He had been excommunicated. Even if excommunication held few terrors for most people, the fact remained that this ultimate weapon had been used against an English prince only once before. No previous monarch had also had to contend with rumours like those which had circulated widely in 1536 about royal plans to tax almost everything in sight, pull down parish churches, and so on. Whether these lurid tales were really popular in origin is beside the point. They were soon spreading like wildfire.

For some of her subjects Mary was evil almost beyond words. She had handed England back to the thraldom of Rome and persecuted 'true' religion on a scale unequalled in English history. For her Catholic subjects (though they were nonetheless loyal), Elizabeth was a bastard and a heretic; and she too was excommunicated. There were agonising difficulties for her more committed Protestant subjects, too. Much as they might see her accession as divine deliverance and much as later generations might idolise her, Protestant zealots of her own day had to come to terms with the disconcerting fact that she was no zealot herself. For example, she could leave the diocese of Oxford vacant for forty years in order to enjoy its income. She sacked an archbishop of Canterbury, Edmund Grindal, who was wholly dedicated to the cause of true reformation. She had little understanding of what fired her Protestant subjects and less sympathy for it. Indeed, it was precisely that apparently unshakeable indifference to the lamentable state of the Lord's vineyard in England and lukewarmness towards suffering Protestants abroad (both of which, of course, may have been *politically* well judged) that drove some increasingly exasperated subjects into increasingly dangerous Puritanism.

All this was hard for those affected to learn to live with.[2] The difficulty was intensified by the major scandal of the period: the failure of the crown to use the wealth that came into its hands as a result of its destruction of the old Church

___

[2] 'Those affected' may have been a small minority, of course. But perhaps never before had so many subjects had to cope with such a variety of crises of allegiance and respect for authority.

for the lasting benefit of society: for education, for the poor and needy, for public works and the like. The truth is that for most of the time the Tudors patronised little of anything, whether the arts (except music), science, universities, schooling, the professions, overseas exploration, social welfare or relief; and with few exceptions the little they did was probably the result more of initiatives from below than of spontaneous interest on their part. Sixteenth-century monarchy in this respect had not much to be proud of. The achievements of Henry VII and his remarkable mother, Lady Margaret Beaufort, are in the best traditions of, and look back to, earlier royal patronage, but the genes evidently failed to survive. It was therefore a tragedy that the wealth of monastic England should have come into the hands of Henry VIII, for few monarchs were less likely to make enlightened use of it.

His failure to bestow more than a token amount on education, his failure to endow schools and hospitals or to tackle the problem of poverty (the fact, indeed, that he put down schools, destroyed hospitals and so on) is well known and need not detain us. We know from the writings of contemporaries like Roderyck Mors, Crowley and others how bitter was the disappointment, how keen the sense of betrayal. The point is this: for Mors, Crowley and the rest that betrayal was another thing that had to be accommodated. Had subjects ever had to cope with such disappointment, such disillusion? It would have been easier to do so had not statute and proclamation waxed indignant against waste, vice and oppression, and spoken fulsomely of royal dedication to learning and the well-being of the subject. Henry had paraded himself as paragon of enlightenment and made clear promises.[3]

It is going to be argued here that what happened in the next reign provided little comfort for the so-called 'commonwealth men' indignant at the betrayal of their cause. Of course, Edward can scarcely be held responsible for events, but the son's regime showed only a little more virtue than the father's.

---

[3] For example, in the preamble to the statute of 1539, written by himself, setting up new bishoprics. See above, p. 78.

We will probably never have a complete picture of the effect of the Reformation on English schools and hospitals, and never be able to draw up a definitive balance sheet of losses and gains. The sources are often so incomplete or difficult to interpret that, for instance, one cannot always be sure that a medieval school which seems to have disappeared did not in fact survive (or that subsequent 'foundation' was not really a refoundation) or that a hospital was still a going concern when it was suppressed and not a mere husk, a sinecure generating an income for a perhaps absentee master whose loss only the latter might have lamented. Secondly, we use the words 'school' and 'hospital' indifferently, as though they were uniform, whereas there was probably enormous variety in size and quality not only between the humblest chantry school and, say, Eton, but between one chantry school and another, one hospital and another. The data, therefore, is pretty raw. Finally, in assessing the effect of the Reformation on schools in particular, we have always to remember that by the early sixteenth century there was a growing number of free grammar schools run by towns or in the charge of lay trustees as well as (presumably) a variety of private tuition, not to mention plenty of opportunities for some elementary education. So the schools attached to religious houses, chantries and guilds were but part of the national whole. How large a part? One can only estimate that they were a fairly substantial proportion (though they did not include the most prestigious foundations, like St Paul's and Winchester).

When we come to assess how they fared during the mid-sixteenth-century tumults, the first fact to be noted is that much survived and there were some absolute gains.

Some monastic schools survived the deluge. At Evesham, for instance, the crown took on responsibility for paying the schoolmaster's annual stipend. Royal grammar schools emerged at the ex-monastic cathedrals of Worcester and Canterbury and elsewhere. Some ex-monastic properties were indeed bestowed on the universities. Trinity College Cambridge hails Henry VIII as its founder. More importantly, perhaps, it is now stoutly maintained that Edward VI's reign was not the educational and social disaster that it was once said to have been. Chantries and guilds were suppressed, but on the whole their schools and hospitals survived. The act of 1547 was aimed against their religious functions, not their good works, and the commissioners sent out to implement the statute of suppression acted conscientiously.[4] So, far from destroying a flourishing system of schools and hospitals, the act, it is now argued, preserved what was worth preserving and allowed for a useful reallocation of resources. Moreover, the other institutions which came within the act's purview were treated with similar care. Some of the remaining colleges (communities of secular priests) were allowed to continue, albeit with reduced staffs and endowments, wherever it could be shown that their churches served a clear pastoral need. The same was true for free chapels: where these were proving useful as chapels of ease they were allowed to stand. Ex-chantry priests were selected and assigned to them, as they (and some ex-guild priests) also were to some parish churches in need of additional clergy. The remaining chantry and guild clergy were pensioned off.

There were some astonishing displays of official scrupulosity. For example, the crown separated out and continued to pay the sum of £6 10s. 6d. to the poor of Cambridge, in accordance with the founder's wishes, from the income of a former obit; the remainder of the endowment (from shops and booths) was forfeit because it supported prayer for the dead. Similarly the crown confiscated one of two tenements given to St Mary Bow in Cheapside because it had been given to 'find' the light in the rood loft called 'le beame light', but carefully continued to pay the church the income from the other tenement for the regular ringing of Bow bell, night and day, as the benefactor had instructed. Banbury was still receiving in 1824 the sum of £10 2s. 10d. a year from the crown for the maintenance of twelve poor people, in accordance with an undertaking made when the guild was suppressed

---

4   See the major work by J. Simon, *Education and Society in Tudor England* (Cambridge, 1966), esp. chs. viii and ix, and her articles on the work of A. F. Leach in *Past and Present*, 13 (1957) and *British Journal of Educational Studies*, xii, no. 1, (1955); N. Orme, *English Schools in the Middle Ages* (1973), esp. chs. 9 and 10. The combined effect of these and other studies has been to discredit much of Leach's work, especially his *English Schools at the Reformation, 1546–8* (1896).

over 260 years before.[5] Everything seems to have been benign and well-intentioned. But this is not the whole truth.

First, the reports of the commissioners who toured the counties to implement the act of 1547 contain many appeals to the crown from towns which had not previously boasted a grammar school that they should now acquire one, i.e. that some of the wealth flowing into royal hands should be directed to endowing new schools. Many of these appeals, such as those of Beverley, Cirencester and Witney, fell on deaf ears. The crown was not willing to bestow ex-chantry and guild lands for this purpose, that is, to give them away.

Next, there were certainly absolute losses (permanent closures). As regards schools, the casualties began in 1530, when Wolsey's ambitious foundation in Ipswich was felled by the king, as his Oxford college nearly was, too. The dissolution of the monasteries certainly swept away a number of schools of varying size and quality, and so did the dissolution of guilds and chantries. The schools concerned were probably small and perhaps informal, but they could have been useful. Lambourn in Berkshire lost its school; so did Ivinghoe in Buckinghamshire, of whose cantarist it was reported in 1548 that he 'dothe teach childerne'.[6]

Similarly, hospitals were destroyed in the 1530s. Perhaps not many were providing a useful service, but some were. London's plight is well known; York lost thirteen of its twenty-two, including St Leonard's, which had forty-five inmates at its end.[7] The Chantries Act of 1547 did not extend to hospitals, as its predecessor of 1545 had done. Nonetheless, hospitals attached to chantries and guilds could be at risk when their parent institutions went down. Fyfield in Berkshire lost its almshouses (still functioning as a hospital) and so did the village of Alkmonton in Derbyshire, where St Leonard's, with seven poor inmates, failed to survive the spoliation of 1547/8.[8] Again, the victims belonged to small rural communities and probably collapsed largely because there was not enough local pressure to save them.

---

5   *CPR, Philip and Mary*, iii, 390; iv, 90–1; *VCH, Oxon.*, x, 125.

6   *VCH, Berks.*, iv, 252; *Bucks*, ii, 386, quoting E301/5, the chantry certificate for Bucks. Some guild priests may also have given informal tuition.

7   Palliser, *Tudor York*, p. 222.

8   *VCH, Berks.*, ii, 94; *Derby.*, ii, 81.

There were other communities, not all of them small, which, though they eventually recovered endowments of former schools and hospitals, did so only after years and a struggle. For example, Bruton was able to get its former abbey school restored some twenty years after the Court of Augmentations had seized its endowment, pensioned off the master and allowed him to retain the schoolhouse and garden wherein 'to live lycentiously at will', as the townsfolk complained.[9] Determined petitioning won the day in 1549. The hospital belonging to Abingdon's guild seems to have closed in 1548, but was restored, as Christ's Hospital, five years later. St John's Leicester, which sheltered six poor men in 1548, ceased then to exist and was not restored until 1589, or so it seems.[10] Lambourn in Berkshire (already mentioned) lost both its chantry school and almshouses in 1548 and re-endowed its hospital, but only its hospital, some forty years later. It took London nearly a decade to begin to recover some of its former hospitals brought down by the Henrician suppressions. It is reckoned that York, which was particularly badly hit by the dissolution of monasteries, had no grammar school at all between 1539 and 1575.[11]

So there were certainly some long-term, but not permanent, closures, as well as some (maybe only a few) absolute losses. Much more important than this, however, is the fact that the crown did not honour its promises to use new-found wealth to set up new schools and hospitals, that is, spontaneously and *gratis*. There were indeed some new foundations; but, as we shall see, they were the result of local initiative and had to be endowed by the petitioners themselves. Apart from a handful of foundations in Henry VIII's reign, there was little sign of royal bounty.

On the other hand, though idealists' hopes of large-scale endowment of new institutions by the crown were dashed, most of the former chantry and guild schools and hospitals

[9] Quoted in Leach, *English Schools*, p. 191. *CPR, Edward VI*, iii, 191–2.
[10] *VCH, Berks.*, ii, 93; *Leics.*, ii, 40. However, Lutterworth hospital survived, even though the master was an absentee, the buildings were in ruins, and there were no inmates (*VCH, Leics.*, ii. 43).
[11] Palliser, *Tudor York*, p. 176. Penrith (Cumbria) recovered the endowment of its former chantry school in 1564, i.e. sixteen years after suppression (*CPR, Elizabeth*, iii, 71).

were rescued. There were some anxious moments and probably some temporary dislocation, but on the whole these institutions survived and by the end of Edward's reign had been fully and freely re-endowed by the crown.

The story seems to have run thus. Though the 1547 act empowered the commissioners in charge of chantries, colleges, guilds and the rest to assign lands for re-endowment of schools, for support of the poor, provision of extra clergy, etc. − an undertaking which doubtless helped to secure the act's passage through Parliament − in the event, the government came forward with annual payments only (payable at the Court of Augmentations), and not with landed re-endowment.[12] In the long run, of course, such an arrangement would have proved very expensive to the crown. In the short run, however, it had the major advantage of allowing a regime desperate for war finance to realise assets and quickly lay hands on considerable sums of money from sales of the seized lands.

So everyone − schoolmasters, inmates of almshouses, clergy assigned to free chapels and the rest − was to receive a government salary or pension. Thus the master of the grammar school at Crewkerne in Somerset was to be paid £8 6s. 8d. a year (exactly what he had been receiving hitherto) and the almsfolk formerly cared for by the fraternity of the Sepulchre in Taunton the sum of 56s. 4d. a year each. The 3s. 4d. a year previously paid to prisoners of Ilchester from the income of a chantry in Ilminster was also to continue. In Southwell the minster of the famous college was to become a parish church, with a former prebendary as vicar and two assistants, all of whom would receive annual stipends from Westminster. The school was to continue, the master receiving a salary of £20 a year. The grammar schools of Alnwick and Morpeth were among the many former chantry and guild schools whose masters were to be provided with

---

12 It is now clear that (almost) all former chantry and guild schools were indeed sustained in this way. A major source of Leach's misunderstanding (and fierce attack on the Edwardian regime) is the fact that the surviving Exchequer records which provide for pensions to be paid to masters, etc., are incomplete. Leach took them (E301/1) to be comprehensive. Joan Simon (see works cited in note 4 above) has finally shown that he was wrong and that many schools not contained in those apparently complete lists in fact received government salaries.

an annual salary from state funds. An ex-guild priest was to become assistant in Chesterfield and three additional clergy (two of them ex-cantarists) were to be appointed to All Saints Derby. In Wisbech £10 13s.4d. was earmarked by the royal commissioners for continued upkeep of seabanks previously maintained by local guilds.[13]

From one point of view this is all very impressive and shows an often astonishing concern for detail and human beings which any bureaucracy would envy. But government salaries were dubious assets. There was no guarantee that they would survive sudden changes of regime. They were liable to fall into arrears. They were not inflation-proofed – and inflation, slow but remorseless, was a major feature of sixteenth-century European life. They had to be collected from Westminster (not a simple thing for, say, almsfolk to arrange). As we shall see, despite the firm statement that the payments assigned in 1549 to named recipients – masters, almsmen, vicars and the like – would continue to be paid to their successors in perpetuity, there could be a hassle when a successor actually came forward to claim what had been awarded to the original grantee. Moreover, though salaries kept bodies and souls together, they provided nothing for maintenance of property and other overheads. Finally, the substitution of direct payments from Westminster for locally administered endowments denied local communities that ownership of their schools and hospitals which civic pride required.

It is not surprising, therefore, that a change of policy occurred. Towns started to petition the crown to re-endow permanently those schools and hospitals which, under the previous scheme, would simply have received personal payments to masters and inmates. By Edward's death in July 1553, at least twenty-six schools and six hospitals which had originally belonged to chantries or guilds had been re-endowed.[14]

---

[13] E301/1, fos. 2, 4, 7, 20 and 21. Extracts relating to schools (only) are printed in Leach, *English Schools*, and described there as 'schools continuance warrants'.
[14] These and other 'global' statistics given below are derived from study of *CPR* for the reigns of Edward and Mary. Since some grants may have failed to get onto the patent rolls, the figures may do a little less than complete justice to the crown. The change of policy referred to (from pensions to endowments) began in 1549, but the main flow of grants came in 1550/1.

The towns received back ex-chantry and ex-fraternity possessions: sometimes these were the former properties of the parent chantries or guilds themselves, sometimes they were a mixed bag of bits and pieces from various (usually nearby) dissolved chantries, guilds, colleges, 'services', obits, lights, plus even an occasional ex-monastic property. Thus in 1551 Sedburgh received ex-guild lands and properties of various chantries in Yorkshire with which to restore the school founded by Roger Lupton, which had collapsed when the chantry was suppressed.[15] Louth gained £40-worth of properties for its school, including 'Our Lady Beadhouse', meadows, arable land and crofts, and the profits of three weekly markets and three annual fairs, all of which had formerly belonged to its St Mary's guild. St Mary's church was to be used as a schoolhouse. In April 1552 Macclesfield acquired lands formerly held by St John's college in Chester, and a chantry there, as well as getting back 'le Scole House' in Macclesfield itself. Boston refounded an almshouse entirely with the lands of two of its former guilds. Abingdon was granted former possessions of both its dissolved abbey, including the Antelope Inn, and of its former Holy Cross guild, with which to refound its almshouse, Christ's Hospital, for seven men and six women. The total value of the endowment was a handsome £65 11s. 10d. a year, so the surplus was to be spent either on repairs of four bridges and roads or on a grammar school. In this case, as in the others, the royal grant included a licence to acquire further lands in mortmain to support the school.[16]

These endowments were genuine gifts. Occasionally the recipients were liable to pay the ecclesiastical tenth (one tenth per annum of the clear value of the land) which the crown still claimed on Church lands when they had passed into lay possession, but that was all. Stratford-on-Avon had even offered to purchase its former guild lands from the crown. Instead it received a free gift of all the former guild's possessions, plus the income of the former college, now the parish church, as re-endowment of its almshouses and grammar school. True, it had to pay £20 apiece to the schoolmaster and the new vicar of Stratford (plus £2 for his tenth), and £10 a year to his assistant minister. In other words, the crown had off-loaded responsibility for paying the salaries of two new clergy. But that still left £38 net for the almshouses, etc.[17] Stratford, like the other beneficiaries of royal bounty, had grounds for gratitude.

On the other hand, they could justly remark two facts. First, they and the others were merely being given back (usually only a part of) what had previously been enjoyed by their communities, although the lands and so on had previously belonged to chantries and guilds rather than directly to the town authorities. Secondly, there was surely only one explanation why these endowments had been conceded: namely, pressure from below. Towns had to take the initiative and petition the crown. They commonly needed to enlist a local magnate or a prominent public figure to lend weight to their requests.

It was not a question, therefore, of a zealous regime spontaneously promoting education of youth and social welfare. On the contrary: success came only to those local communities who had the necessary worldly knowledge, tenacity of purpose, cash and influential patronage to enable them to undertake anything as sophisticated as a petition to the monarch. Moreover they came up against a crown which fought every inch of the way and not always cleanly. Take the case of Southwell: as has been noted, in 1549 an annual salary was awarded to its schoolmaster. When he moved on to another post, however, the Court of Augmentations refused to pay his successor. Only after the town had protested was it agreed that the salary had been allotted to the master 'for the time being' (i.e. for ever), and all was well.[18] Another example is Stockport's grammar school, set up by Sir Edmund Shaw, together with a chantry, in 1488. The school survived, stripped of its 'superstitious' activities, only because the Goldsmiths' Company, whom Sir Edmund had appointed as his trustees, made a substantial

---

[17] Ibid., v, 279–80.
[18] *VCH, Notts.*, ii, 188–9.

donation to the crown to save it.[19]

We have already seen how Coventry was misused and how strenuously it had to fight to acquire what had been promised to it. The story of Ludlow's dealings with the government is scarcely less revealing. According to the act of 1547, no lands of any institution 'mentioned or expressed' in the act were to fall within its scope if their possession had been confirmed by either Henry VIII or Edward himself. Ludlow was one of several towns which had received royal confirmation of their guilds' possessions and could therefore have presumed that they had little to fear from this new measure. Once the act was passed Ludlow claimed immunity for the possessions of its famous Palmers Guild. Its properties, they said, should pass to the corporation. They had the law on their side. They sent a delegation to the Court of Augmentations to put their case, and even took the trouble to consult some of the king's judges, who, they alleged, shared their opinion. Faced with this deputation and realising what an expensive precedent was at stake, the chancellor of Augmentations did what any bureaucrat would do and referred the townsmen to his superior, Protector Somerset. Somerset did what anyone in his position would be tempted to do — nothing. That was in June 1548. Ludlow, anxious and angry, and fearful that Parliament would be used to pass another act which would bring 'our saide gilde within the compas of the same', kept up the pressure. Eventually, in May 1551, the Privy Council indicated that a settlement was at hand and ordered a 'booke' to be prepared by Augmentations listing what the town would recover and on what terms; but still nothing happened. At this point Ludlow addressed a splendidly robust petition to the king himself, quoting the statute at him and pointing to the guild's venerable history and numerous good works (as well as to the town's loss of rents from dissolved religious houses and the expense of

---

19 *VCH, Cheshire*, iii, 249. Even when the crown made amends, trouble could come from another direction. Stafford lost its chantry school in 1548, and two years later the burgesses successfully appealed for royal restoration. A disused chapel was turned into a schoolhouse to replace the lost one — whereupon Henry Lord Stafford claimed the property was his. It took nearly fifty years to settle the matter and finally extinguish the Stafford family claim (*VCH, Staffs.*, vi, 164).

maintaining walls, pavements, conduits and three stone bridges). At last, in April 1552, they were granted what they believed had been rightfully theirs all along. All the former guild's buildings and lands were handed to the town (since there had been near-identity of municipal and guild officers one could almost say handed *back* to it). The grammar school and hospital had been saved, but the town now had to pay for the schoolmaster, maintain the almshouses and give the thirty-three inmates 4*d.* a week each. The old guild had employed three priests. In their place the town was to maintain a preacher 'to interpret the pure Gospel and minister the sacraments', and a perpetual assistant in the parish church. Thus the crown encumbered the town with payments which it would itself have incurred, and after a long, wearing and expensive battle Ludlow might also meditate ruefully on the fact that the restored lands came to them with an annual rent of £8 13*s.* 4*d.* attached, payable to the Court of Augmentations.[20]

Nonetheless, this story, like most of the others, had a fairly happy ending. So the 'catastrophic' view of what happened in Edward VI's reign is still erroneous. On the other hand, Edward VI is still no convincing patron of learning (or of almshouses, for that matter), and the irony of having his name adorn some of England's most prestigious schools, as though he were their true founder, little less acute.[21]

---

[20] For all this see T. Wright, *A Historical and Descriptive Sketch of Ludlow Castle and the Church of St Lawrence, Ludlow* (18th edn, Shrewsbury, 1929), pp. 367–72.

[21] Hence, while accepting much that Joan Simon has established, I still regard as over-generous (and somewhat misleading) her basic thesis that the commissioners of the 1540s were engaged 'in much the same kind of undertaking as the charity commissioners of three centuries later' (*Education and Society*, p. vii). Could this be as unguarded as her claim that royal rhetoric about 'particular love and affection' for learning and the Church, etc., was genuine (ibid., p. 192)? The commissioners of the 1540s may not have been philistines, but they were certainly agents of a regime hungry for cash — so hungry that it is difficult to see them as wholly disinterested servants of education. Some of the literary evidence which Miss Simon herself quotes perhaps conflicts with her rather optimistic view of things.

While towns like Coventry and Ludlow were struggling to rescue some of their past, an avalanche of sales of ex-chantry, guild, college and obit lands was taking place at the Court of Augmentations. Much went to syndicates who bought on speculation or acted as agents for others, in the same way as much ex-monastic property had been handled. The sales were under way by mid-1548; by March 1549 they reached £18,000 a month. There were some prodigious purchases. To take some random examples: in May 1549, Sir John Thynne and Thomas Throckmorton paid £4,340 for the possessions (including livestock, cottages, stables, barns, wind and water mills, rents in kind as well as much land) from sixteen former chantries, three 'services', two guilds, one college, one chapel and a 'lamp'. The possessions were scattered over six counties. The two Partridge brothers of Amesbury spent £4,258 on the possessions of thirty-six former chantries and 'services', five obits and three guilds. The total annual value of the properties (in five counties and London) was £383, so they had bought at a bargain price: eleven years' purchase. In March 1550 two merchant tailors of London came to the Court of Augmentations in Westminster with the massive sum of £1,142 in *ready money* to buy numerous bits and pieces which had previously endowed four fraternities, two chantries, two colleges, three obits, etc. in London and nine counties. There were meadows, tithes, an orchard and other lands stripped from the partially disendowed Southwell College; houses, shops, cellars, lofts and the like which hitherto sustained 'service' priests in two London parishes; 'the brothred house' of the former guild in Potten End (Bedfordshire), and stone, timber, iron and glass from a chapel there, the house of the dissolved Holy Trinity guild in Daventry, and much more.[22]

Four months later two aldermen of London and a 'common clerk' parted with no less than £18,744 in order to acquire an astonishing collection of hundreds of endowments for anniversary masses administered by the liveried companies of London. As has been said, these companies had originally been threatened with extinction along with the religious guilds,[23]

22 *CPR, Edward VI*, ii, 102–12, 255–7, 329–34.
23 See above, pp. 36, 67.

but the government had drawn back from so provocative a deed and they had escaped: that is, they were to lose only endowments made for explicitly 'superstitious' purposes. These, as the sale of July 1550 shows, were cut away with merciless precision. Thirty-three companies, from mighty Mercers and Goldsmiths to Fletchers, Saddlers and Pewterers, felt the surgery and parted with income from lands, houses, shops and the like (mainly in London) which yielded £939 a year for masses for deceased members and their kin.

The accounts of the sale show vividly how wide was the range of facilities which a large company could offer and how dangerous it is to draw a sharp dividing line between the religious and the 'secular' guild. These companies had been acting as trustees for hundreds of deceased freemen who had bequeathed messuages, shops, inns, etc. for anniversary masses to be said for them, their wives and families in (usually) various parish churches all over London. Thus the Haberdashers' Company had administered lands worth £16 a year for masses to be said at the altar of SS Matthew and Mary Magdalen in St Paul's for two former freeman, 24s.8d. and 16s.8d. from messuages in Wood Street for two other obits, and 22s. from a tenement in Aldgate Street for the anniversary mass of Stephen Smith, and so on. As well as funneling a large stream of cash into London parishes, the company had been responsible for assigning 16s. a year in rent from 'The Three Nuns' in St Mary Woolchurch to the hospital of St Mary without Bishopsgate for the anniversary mass of John Goodwin, and £7 a year to Reading Abbey for masses for Sir Stephen Peacock, a former master. All this was typical. The companies had often leased the properties to churchwardens of the churches concerned, and thus, as trustees, simply paid back the income to fund the requiem masses. Sometimes these 'foundation' masses, as we would call them today, were annual obligations incurred by a company as a result of a one-off donation — to build the hall, for instance. Sometimes a company had directed the income entrusted to its care to a religious fraternity. The Salters' Company, for instance, had been making an annual payment for a deceased brother to Corpus Christi guild in the church of All Hallows. The Founders had paid a pound a year to the guild of St Mary in Queenhithe for the anniversary mass for a benefactor who had helped them build their hall. There had been money for numerous lights and lamps, as well as masses, and among those whose ordeal in Purgatory was thus to be reduced — for that had been the whole purpose of this complex network of arrangements — there had been many wives and widows of freemen.[24]

Such lists of scales — showing, page after page, past piety disowned and memorials to ancestors and spouses despoiled, apparently without a thought for benefactors or intended beneficiaries — make dispiriting reading. But we cannot know how much local communities succeeded in hiding from royal commissioners and adapting endowments to new uses by turning a guildhall into a townhall or, as at Whittlesford in Cambridgeshire, into a workhouse, then a poorhouse and even a schoolroom.[25] As has been said, concealed lands of former chantries, guilds and the rest were being discovered well into Elizabeth's reign, seized and sold off by the crown.[26] More importantly, we cannot know how much of what the crown seized found its way back to the towns and villages whence it had come, because we cannot trace (except occasionally and by accident) what the speculators or agents subsequently did with the sackfuls of purchases they made at the Court of Augmentations. Maybe they in turn sold some of their newly acquired properties to the town where the chantries or guilds or whatever had previously stood. Maybe they had been acting as agents for those towns from the start. It is possible, for instance, that the huge purchase of former religious endowments administered by the London companies was made possible only by capital provided by the companies themselves. They could have been interested in recovering what were doubtless often some of the choicest properties in the city.

We know that the towns had an interest in making such acquisitions, because, at the very time that some were pressing the crown to re-endow (free of charge) former chantry and guild schools and almshouses, some of these (as well as several others who had no such institutions to revive), were

---

24 For all the above, see *CPR, Edward VI*, iii, 386—401.
25 *VCH, Cambs.*, vi, 272.
26 Cf. C. J. Kitching, 'The Quest for Concealed Lands in the Reign of Elizabeth', *TRHS*, 5th ser., 24 (1974), 63—78.

also making direct purchases from the crown of other newly confiscated lands. Thus in August 1548 the burgesses of Dorchester paid £149 for the possessions of a former chantry in the town. Stamford paid a little less for a cottage, messuages and barns belonging to three of its former guilds. York paid £212 for lands and buildings of two of its dissolved guilds; Newcastle £144 for a suppressed free chapel/chantry.[27] By the end of Edward's reign some towns were also leasing lands from the crown, presumably because the capital for purchase was not to hand: the small town of Giggleswick in Lancashire acquired lands of a dissolved college and a chantry for 63s. a year; Bath some of the former abbey's possessions for £10.[28]

We must distinguish three categories of towns. First, there were those which were simply asking that their former schools or almshouses be re-endowed, and were indeed granted the necessary lands *ex gratia*. Such were Abingdon, Burton, Chelmsford, Grantham, Guildford, Louth, Macclesfield, Morpeth, Sedburgh and Shrewsbury, etc.[29] Next, there were a few towns which, though they were restoring former institutions, had to pay the crown a lump sum or substantial annual rent because they had acquired much more than was needed to support former schools or hospitals. Coventry, Wisbech and Ludlow are in this category. Thirdly, there were some nineteen towns which had no pre-Reformation foundations to restore but bought up lands and the like which had come into the crown's possession thanks to the 1547 act. The mayor and commonalty of Bristol, for instance, paid £51 for the chapel (and its ornaments) formerly belonging to the fraternity of the Assumption. Maidstone spent £205 on recovering its Corpus Christi fraternity's guildhall, many of its other possessions and nine houses for the poor, as well as lands of a dissolved college and a free chapel, the income from which was also to support a new grammar school.[30] A

[27] *CPR, Edward VI*, i, 309–10; ii, 173–4, 253; iii, 31.

[28] Ibid., iv, 439–40; v, 68–9.

[29] There are, however, one or two exceptions. Thus Birmingham received £21-worth of former guild lands for a grammar school — a new one. There had been no medieval school, so this was not a re-endowment. I cannot explain why Birmingham was so lucky. The list of *ex-gratia* refoundations includes several ex-monastic schools, e.g. Bury St Edmunds, Bruton, Sherborne (as well as Abingdon).

[30] *CPR, Edward VI*, ii, 174–6.

few weeks before the massive purchase, already discussed, of former endowments entrusted to London's liveried companies, the mayor and citizens of London had come forward with £456 13s. 4d. with which to purchase the guildhall that is now *the* Guildhall, the nearby chapel, 'le librarie' and all the former guild's halls, kitchens, cellars and so on (but no bells, plate or ornaments). They also acquired properties in Holborn.[31] There were similar purchases, just mentioned, by York and Newcastle and other towns. The message was clear. If a town wanted to recover former chantry, guild, college, or obit lands for any purpose other than re-endowment of a pre-Reformation school or hospital — even for endowment of a new school, as in Maidstone's case — it had to pay. The community had to find the money to re-acquire what, at least in the case of suppressed guilds and obits, had previously belonged to and been administered by the community, albeit by guild officials and churchwardens rather than municipal officers (but the distinction might not have been great in many cases) and which had been providing that community with perhaps considerable practical and material amenities for decades.

The total number of towns in these three categories is forty-three. One way or another and at varying expense to themselves, forty-three towns successfully petitioned the crown during the reign of Edward VI for grants of former possessions of the religious institutions brought down by the act of 1547 (and there were one or two bids for ex-monastic properties as well).

Two of these towns received further awards in the next reign: Abingdon recovered some more of the former possessions of the abbey and Holy Cross fraternity, plus some local ex-obit and chantry lands; Boston received a further £60-worth of the possessions of three of its suppressed guilds with which to provide for a grammar school, extra parochial clergy and four poor folk.[32] Fifteen other towns made successful bids in Mary's reign, such as Bridgwater (which recovered former chantry and obit lands), Clitheroe, Mansfield and Sheffield. Walsall obtained ex-chantry lands for its

---

31 Ibid., iv, 19.
32 *CPR, Philip and Mary*, ii, 153—5; iii, 380—5.

grammar school. Basingstoke recovered lands, mills, barns, etc., which had belonged to its Holy Ghost fraternity, for the refoundation of that guild. The largest of Mary's grants went to Derby: £77-worth of lands from Derby abbey, Holy Trinity guild, chantries and chapels, to support a grammar school and three new perpetual vicarages in the town. Derby had to pay handsomely for this (£266 down and £41 15s. 11d. in annual rent thereafter), and so did Abingdon for its grant.[33]

For the rest, however, Mary was more generous than her half-brother had been. She gave away properties for which Edward would have charged. On the other hand, her gifts were often minuscule. The truth is that she probably had little to give: the bulk of the chantry and guild lands and so on had passed out of royal hands by the time she arrived on the scene. Hence she was able to do Boston a favour probably only because the disgrace of the marquis of Northampton, William Parr, who had bought enormous quantities of the former possessions of Boston's guilds in Edward's reign, happened to make this possible.[34]

This probably explains another feature of her reign. She endowed only a few grammar schools (Bromsgrove, Ipswich and Walsall among them), but granted licences for at least sixteen more to be set up by towns or individuals from their own resources. Similarly she re-endowed five or six hospitals, but granted licences for seven more. Thus the town of Thaxted received royal assent to a petition to set up a school and almshouses, but no endowment. Owen Oglethorpe, bishop of Carlisle, was licensed to acquire lands up to £40 in annual value to endow a grammar school and almshouse in his native Tadcaster, but the lands were to come from him.[35]

We have been tracing how local communities responded to government policies: how they salvaged, built and rebuilt. Attention has focused so far on the reigns of Edward and Mary, but the story really begins in their father's time.

[33] Ibid., i, 170–2, 193, 204; ii, 192; iii, 262–3; iv, 168–9.
[34] Ibid., ii, 153–5.
[35] Ibid., iii, 154–6, 166.

Despite Thomas Cromwell's alleged zeal for 'urban renewal' and despite the urgent pleas on behalf of communities like Northampton and Coventry by Dr John London, one of the royal agents employed in the later stages of the dissolution of monasteries and a man with a genuine concern for the 'commonwealth', little was done in the 1530s to relieve the worst hit of the many older towns which were then in economic difficulty. Dr London repeatedly pleaded that conventual churches be allowed to stand and suggested that, for example, ex-friary buildings and sites be handed over to towns to relieve poverty and unemployment, and to halt urban decay, but without success.[36] Cromwell's ears may not have been stopped, but his hands did not move.

Some towns began to take the initiative in the next decade. Several put in successful bids for ex-monastic properties — Norwich, for instance, acquiring a former hospital for use as a poorhouse, plus lands to support a school.[37] During the 1540s, in the wake of the monasteries, the colleges of secular clergy (some of them mighty establishments) were tumbling to the crown. Several towns took action to save at least something from the wreckage: Warwick redeemed its collegiate church and some of the latter's former endowment; Crediton paid the crown £200 for its college.[38] In 1543 the inhabitants of Southwell managed to secure an act of Parliament which restored their college in its entirety, three years after suppression — a remarkable feat.[39] Perhaps the most remarkable of all, however, were those purchases from the crown by townsfolk of the churches of former religious (Benedictine monks and nuns, for they had tended to be urban-dwellers) which saved for posterity such glorious fanes as those of Great Malvern, Romsey, St Albans, Sherborne and Tewkesbury (rescued whole and entire for £200, £100, £400, £66 13s.4d. and £453 respectively) and parts of former conventual churches, like those of Boxgrove, Malmesbury and Pershore, which also still stand today as parish churches, truncated but magnificent.

[36] See, e.g., *LP*, xiii, i, 1342; ii, 346, 367; xiv, i, 3 (5), 42.
[37] Finally granted a few weeks before Henry VIII's death (*CPR, Edward VI*, i, 13—17).
[38] Ibid., i, 43—4. For Warwick, see below, p. 130.
[39] It was certainly the result of local initiative, though introduced via the Lords (House of Lords original acts, 35 Henry VIII, no. 42).

Londoners were fairly conspicuous in this story. They bought the conventual church, shorn of its nave, of St Bartholomew's in Smithfield. They leased St Mary Overie from the crown until 1614, when they bought it outright for £800. And, of course, by the end of Henry VIII's reign they were hard at work recovering some of their lost hospitals.

Many similar examples could be cited. Towns had begun to flex their muscles and to learn how to rescue something from the past well before the surge of bids which got under way in 1549 and continued into Mary's reign. They had also perceived how these transactions might require the less sophisticated among them to take an important step forward in their own constitutional development.

Mention was made above that Thaxted in Essex was granted a licence by Mary Tudor (in 1556) to found a school and almshouses. At the same time the town was given its former guildhall (alias 'le Mote Hall') to be the common meeting hall for the borough government. Thaxted had been granted incorporation. It was one of no less than thirty-five towns which achieved corporate status or had royal confirmation thereof during Mary's reign. The initiative for this came from below. It was intimately connected with the whole story of the efforts of towns to claw back some of the local endowments seized by the crown, because, though the refounded schools could be and often were handed over to the charge of newly appointed local trustees, towns could more easily take on responsibility for schools and almshouses, and acquire former guild and chantry properties, when they had themselves achieved legal identity. Incorporation was a necessary precondition.

We can see this fact at work in Edward's reign. Maidstone, for instance, was incorporated at the same time as it bought ex-guild and college properties. Similarly, Wisbech and Stratford-on-Avon, deprived of religious fraternities which had previously provided some *de facto* corporate identity, sought royal grants of borough status when they recovered the possessions of the former guilds and became responsible for the schools and almshouses those guilds had run.

In fact the story of incorporations also begins in the previous reign, in 1542, when Reading received royal incorporation together with the grant of the former Greyfriars church in the town.[40] Three years later Warwick concluded its elaborate bargain whereby, in return for substantial payment, it was granted a charter of incorporation, together with some of the possessions of the former college of St Mary, a rich collegiate church which had come into the crown's hands but was now to be reinstated as a parish church. The burgesses, collectively invested with the rectory, would henceforth be responsible for paying the vicar, two curates, a clerk and a sacristan. A licence to found a free grammar school was also granted. The town was to pay the master his annual stipend of £10 and provide him and the vicar with a dwelling. So the burgesses acquired a church, endowments and a school — as well as, and thanks to, taking a major step towards municipal status and self-government.[41]

Many of Mary's grants of corporate status were unconnected with recovery from the crown by the towns concerned of former religious lands. Indeed, in seven cases the grants were allegedly gracious rewards for loyalty during the Lady Jane Grey affair. But in several cases the pattern discernible in the previous decade is still to be seen: Leominster, for instance, incorporated in March 1554, was thus able to acquire £36-worth of former chantry and obit endowment in the town. Launceston's borough status was confirmed, and the mayor and commonalty appointed as warden and governors of the hospital of St Leonard there. Abingdon's large-scale recovery of its former guild's lands (and other properties confiscated under the 1547 act) required and was consummated by its elevation to full borough status in November 1556.[42] And, of course, those new boroughs which had received nothing directly from the crown would now be able to buy from those who had — the first grantees and speculators.

Doubtless the motives for these purchases would have

[40] *LP*, xvii, 285 (1).
[41] *LP*, xx, i, 846 (41). Purchase of a former monastic church for use as a parish church could also be the occasion for incorporation, as was the case with Romsey in 1544. See *LP*, xix, i, 141 (57).
[42] *CPR, Philip and Mary*, i, 395—8; iii, 174—8, 380—6. For a study of incorporations during the reigns of Edward and Mary see R. Tittler, 'The emergence of urban policy, 1536—58', in J. Loach and R. Tittler (eds), *The Mid-Tudor Polity, c.1540—1560* (1980), pp. 74—93.

been various, including resentment of intrusion from outside and fear of 'foreigners' who would bleed the community of cash and neglect upkeep of properties. Civic pride would have played its part. Schools and hospitals of former chantries and guilds might have been rooted in superstition; but they were also rooted in the community and served it. Guildhalls were useful, often handsome, buildings. The royal grants, even of mere licences to found schools or hospitals, gave new authority to town governments, new scope, new responsibilities.

It had been a worrying and expensive time; for places like Ludlow and Coventry a nerve-wracking time. For a place like Leicester the struggle had scarcely begun: the charter of full incorporation and the return of over 200 town properties formerly belonging to colleges, chantries and Corpus Christi guild was not wrung from the crown until the late 1580s.[43] For others, however, the crown's assault on the guilds, chantries and so on had set in train a series of events which, in the upshot, affected them deeply. Maybe the lands and buildings that towns recovered was a small fraction of the original total, but the centralist policy of paying annual salaries to local functionaries from the Court of Augmentations had been defeated and replaced by local endowment and re-endowment, locally administered. The administration of these endowments, which had previously been distributed among a variety of local agencies such as guilds and churchwardens, had been transferred to the single control of borough governments. Power and responsibility were moving upwards and being concentrated into fewer hands. For some, therefore, the story had a happy ending after all.

A handful of religious fraternities were restored under Mary and five hospitals re-endowed, notably the Savoy hospital in London and St Leonard's in Newark. Some half-dozen religious houses had been reopened by the end of her reign. A few other religious foundations — two colleges, chantries and free chapels — had also been put back, and five new chantries licensed.[44] The numbers are strikingly low. Why?

[43] M. Bateson (ed.), *Records of the Borough of Leicester, 1103–1603*, iii (Cambridge, 1903), 234–52.
[44] Again, the statistics are from *CPR, Philip and Mary* and may not be complete.

The answer is not so much that Catholic fervour was a thing of the past as that the circumstances of the times made faster progress difficult. To take Mary's position and that of Cardinal Pole first: for both it was a question of restoration rather than innovation. The old order was to be put back as it used to be, as exactly as possible. As far as former religious houses were concerned, therefore, that meant finding not only buildings that were available and inhabitable, but also at least the remnant of the former community. Syon could be restored because the crown happened to be able to give back the late abbey to a surviving community, returned from exile, of English Bridgettine nuns and monks. Seven Dominican nuns formerly of Dartford priory and twelve Carthusians who petitioned for restoration could be given their erstwhile houses, and so on. But so much had happened since the dissolution nearly twenty years before: lands had changed hands perhaps several times, former religious had died, found alternative employment, perhaps married, etc. So there was never a chance of more than a very partial restoration. Similarly, Savoy hospital could be restored because of the disgrace of the man who had acquired the site and lands in the previous reign.[45] Wolverhampton college had come back into the crown's hands thanks to the fall of John Dudley, duke of Northumberland, and could therefore be reunited with St George's Windsor.

As ever, a good deal of the initiative, such as it was, came from below, and not just from surviving remnants of former religious communities. For instance, the earl of Pembroke, who had the reversion of the site of the former Dominican house in Southampton, persuaded the crown to buy out the existing lessee, a London merchant, by granting him a licence to export up to 40,000 kerseys over two years free of customs duties in return for surrendering the lease. So the crown sacrificed revenue in order to allow the earl to restore the friary.[46] It so happened that the land given to the guild of St Thomas in Hempstead (Essex) in 1514 to maintain a priest was still in crown hands in 1555: so a former feoffee of the guild lands could petition for the land and use it for

---

[45] John Gates, executed for complicity in the Lady Jane Grey plot.
[46] *CPR, Philip and Mary*, iii, 360–1.

support of a priest and relief of the poor in accordance with the benefactor's will.[47]

Nevertheless, these and the bids to found new chantries and the like were but a trickle. It inevitably took time for new foundations to be planned and petitions put together. It presumably took time for people to realise that the Marian restoration of the old religion was a reality and secure, and for layfolk to begin to feel confident enough to start endowing chantries, guilds and obits once more. In view of recent history, only a rash man would have been in a hurry to bestow his worldly wealth on pious foundations.

Furthermore, Mary's first concern and a substantial achievement of her reign was to lavish gifts on the secular church, especially bishoprics, and hence make good some of the depredations of previous years. She released her new (or restored) bishops from their predecessors' debts to the crown for first fruits and tenths and excused newcomers their own dues. She rescued for Durham all the possessions which John Dudley had been planning to seize by virtue of an act of Parliament passed just before his fall. The diocese of London received grants of lands and rectories, etc., to the value of £526 a year. She made grants to Winchester and Exeter. Archbishop Heath of York was massively compensated for what his Protestant predecessor had been forced to surrender to the queen's predecessor and was given a new London residence — part of the former possessions of the disgraced Charles Brandon, duke of Suffolk — in recompense for York Place, which her father had unlawfully seized from Wolsey twenty-seven years before and turned into the royal palace of Whitehall. To Reginald Pole was given over £1,000-worth of former possessions of the see of Canterbury and St Augustine's abbey, much of which had come back into the crown's hands via those of Thomas Cromwell, Thomas Wyatt and John Dudley.[48]

Mary brought brief respite after two decades or so of spoliation. Wealth was flowing back into the Church and being transferred from layman to cleric. A tide had turned.

---

[47] Ibid., ii, 119.

[48] Ibid., i, 119–20, 232–3, 329, 377–8; ii, 168; iii, 68–72, 187, 264–5, 276, etc. Cf. ibid., iii, 513–15 for the re-endowment of Manchester College.

The queen was also keen to transfer back to the clergy as much as possible of former clerical patronage and the income from appropriated livings (i.e. the rectorial tithes which monasteries had enjoyed from parish churches 'appropriated' to them and which had passed into the crown's hands at the dissolution). Mary consistently included gifts of rectories and their attendant vicarages in her grants to her bishops. She wanted to concentrate ecclesiastical patronage in bishops' hands. She endowed Oxford colleges by granting them ex-monastic rectories (tithes and the right to nominate vicars).

She also licensed laymen to use rectories to endow religion. The appearance on the scene of the *lay* rector, i.e. a layman who enjoyed the share of tithes from an impropriated living which he had acquired via the crown at the dissolution of the monasteries, could be seen as one of the more remarkable and shocking results of the Henrician Reformation, not least because it gave laymen a new and, in the case of many of the dependent vicarages, virtually untrammelled patronage. Interestingly enough, by the end of Mary's reign the unease which one would expect the more conscientious laymen to feel about all this was beginning to show itself in action. In November 1556 two laymen, one a serjeant-at-law, petitioned to be dispossessed of a rectory and allowed to return the income to its parish church. In the following February Sir Francis Englefield shed three rectories, using two to endow an obit for himself, his parents and benefactors. In June 1557 Anthony Browne, Viscount Montague, 'being piously moved', extinguished ten appropriations, that is, surrendered the rectories, and used them to found two chantries in Sussex.[49]

Had Mary lived longer, there might have been many more examples of laymen's consciences being pricked. Indeed, the crown itself might have eventually led the way. An act of Parliament of 1556 allowed Mary to bestow on the Church all the rectories and the like which had come into royal hands since 1538 and for Cardinal Pole to allocate the income to subsidise poor livings, preachers and clerical education. Some £7,000 a year would have passed back into clerical hands; but

[49] Ibid., iii, 320, 356, 440–2. Laymen also transferred rectories to Oxford and Cambridge colleges. Sir Richard Southwell handed over some to newly refounded Syon abbey (ibid., iv, 439).

the plan miscarried. Such were the demands of war (once again) that the bishops decided — voluntarily, Pole insisted — to forgo this windfall and to offer it back to the crown for the defence of the realm. Something, however, was gained. The advowsons (i.e. the right to appoint to the livings concerned, as distinct from the income thereof) were indeed transferred to the bishops.[50]

With Mary's death, of course, these new beginnings were snuffed out. The newly refounded monasteries, chantries and guilds were swept away again, along with the Catholic hierarchy, the altars, the mass — everything which Mary had restored. Clerical first fruits and tenths were immediately restored to the crown. Another act of Parliament, clearly designed to take advantage of the deprivation of the surviving bishops from Mary's reign, empowered the crown to exchange the rectories it still held for episcopal lands (a transaction which would be disadvantageous to the Church because the income from rectories was less easily adjusted to keep pace with inflation). The act also imposed a strict limit on the length of any lease any prelate might grant in the future. Since long leases were best avoided by landlords in a time of inflation, this measure seemed to provide useful protection to episcopal incomes. But the act went on to say that the restriction should not apply when the beneficiary was the crown itself.[51] Like father, like daughter. A predatory crown was on the prowl again.

---

[50] Ibid., iv, 399–400, 402, 420, among others. Cf. F. Heal, *Of Prelates and Princes*, ch. 6.
[51] Heal, *Of Prelates and Princes*, pp. 202–4.

7

Survival and Revival
of the Old Faith

One of the notable things that has been happening to the
study of Tudor history in recent years is the accumulation
of evidence by people who have no ideological axe to grind
that Mary Tudor's reign was not so unsuccessful after all.
There was a disastrous marriage; we today are horrified by
the burnings and one may wonder how long it would have
been before English Protestants on the Continent counter-
attacked with a full-scale missionary effort to deliver the
homeland from the clutches of Antichrist. All the same, in
1553 there was a real sense of a fresh beginning after years
of confusion and upset — not unlike the mood of 1660.
Mary's regime tried to be broad-based, to be sensitive to
the political nation, and to face up to urgent problems —
financial, administrative and military. It produced a good
deal of sensible housekeeping and reform. Reginald Pole
now looks less anachronistic and clumsy than he used to.
He and his brother bishops would stand up to comparison
with any bench of bishops the *Ecclesia Anglicana* could produce from its previous history (and much of its subsequent?).[1]
So, if we muse on the chances of success for Protestant
missionaries from Strasburg, Frankfurt and Geneva of cap-
turing officially re-Catholicised England, we should also
consider the suggestion that, had she lived, Mary might

[1] Cf. J. Loach and R. Tittler (eds), *The Mid-Tudor Polity*, esp. introduction and
articles by Tittler and R. H. Pogson; Pogson, 'Revival and reform'; D. Loades, in
The Reign of Mary Tudor (1979) is less enthusiastic but gives credit for the positive
achievements of the reign. A major advance in understanding of the religious
policies was taken in P. Hughes, *The Reformation in England*, ii (1953).

have accomplished a restoration of the old faith as enduring as that in Southern Netherlands or even Poland.

Much of the flowering of recusant history (post-Reformation Catholic history) in recent decades has tended to show how tenacious and widespread was the survival of the old religion during and after Elizabeth's reign. It was not merely that Lancashire, much of Yorkshire and the north-east were steeped in recusant conservatism. Nonconformist popery was powerful in Northamptonshire and Hampshire ('Southamptonshire') Hereford and Worcester, much of Warwickshire, and some of Sussex. Even East Anglia and Essex showed signs of dogged allegiance to the old ways.

There remains, of course, the Protestant 'walkover' of 1558/9.[1a] Anyone who wants to draw a firm straight line from the rehabilitated Marian Catholicism to the triumphalist recusancy of the 1580s has a major problem. The whole affair is ill-documented and obscure. Doubtless there was much confusion and much indifference. Whatever the explanation, there was a large-scale collapse when Elizabeth put the old order to the test. The bishops stood firm — but not many other people imitated them, it seems.

That said, three things should be added. First, the Elizabethan government's intention was to pick out only the more obvious and aggressive opponents and to 'include in' the rest and hope for the best. Contrary to what some have supposed, the official desire was to woo and win over, not to exclude. Issues were deliberately blurred. Secondly, there are all manner of difficulties in assessing the oaths of supremacy which were taken to the new regime. There was evasion. As the bishop of Chichester complained in 1577, lists of oath-takers were returned which named folk who had never complied.[2] Then there is the intriguing question as to how much oaths mattered anyway. Some years later a Lady Throckmorton was to argue that Catholics could say and swear whatever they or anyone else liked, 'without touch of

---

[1a] For the story of the 1559 Parliament, see N. L. Jones, *Faith by statute: Parliament and the settlement of religion, 1559*, Roy. Hist. Soc. Studies in History, 32 (1982). Dr Jones shows that, contrary to our previous belief, that settlement was largely the work of the crown and gives new support for the idea of Reformation 'from above'.

[2]   Sp 12/111, no. 45.

conscience', if they were swearing on English (heretical) Bibles. 'These', she judged, 'were but the bookes of heretiques and of no force before god.'[3]

If that was the attitude of many clergy in 1559, how valuable were their oaths of supremacy? How valuable were the subscriptions of JPs and the like later on? We have here a fierce statement of the principle that faith is not to be kept with heretics and a lay moral code which makes later clerical casuistry look rigorous.

Thirdly, there were whole communities which did not take much notice of the new religion for a long time, but carried on more or less regardless, and there were indeed clergymen who compromised by celebrating both the new communion service and the old mass. Cardinal Allen himself said there had been such people. Thomas Morren, former chaplain of the deposed Marian bishop of London, Edmund Bonner, in 1561 thought it necessary to denounce such priests as traitors, and worse, in a tract which he himself distributed in Chester.[4] As late as 1584 a Miles Yare, a parson in Suffolk, was reported to be saying mass (though still a parson) in his parlour.[5]

All this no doubt helped to obscure issues and ease the change-over. Nonetheless, what happened in the early years of Elizabeth's reign throws unflattering light on the quality of Marian Catholicism. We will never get clear exactly what happened.[6] But it may be worth noting one or two intriguing details.

There are indications — they are tantalisingly few — that some of the deprived Marian bishops, though in confinement, were not inactive. David Poole, for instance, deposed bishop

[3] SP 12/173, no. 26(1).

[4] We know this from Bishop Pilkington's discussion in his *Answers to Popish Questions*, of 1563 (*Works*, PS, 3 (1842), 630—1). Cf. *CSP Addenda, 1547—1565*, p. 521.

[5] SP 12/169, no. 19. He was said to have been among many people in Suffolk who aided popish priests, having been given the living in 1565 by a Catholic patron, Thomas Cornwallis. See D. MacCullough, 'Catholic and Puritan in Elizabethan Suffolk', *Arch. f. Ref.*, lxxii (1981), 253.

[6] The whole matter has been hotly debated, of course, in the past. The truth seems to be that there were few deprivations at the beginning of Elizabeth's reign but that the significance of this fact is as difficult to interpret as the lack of much open resistance.

of Peterborough and under virtual house arrest, in 1562 or thereabouts received a priest called John Felton who had been ordained probably in the 1530s, had initially conformed under Elizabeth and then decided to quit. The bishop heard his confession, absolved him from schism, imposed suitable penance (some fasting) and sent him on his way.[7] Felton became thereafter a vigorous papist missioner. It was said that Poole received many clerics in this way, restored them to communion with Rome and presumably despatched them, like Felton, to oppose and undermine the Elizabethan settlement. All of this reminds us, incidentally, that, though the number of deprivations of clergy in 1559/60 may not have been great, there was perhaps quite a considerable number of clerical defections from the Established Church in the following years (as well as examples of clerics who did not leave the fold but were of very doubtful loyalty). But to return to the bishops: the former bishop of Lincoln, Thomas Watson, also kept in contact with his co-religionists. He lived in semi-confinement until the early 1580s. In 1583 an agent from the English college in Douai, despatched to England to collect money for the college, was being interrogated about his contact with Watson, when he had last seen him and what he had reported about the bishop's circumstances.[8] Watson was clearly in touch with the seminary priests, because one of them, the ardent anti-Jesuit Thomas Bluet, could claim that the bishop was one of the old guard who was worried by the arrival of the Jesuits on the English scene in 1580 and predicted that they would inevitably provoke the government into imposing harsher laws on all English Catholics.[9] Since Bluet himself had been arrested in 1578 just a few months after he returned to England from Douai and had been sent from the Marshalsea to Wisbech in 1580, we have the interesting possibility that old Bishop Watson was in contact with the whole group of secular priests who had been rounded up and interned in the bishop of Ely's bleak residence in Wisbech.

Meanwhile Bishop Bonner, ex-bishop of London, had

---

[7] SP 12/156, no. 29(i).

[8] SP 12/157, no. 49.

[9] T. Bluet, *Important Considerations which Ought to Move all True and Sound Catholics...* (1601; 1831 edn), p. 47.

made a brief reappearance on the scene. Since his deprivation he had been lodged in the Marshalsea and been able to watch several former members of his entourage, like Dr Morren and the future Jesuit, Thomas Derbyshire, play a notable part in the early resistance to Elizabeth's religious policies. Bonner may well have been actively involved himself: it is difficult to imagine that so aggressive a man would have lain dormant in prison. That is simply speculation, but there is no doubt that in 1569 he received a visit in prison from the mysterious Dr Michael Morton, an envoy from Pope Pius V and one much involved in the Northern Rising later that year.[10] That was surely not just a goodwill visit. Was Morton seeking Bonner's advice and help, and perhaps alerting the old bishop to the possibility that he might emerge from prison a second time and take over the diocese of London once more? Bonner had done just that once before, against most of (if not all) the odds.

So the old hierarchy kept up some flickering *episcope* over their flock and English Catholicism in the first decades of Elizabeth's reign was not completely bereft of leadership (other than Allen's). And perhaps a man like Watson was young enough in 1558 to speculate whether he might live to see another sudden change in the direction of English religious affairs and himself be reinstated in Lincoln. Meanwhile at Mr Yates's house (Lyford Grange) near Wantage in Berkshire lived the hidden remnant of English monasticism, a group of Bridgettine nuns still following the religious life as late as 1581. Some had survived as a community at Lyford when their house, the famous abbey of Syon in Middlesex, was dissolved in 1539; another group had fled abroad. The two groups came together when Mary restored Syon. When their house was dissolved a second time, some took to the Continent once more, some returned to Lyford.[11] They were still in residence when Edmund Campion was captured there twenty years later, doubtless waiting like their sisters across the water, and the other English communities (notably the Dominican nuns from Dartford priory), for the moment

[10] G. E. Phillips, *The Extinction of the ancient Hierarchy...* (1905), p. 327.
[11] SP 12/168, no. 25 (ii), the confession of a seminary priest made in 1584. The story of the community after its dissolution in 1539 is told in SP 12/146, no. 114, as well as, e.g., Knowles, *Religious Orders*, pp. 440, 441–2.

when their house in England might be restored again.

In Mr Yates's moated house, then, existed a clandestine nunnery. In his house and many others', in churches and parsonages, were caches of mass vestments, missals, agnus deis, and all the rest of what was described as 'popish trash' — not to mention the altar slabs and holy-water stoups hidden in gardens and rubbish tips. We know that a great deal survived because, when recusant houses were ransacked, the searchers repeatedly found hordes of vestments, beads and books and so on.[12] As has been said, priests arriving to say mass in country houses usually found everything necessary for the liturgy. Church court records suddenly throw up stories of sets of vestments hidden in lay homes, of popish items handed down from father to son, or even from parson to Catholic neighbour.[13] In 1576 Archbishop Grindal was asking that throughout his province there be enquiry whether all altars and rood lofts were taken down, massbooks and grails 'utterly defaced, rent and abolished', vestments, albs, stoles, crosses, images and so on 'utterly defaced, broken and destroyed' — and if not, who had custody of them. He had asked these questions, with good reason, five years before when he arrived in York. Translated thence to Canterbury, he had the same anxieties. He also asked some revealing questions about whether ministers used any 'crossing or breathing or elevation of the bread and wine, any oils, chrism, tapers, prayers for the dead, excessive tolling of bells, illicit banners, torches, beads or popish primers'.[14]

All this and much else about the survival of Catholic rites and practice (including pilgrimages to wells and shrines, even to Canterbury) is well known. It paves the way for the claim that we have hitherto underestimated the contribution

---

[12] E.g. SP 12/156, no. 29(i); 164, no. 14; 167, no. 47, among others. SP 12/158 no. 9 lists a formidable amounts of popish vestments, etc. and books (including one by John Fisher) found in recusants' cells in Winchester gaol in 1583.

[13] In 1584, for example, one Oxfordshire man was presented for keeping 'coopes', another for having relics given to him by a vicar on his deathbed, a third for possessing vestments. A fourth told of vestments, crucifixes, bells, and cloths galore in the hands of locals. E. R. Brinkworth, *Archdeacon's Court: Liber Actorum 1584*, Oxf. Rec. Soc., 24 (1942) 200, 1, 5, 9. There are many similar stories of survival of Catholic 'gear'.

[14] Grindal, *Remains*, PS, 8 (1843), pp. 124–42, 151–70.

of the so-called Marian priests to the story of post-Reformation Catholicism ('so-called' because many of them, like John Felton, were in fact ordained before Mary's time). These men played a crucial part in sustaining the old faith through Elizabeth's reign — indeed, beyond. A Marian priest was still alive and active in 1616, supplying money and books to a nephew about to set out for the English College in Rome. He holds the record among his fellows for longevity.[15]

Marian priests were pioneers in the work of sustaining the officially proscribed creed. They were the first to 'convey themselves secretly from one papistes house to another', as the Bishop of Llandaff complained in 1579, mentioning as a particular offender a certain George Morris BD, who was another of Bishop Bonner's former brood.[16] They learnt how to disguise themselves as serving-men and the like. The first missionaries to England were not the alumni of Douai in the 1570s but an extremely interesting mixture of men who had gone abroad much earlier and came home in the 1560s after exile in Louvain — or, like Dr Morton, in Rome.[17] Marian priests set up as chaplains in gentry houses and as tutors to the children. Some stomped the highways and byways from one mass-centre to another, itinerant and fugitive. Many of the houses (Fitzherbert, Wharton, Wiseman, Paulet) which were later famous for the seminary or Jesuit priests whom they entertained had previously been, and continued to be, served by Marians. Like the later clergy they were sometimes imprisoned and even martyred. They worked closely with the new clergy from the Continent: for example, no less than 228 people were said to have been converted in Staffordshire in three months in 1582 by three

---

[15] He was Valentine Tayler. A. Kenny (ed.), *The Responsa Scolarum of the English College, Rome*, CRS, 54 (1962), 292. Of the scores of known Marian priests, a remarkable number survived until the early seventeenth century.

[16] SP12/139, no. 30.

[17] Thomas Wright, arrested at Boroughbridge in 1579, in the company of Thomas Mudde (former monk of Jervaulx who fled to Scotland, returned in Mary's reign and died in Hull prison in 1583) was one. Henry Henshaw, ex-rector of Lincoln College Oxford, fled in the early 1560s and then returned to England. See SP 12/98, no. 10 for a priest come from 'beyond' the seas before 1574. Thomas Heskins, ex-chancellor of Salisbury, fled to the Continent *c.*1560, became a Dominican and was back in England before 1565 (W. Grumbly (ed.), *Obituary Notes of the English Dominicans from 1555 to 1952* (1955), p. 3).

priests. One was Dr Henshaw, sometime rector of Lincoln College, Oxford, and by then a devoted papist; the second was Oliver Heywood, a Marian priest; the third was William Holt, a Jesuit just arrived from Counter-Reformation Europe.[18] New and old overlapped.

Marian priests had their share of 'cloak-and-dagger' activity. One Roger Johns MA used an altar allegedly erected by a Glamorganshire gentleman 'in a wood'.[19] The future Jesuit, John Blackfan, began a long and colourful Catholic career by being told to meet a Marian priest secretly in a similar place, where, after interrogating the young man, the priest performed an extraordinary ceremony of reconciliation by dubbing him with a bough from a nearby tree and reciting a psalm over him.[20]

Priests ordained before the Elizabethan settlement had practical advantages. Lord Montague of Cowdray in Sussex, a famous centre of popery, would allegedly allow only a Marian priest in his house — not a Jesuit or a 'seminary' from Douai — to act as chaplain.[21] Why? Partly because a Marian priest was less provocative; partly because he was less rigorous and allowed the viscount to put in an appearance at the local Anglican church from time to time and thus escape the full oppression of the recusancy laws. His chaplain deemed it expedient to make this concession now and then, and said that such occasional conformity would not be a sin. Likewise the defiantly papist house of the Wisemans at Braddocks in Essex was served by 'an old priest' (i.e. a Marian) because that way it could avoid molestation. Marian priests were not liable for the fierce penalties which awaited the missionaries from Douai, Rome and later English seminaries in Spain.[22] They knew their way round better than did newly arrived clerks from overseas.[23] As well as

---

[18] SP 12/156, no. 29. Heywood was ordained in Henry VIII's reign and died in 1586, in prison (SP 12/195, no. 34).

[19] SP 12/118, no. 11 (ii).

[20] *Foley*, ii, 625–6. His subsequent career was equally colourful.

[21] SP 12/245, no. 138.

[22] As Dr MacCullough has shown (in 'Catholic and Puritan'), Marian priests could also be presented to livings in the Established Church by recusant gentlemen.

[23] And were skilful at eluding detection. Thus William Battie, deprived vicar of Halton (Lancs.), was reported as having died long before but in 1589 was 'secretly kept' and saying many masses (SP 12/229, no. 26).

being less dangerous to 'entertain', because they had been lawfully ordained in England, they could (it was eventually decided) solemnise marriages which the Established Church would recognise. So if a marriage could take place before a Marian priest there was no pressure on a Catholic to take the first step to apostasy and no doubt about the civil validity of the contract.

Later Catholicism had ample grounds for gratitude to often heroic Marian priests.[24] Of course, their fatal shortcoming was that they had no way of replacing themselves until William Allen founded the seminary in Douai which, even if this was not its original intention, became the source of missionaries to England. Old Thomas Goldwell, Marian bishop of St Asaph and subsequently an exile in Rome, continued to ordain Englishmen for the English mission up to his death in the 1580s. But none of the few deposed Marian bishops who still lurked in England seems to have dared to go as far as clandestine ordination. Like many others, they were either numbed by defeat or simply waiting passively for the old order somehow to be restored.

The old clergy had another, but lesser, limitation. They doubted whether they had the power to recognise fellow-countrymen who had fallen into schism by attending non-Catholic services, since this was a 'reserved' sin. Until a Marian had been granted additional power to grant absolution for this, his work would be confined to that inevitably dwindling number of Catholic laymen who had never conformed. The authority to reconcile had been conferred by Rome on the leading English Catholics in Louvain, Nicholas Sander and the celebrated Dr Harding. Later William Allen had it, too — and these in turn could authorise others. The Dr Morton mentioned above, who came to England from Rome, with a companion, in 1569 was also empowered to confer what was essentially an episcopal faculty to reconcile. A Marian priest could acquire the necessary authority, but not all did. Hugh Hall, a priest who was active in Warwickshire and Northamptonshire, said he never reconciled anyone,

---

[24] Though I would still plead that the arrival of the seminary priests from abroad was crucial to Catholic survival, I agree with Dr Haigh's recent reassessment of the Marians. See his 'From Monopoly to Minority: Catholicism in early modern England', *TRHS*, 5th ser., 31 (1981), 129—47.

but heard confessions only of those who were practising Catholics already.[25] Several priests claimed that they had not even said mass, or very rarely. They had acted as tutors or wandered from house to house, hearing confessions occasionally (especially of the dying), administering the occasional baptism or officiating at a wedding, but had never been real 'massing priests.[26] One rather pathetic man was caught carrying popish equipment, including an *agnus dei* in which were hidden two hosts consecrated years previously in Mary's reign. Perhaps he had never said mass since.[27]

These were doubtless the exceptions. Many Marian priests were very active and bold, and had no doubts about themselves. But there was great variety among them, and it is difficult not to see the arrival of the priests from Douai and then Rome as anything but a powerful transfusion of new life and confidence into the Catholic community. Nevertheless, Marian clergy had laid the foundations of the Catholic mission.

There is another important thing to say about those early days. The Northern Rising of 1569: what a serious event that was, and how much more than a wild fling by a couple of crazed earls. The main actors may well have been a rather unconvincing lot. Everything misfired badly. But, in the first place, the rebellion revealed to the government with shocking clarity how lamentably the new regime had failed to take root in the north-east. 'Not ten gentlemen in all this country favour the queen in the matter of religion', wrote Ralph Sadler to Cecil in December. 'The common people are ignorant, superstitious and altogether blinded with the old

[25] SP 12/164, no. 77. He claimed not to have said mass for five years. Cf. SP 12/168, no. 25 (ii).
[26] See, e.g., SP 12/156, no. 29 (ii) and note 25. One Anthony Atkinson, when caught in 1585, said he had celebrated mass only once since expulsion from Magdalen College, Oxford, in 1559 (SP 12/197, no. 1 (i)). Simon Southern, ordained in 1533, alleged in 1582 that he had not said mass since it was outlawed (1559) and had heard confessions only (SP 12/156, no. 29 (ii)).
[27] SP 12/179, no. 7 (i). But he had been a minister in the Elizabethan Church before quitting for conscience's sake around 1577.

popish doctrine.'[28] When Sir George Bowes tried to defend
Barnard Castle for the queen, over 220 of his men leapt the
walls to join the rebels, while others eventually mutinied
and opened the gates to the enemy. Though the rebellion
collapsed quickly, when it was over the leaders stayed only
just across the Scottish border and their return was expected
daily by their supporters in England. Meanwhile the government could ponder the fact that, had not the earls and Lord
Dacre been flushed out of their territories from the Trent to
Berwick and across to Carlisle, royal control might have been
lost. 'All things in Lancashire savoured of open rebellion',
the bishop of Carlisle reported. Men, armour, horses and
munitions were gathered.[29] London later discovered how
Sir Thomas Fitzherbert would have raised his tenantry in
the Peak and uncovered the full extent of conspiracy in
Norfolk — allegedly to proclaim Norfolk king, link up with
the northern rebels and set up idolatry again.[30] How much
the Spanish were really implicated is not relevant here; the
plotters claimed they were. And there could be no doubt
about Rome's involvement. Pius V knew about the intended
northern rising and encouraged it. He sent a priest to England
to persuade the earl of Northumberland and 'many others'
to rebel.[31] Nicholas Sander in Louvain may well have been
an intermediary in negotations; other priests were conspicuous ringleaders during the rising. It is wrong to see this
rebellion as just the death of feudal Catholicism: 'these
troubles are but a beginning', someone rightly told Cecil.[32]
They destabilised the whole situation, not least because for
several years afterwards there was constant fear that the
earl of Westmorland and his companion who had escaped
to the Low Countries would return, with Spanish/papal
backing and no doubt the formidable Nicholas Sander in

[28] *CSP, Addenda, 1566–79*, p. 139. To read the pages covering these events is
to get a vivid sense of the crisis, and of how much Elizabeth owed to the earl
of Sussex, her lieutenant in the north. See W. MacCaffrey, *The Shaping of the
Elizabethan Regime* (1969) for an account of events.

[29] Ibid., p. 321.

[30] SP 12/194, no. 75; SP 12/71, no. 61.

[31] *CSP, Addenda, 1566–79*, p. 390; SP 12/85, no. 27.

[32] *CSP, Addenda, 1566–79*, p. 170. Cf. the warning that many 'hollow heads'
remained in the north (ibid., p. 209).

the van. Secondly, it showed that Catholics were ready to invoke the temporal arm, to turn to violence. It inaugurated a new phase in the struggle between Reformation and Counter-Reformation. It was followed directly and obviously by the armadas against Ireland mounted by Nicholas Sander and others, by Morys Clynnog's proposals, put to the pope in 1575—6, for an assault on Wales, and, of course, by the events of 1588.

For whatever reasons, recusancy increased in strength and confidence during the 1570s. Maybe the bull of 1570 was more effective than has been supposed. The bishop of Carlisle (already quoted) reckoned that it had a major impact on Lancashire. It caused a man like Edmund Plowden to stop conforming.[33] So it may have greatly clarified issues for both sides. Thanks also to the Marian clergy, the increase in popish nonconformity was under way before the seminary priests from Douai started to arrive. It defeated government counter-measures — increasing use of imprisonment, bonds for good behaviour, restriction of movement of known dissidents. It forced the government to think again about its tactics for uncovering and suppressing disobedience.

By the mid-1570s, however, English Catholics were shifting their ground. Their leading spokesmen were now talking less of violence and rebellion and much more of the temporal (i.e. civil) obedience which Catholics owed and would give their queen. At least for the moment, Elizabeth's Catholic community was apparently ready to pledge itself to loyalism and non-resistance. This new turn of events came to a climax in the early 1580s when a group of Catholic laymen, eager to break the impasse between a government heading for increasingly bitter and bloody persecution (as the 'seminaries' and then Jesuits began arriving) and Catholic recusants who, while unable to comply with the queen's religious policies, were in other respects model and devoted subjects. They decided to try to end deadlock by formally asking for toleration.

The details are scanty. The first mention of the plan dates from late 1581 or early 1582. It is a story relayed by a third

[33] SP 12/144, no. 45.

party of how a Mr Thomas Skinner, a fairly prominent Catholic layman of Warwickshire, said that he had good hope that a decree allowing some religious toleration would soon be forthcoming.[34] The terms to be offered by both sides were not explained. In mid-1583 a draft supplication to the queen was in circulation which pleaded that Catholics be granted 'free libertye' of their consciences in quiet use of the 'Catholyke relygion' and allowed a specified number of churches in every shire and town. In return for this and the repeal of the anti-Catholic legislation, the Catholics would offer the queen an annual subsidy. The next step was the incident in 1585 when one Richard Shelley of Warminghurst in Sussex actually presented a petition signed by leading Catholic laymen to the queen as she was walking in her garden at Greenwich.[35]

Of course the *démarche* failed. Catholics were asking the impossible — and, be it noted, something which their co-religionists elsewhere in Europe had not yet begun to concede to others. Those who presented that petition in 1585 were making a bid to escape what could be appalling consequences for them of the recent new legislation. It is tempting to wonder, however, how far the decision to seek toleration when first mooted (in 1581) had some connection with the arrival of Campion and Persons in England in 1580. For, though the seminary priests who preceded them had also tried to avoid embroilment in secular matters, the most vaunted feature of what quickly became a very public mission was its claim to be concerned solely with matters spiritual and to have no concern with matters touching the state or the prince. The eirenic Campion wanted to be quite unlike a Dr Morton or Nicholas Sander — or a William Allen, for that matter — and both he and Persons had close contact with the leading figures involved in that petition. Of course all this was quite unrealistic. Whatever their intentions, the arrival of those two, as Thomas Bluet was later to complain, 'like a tempest, with sundry great brags and challenges', predictably resulted in fierce reprisals in the form of that

---

[34] SP 12/167, no. 21 (v). P.Holmes, *Resistance and Compromise: the political thought of Elizabethan Catholics* (1982) analyses the twists and turns in recusant attitudes to the government.

[35] SP 12/162, no. 14 (i).

new legislation from which these petitioners were trying to escape. What old Bishop Watson had allegedly foretold had come to pass.[36] Toleration was out of the question. It was naive to have expected it. On the other hand, the government's harshness itself helped to generate the new militancy among Catholics (a militancy, it should be noted, which never followed that of the Catholic League in France into calling upon the faithful to take up arms against their sovereign).

However, the quest for toleration had not been forgotten. It was resumed in the 1590s. By then, however, the terms of the bargain were eventually to include withdrawal of the Jesuits from England by Rome at the request of English secular clergy.

The lay initiative for toleration taken in the early 1580s reminds us of that important and well-known fact of post-Reformation English Catholicism, namely, the large part played by lay men and women. The survival of the old faith would have been impossible without the country houses which acted as mass-centres, created communities of Catholics consisting of families, servants and dependants, and sheltered priests as tutors, chaplains or itinerant missionaries smuggled in or hidden from ransacking pursuivants, and sent on to their next destination with food, money and possibly escort. The laity nourished and protected their clergy. They subscribed for their relief in prison, for the seminaries and English religious houses (male and female) which were being set up on the Continent; they sometimes rearranged their landed possessions to enable missionaries to go on their rounds without passing outside Catholic 'territory'. Some, like Anne Vaux, could even buy a house to provide shelter, or, like the celebrated Mrs Wiseman, lease properties for clergy to use (in her case a house in Golden Lane in London for the Jesuit John Gerard).

Then one thinks of the famous 'Catholic Associaton' founded by George Gilbert and joined by young men with names such as Stonor, Throckmorton, Tichborne and Vaux,

[36] See above, p. 139.

whose purpose was to plan the missioners' itineraries (including preliminary 'sounding out' of nominal Protestants who might be ready to consider reconciliation), escorting the priests, providing them with horses, clothes, mass equipment, breviaries and cash (from a common fund into which Gilbert contributed much of his own wealth). They made sure that missionaries were sheltered by loyal Catholics. They visited priests in prison. Gilbert bought a printing press for the newly arrived Jesuits. Closely associated with the Society, he took a vow of chastity 'till the Catholic religion should be publicly professed in England'.[37] He died in Rome in 1584 aged twenty-six.

Gilbert was a rare spirit, indeed; but there were many others who played a less heroic role aiding the priests, harbouring them, secretly ferrying future priests and eventually an astonishing number of future nuns across the Channel, selling Catholic books, acting as tutors and schoolmasters, and so on. It has more than once been remarked how close the devout recusant household, with its steady round of mass, family prayer and religious observance, came to the Protestant model of domestic godliness. It could be added that post-Reformation Catholicism, winnowed and strengthened by persecution, had the character of a lay-dominated, de-institutionalised 'Church of the Diaspora' which was exactly what some Protestantism in its purest form sought.

Layfolk suffered for their faith. They were indicted and fined. They went to prison in plenty. Some suffered death. Of the twenty-two people in prison in Hull for recusancy in 1577, for example, sixteen were laymen.[38] Three years later the Gatehouse in London held eighteen religious prisoners, of whom the majority were lay, and had discharged under bond since 1577 another twelve lay people.[39] To jump ahead some decades: in January 1615 the Clink held twelve priests and ten layfolk; in the Gatehouse there were six priests and seven laymen (including one Italian).[40]

Finally, it is clear, as has more than once been noted, that women played a conspicuous part in sustaining recusancy —

[37] *Foley*, iii, 662–3.
[38] SP 12/117, no. 23.
[39] SP 12/140, no. 36 — printed by Pollen in CRS, 1 (1905).
[40] SP 14/80, fos. 119v–20.

partly because 'household' Catholicism gave them obvious importance, partly because their husbands often conformed in order to save inheritances and careers, partly because they were less vulnerable to the law, partly because women are perhaps anyway more serious and responsive to religion — and possibly for several other reasons as well. Whatever the explanation, the fact is clear: out of a list of 157 recusants dating from 1577, 91 were women.[41] The recusants indicted in Newcastle in 1605 consisted of ten men and fifteen women.[42] A major round-up of recusants a decade or so later resulted in 820 being newly indicted. Of these, 532 (65 per cent) were women, including 211 spinsters.[43]

There were well-known individuals, like Anne Line, hanged at Tyburn in 1601 for harbouring priests, and Mary Cole, in prison in the Clink at the age of twenty-one for non-attendance at church, while her mother was in the Gatehouse. Old Mrs Wiseman, whose children included one priest and four nuns (plus another son in the Clink), whose Catholic household was a haven for numerous missionaries, and who took food and vestments to priests in Wisbech prison, was caught at mass in 1594, condemned to death by crushing (the fate of Margaret Clitherow in York) and eventually reprieved.[44]

Many other individual cases could be added. Two must suffice. First, there was Grace Babthorpe who, having spent five years in prison for her faith, been released and widowed, went to Louvain in 1617 to join a community of English nuns there. Her son, a Jesuit, preached at her clothing. Her family, incidentally, by the early eighteenth century had produced five Jesuits and eight nuns.[45] Next, a nun from

[41] SP 12/117, nos. 2, 10. 14, 17, 23 (recusants in Rochester, Hants., Surrey, Berks., Yorks. only).

[42] SP 14/16, fo. 212.

[43] SP 14/16, fo. 214 (calendared late 1605, but probably dating to *c*.1615). Many of the 'spinsters' would have been house servants. Women are conspicuous in other (and unexpected) roles, e.g. as purveyors of Catholic books. In 1574 an informant said he had seen more popish books in a female Londer's house 'then in any place else'; nearly fifty years later the apostate John Gee listed four women among the Catholic 'booksellers' in London (*Foley*, i, 675).

[44] Their stories are told in *Foley*, i, 414–16; ii, 576–9; CRS, 60, p. 62. For other remarkable stories, see Sr J. D. Hanlon, 'These be but Women', in *From the Renaissance to the Counter-Reformation*, ed. C. H. Carter (1966), pp. 371–400.

[45] *Foley*, iii, 192–3. The Bedingfield family had produced no less than twenty-nine by the late eighteenth century.

much earlier times, namely, one Isabel Whitehead, a member of the pre-Reformation community in Chester. After the dissolution she had found refuge in a nearby country house and had thence 'wandered up and down doing charitable works', including visiting Catholic prisoners. She was eventually captured while in bed, when the president of the Council of the North and his men burst into the house where she was staying. They stood over her with swords and rapiers demanding to know the whereabouts of wanted papists, and then took her to York with her hostess. She died in prison in York Castle in 1587, presumably one of the last female survivors of English religious life brought to an end some half-century previously, and also, to the best of one's knowledge, unique in having subsequently carried on a lone apostolate in this way among her co-religionists.[46]

We know now, of course, how inefficient, erratic and casual the enforcement of the recusancy laws usually was. But they were always hanging over people, and could sometimes cut into them ruthlessly and suddenly. Many women, like Grace Babthorpe and Isabel Whitehead, suffered long periods of imprisonment. Of the thirty recusant women in Ousebridge gaol in York between 1579 and 1594, eleven died in prison.[47] Prison took its toll in other places, too.

Naturally, mothers (even grandmothers) often had decisive influence on sons in heading them towards the priesthood. Sisters influenced brothers. At least one schismatic (i.e. conforming) husband was persuaded by his wife to go into exile. One mother had converted her husband and all the rest of the family by the time her son went off to Rome to become a priest.[48] True enough, wives and daughters could also apostatise; but the impression is that female defiance and constancy were more common than female submission. Perhaps the story of the mother of the seminary priest, Thomas Darcy, sums things up. Her stepson Conyers Darcy, an ardent Puritan, fell on the family after his father, a convert

---

[46] *Foley*, iii, 731–2. In 1561 three women listed as obstinate Catholics, but at liberty, included two ex-nuns: Elizabeth Worlington of Shaftesbury, and Margaret Pierpoint, formerly of the Minories, Aldgate (London). The third, Mary Felton, may also have been an ex-religious (*CSP, Addenda, 1547–65*, p. 510).

[47] *Foley*, iii, 800.

[48] CRS, 55, pp. 466–7. Ibid., 54, pp. 287–8 for the preceding example.

to Catholicism, died. He tried to have two of his father's servants hanged for converting people to the old faith, allegedly deprived his mother of everything that was due to her, had her put in prison and wanted her put to death, too. But she escaped from gaol and fled to Staffordshire, where she still lived twenty years later.[49]

It has been powerfully argued that post-Reformation English Catholicism — when it emerges into the light of day in the middle of Elizabeth's reign — was essentially a 'seigneurial', household religion, that it turned its back on the outside world and retreated into the country house; that this lay-dominated religion came into conflict with new Counter-Reformation Catholicism, brought in by the missionaries, that was Hildebrandine and clerical; and that the conflict between Jesuits and secular priests which broke out at the end of the sixteenth century and inflicted much damage on English Catholic life in the next century reflected this antithesis, this deep ideological division between a loyal, English, traditionalist Catholicism and the Jesuit-inspired militancy that was ultramontane, pro-Spanish and violent.[50]

A number of comments suggest themselves. First, the 'hot' Catholicism of William Allen or Robert Persons in the later 1580s, and the overt support of Spanish invasion, were not new. We have seen it all before, in 1569, with Dr Morton and Nicholas Sander. What was perhaps most striking about the 1580s was the forlorn attempt to liberate Catholics from damaging involvement in disloyalty and treason. Campion's failure proved to the proponents of violence that they had been right all along.

Next, there is no clear-cut distinction between lay (and especially gentry) Catholicism and the 'hot' clerical brand. Thomas Skinner, the man we have heard talking about toleration for Catholics, was a notorious, hard-line papist. He told the parish clerk of his village (Rowington, in Warwickshire) that the royal supremacy was untenable, that Peter was pope of Rome and 'thence cometh the true succession' and

[49] CRS, 55, pp. 390–1.

[50] J. Bossy, 'The Character of Elizabethan Catholicism', *Past and Present*, 21 (1962), 39–59, and his *The English Catholic Community, 1570–1850* (1976).

that the Anglican bishops were no more lawful than 'a lease made under the bush'. He ended his discourse with the following: 'thou art a fool, dost thou think that this religion [of yours] is the truth?'[51] Is that not pretty 'hot'? What about the well-to-do Mrs Pauncefoot, who was said in 1590 to be visiting recusants in prison daily and providing for their necessities, and to have a house full of massbooks, relics and persons sought for treason? Her husband was still in the Netherlands with the remnants of the Northern Rising of 1569, and she prayed daily for the coming of the queen's enemies to England in order to subdue the realm. When churchwardens tried to present her for non-attendance at her parish church, the presentment disappeared and her son John threatened to run a dagger through anyone who dared to proceed against her.[52] What about Sir Thomas Fitzherbert, an untameably militant papist? The examples can be multiplied almost endlessly (though it is fair to add that there are also plenty of stories of gentlefolk who were much less outspoken or aggressive).

Similarly, when we look at such evidence as there is concerning relations between gentleman (or gentlewoman) and clerk, one can find stories which support almost any theory. Old Lord Montague preferred Marian priests who did not press on his conscience too hard, but when a new chaplain summoned him back to the straight and narrow he immediately (we are told) doffed his hat, fell on his knees and promised never to err again.[53] You can make of that what you will, as of the story of the chaplain who was sent packing by the lady of the house after he had been so exasperated by the barking of her dog while he was saying mass that he kicked the creature downstairs.[54]

---

51 SP 12/167, no. 21 (v).
52 SP 12/130, no. 34. Cf. the Catholic clique in Colchester, who included a saddler who 'rebuked poore men for goying to divine lettures' and gave money to some 'to bynd them to frequent them no more' (SP 12/120, no. 25). Cf. also the way John Norton of Co. Durham fired at a pursuivant with his fowling-piece to protect Thomas Palaser, a priest hiding in his house. Both Norton and the priest were martyred in Durham in 1600. See G. Anstruther, *The Seminary Priests*, i (1968), 268.
53 W. R. Trimble, *The Catholic Laity in Elizabethan England 1558—1603* (Cambridge, Mass., 1964), p. 102 and n.; *Miscellanea IV*, CRS, 4 (1908), 4—5nn.
54 SP 12/251, no. 13. Another *mulier fortis* called her resident seminary priests 'her chicken'.

The difficulty of making distinctions between different types of priest and gentlefolk is heightened by the fact that Marian priests, seminary priests and Jesuits often worked in the same country house and were even sheltered there at the same time. And though, later on, a pattern emerges (some families tending always to have a Jesuit or secular or whatever) it is not easy to see that these are differing sorts of people who have differing 'world-views', so to speak. We must always remember, too, that even when Jesuits were being most roundly attacked by their secular brethren, their work among layfolk and in the seigneurial homes went on. Layfolk like Tresham certainly had fierce rows with Jesuits; but no case is recorded of any gentleman's house being deliberately closed to the Society for ideological reasons.

Government returns make the distinction between the wilful or obstinate recusants, those who were 'great seducers of her majesty's subjects', the 'ignorant and lewd', the 'conformable' and so on. There were many shades between the recusant so obstinate that authority decided he must feel the weight of the law and the church-papist or fully conformable ex-papist. These distinctions cut across differences of class and sex — and even, to some extent, across the division between cleric and layman. There are plenty of examples of timorous clerics, and even apostates, as well as of heroes among both secular and regular clergy; just as there are plenty of examples of zealous layfolk, lukewarm ones and apostates. One can find many different 'kinds' of Catholicism, but none was the exclusive prerogative or distinguishing mark of either clergy or laity. To complicate matters further, the terms 'church papist' and 'schismatic' themselves could cover a wide range of religious attitudes. Many 'church papists' were indeed 'conformable' and docile, if not well on the way to complete acquiescence in the new order. Others, though outwardly conforming (perhaps to save skins or property), remained stoutly papistical at heart and encouraged wives and children to remain loyal to the old faith. 'Schismatics' not only gave cover for recusancy but could 'do most mischief, havinge dispensacion to entertaine priestes when manie recusantes dare not for feare of penall statutes'.[55] They could be more dangerous, then, than known obstinate papists.

[55] SP 12/168, no. 35.

It does less than justice to post-Reformation Catholicism to describe it as simply a 'seigneurial', country-house creed. Of the six women imprisoned in York Castle in 1577 three were wives of butchers (including Margaret Clitherow), two wives of tailors and one the wife of a gentleman. In Hull at the same time the twenty-two prisoners included one labourer, a yeoman, a blacksmith, a saddler, a tiler, a carpenter and a weaver, as well as five gentlemen and three ex-schoolmasters. The Catholic prisoners in Salford gaol in 1582 consisted of one knight and four others of the gentle class, six priests, one schoolmaster, three husbandmen and five unmarried women. The big round-up for indictment of recusants in 1615 brought in 820 new names. As has been said, 532 were women. Only 50 were gentlemen. Some 239 were described as 'yeomen, labourers and mechanicals'.[56]

Certainly the gentry provided the main mass-centres, but in 1593 one seminary priest, Thomas Clarke, confessed to having said mass also in a 'poor man's house', to which one Richard Tailford, a mason, had brought him, and to having heard many confessions, mostly of poor folk.[57] Eleven years before, Whitgift had complained of two brothers (one had been a porter of Bishop Bonner in Queen Mary's time) who were watermen on the Severn near Tewkesbury and to whose presumably humble house many papists resorted for mass and 'to have other conference'. The bishop judged that there were 'not two worse affected' than this pair, 'nor that doo more harme'.[58] Similarly, though Gilbert's associates who escorted priests around the country were scions of famous recusant families, much humbler folk were also involved in like work. A Mr Phillips in a doctor's house in Chancery Lane was reported to be 'the greatest dealer with priests here in London, and by his meanes they are directed from place to place.' He was apparently planning itineraries, therefore. So was a Mr Ingrams of Gray's Inn. The 'seminary' Bernard Pattenson was accompanied by a 'base-born desperate and villainous fellow' who carried in a cloak bag behind him on his horse the priest's mass equipment and books. He was

[56] SP 12/162, no. 14 (i); SP 12/155, no. 76; SP 14/16, fo. 212.
[57] SP 12/244, no. 5.
[58] SP 12/156, no. 29.

captured with the priest and was a prisoner in Durham Castle in late 1593.[59]

Humble folk gave priests a roof over their heads in inns and lodging houses, especially at the ports. They conveyed letters and messages among English Catholics and between England and the Continent. They must have had a major hand in the remarkable spread of Catholic books and pious objects from abroad. The Privy Council, worried by this underground network of communication, was constantly on the alert for 'purveyors' of papist books and articles of piety, and eager to track down people like Lucy, a 'common messenger' among papists, who had been spotted in St Paul's churchyard.[60] In 1624 an apostate Catholic, who was presumably well informed, listed no less than twenty-two Catholic booksellers in London. Four were women (including a Mrs Fowler of Fetter Lane, who 'tradeth much to St Omer's', and one Widow Douce, 'a famous dealer'). He reported twenty-six Catholic physicians in the capital, eight surgeons and apothecaries (four in Fleet Street alone) and said that of the numerous barber surgeons very many were 'popish'.[61] So London's recusancy was not confined to the houses of well-to-do or foreign ambassadors, or the Inns of Court.

There was also an impressive network of people involved in collecting money for the English seminaries and religious houses (which was conveyed out of the country) and for the relief of Catholics in English prisons. The more affluent contributed; humbler layfolk (and clergy and even nuns) collected and delivered the cash.[62] And when it came to imprisoning recusants there were certainly some who could

---

[59] SP 12/168, no. 34; *CSP, Addenda, 1580—1625*, p. 356. Concerning the social structure of recusancy, note that the Catholic prisoners in York Castle in 1635 included a 'poor tailor' who had been there for twenty-eight years, a 'poor weaver' (there eleven years), a 'poor lame man' (there fourteen years), and a James Wallis, 'poor man' who had been there twenty years for carrying 'beads and crosses' (*Foley*, v. 764). One would like to know about many other humble laymen and women, e.g. one 'Greene', a carpenter who made 'beades', and all the 'secrete places', very difficult 'to bee discerned' in Derbyshire (SP 12/251, no. 13).

[60] SP 12/240, no. 105 (ii). Cf. SP 12/120, no. 64.

[61] *Foley*, i. 670.

[62] See, e.g., SP 12/168 no. 31 (listing huge sums for Catholic prisoners); SP 12/169, no. 19; SP 12/256, no. 116.

not pay their way at all (as prisoners had to) and therefore were allowed to go free. It is not just that there were Catholics too poor to be worth trying to fine for non-attendance at their parish churches; there were some too poor even to go to prison.[63] It was said that, in London at any rate, poor papists repaired to Catholic houses at regular times for 'their diet' (i.e. for handouts) and that some were left money to say prayers for recently dead recusants which was paid in weekly doles; an interesting glimpse of how, in these changed times, the doctrine of Purgatory could continue to result in benefits for both the living and the dead.[64]

Early in James I's reign the Exchequer's records, the recusant rolls, list many more names than do their predecessors and give more information of social status. To take three short examples: in the village of Lowick in Northants in 1606 ten recusants were named. Six were women (including four spinsters and one widow); two of the men were described as 'yeoman', two as 'labourer'. In Hathersage in north Derbyshire there were seventeen women out of a total of twenty-seven recusants. Six of the men were 'yeoman' and four 'husbandmen'. Some eighty women were listed for Warwickshire, many of them wives of blacksmiths, butchers, weavers, tailors and the like; and among the men there were also joiners, glovers, barbers and so on.[65]

Some of these and the other women may have been domestic servants in nearby Catholic houses; others were probably not. The nearby Catholic country house would presumably have provided recusant blacksmiths, weavers and similar people with their only access to mass and the sacraments. It may have favoured them with its custom. Doubtless the Catholic squire gave some protection from over-intrusive sheriffs and churchwardens; in some parts that protection would have been complete, in others far from perfect. But the point is that these recusant village craftsmen and husbandmen who sheltered under the local Catholic magnate's wing did so without necessarily being members of his household or his economic dependants. There were even some villages which contained communities of fairly humble

---

[63] SP 12/243, no. 76 at fo. 204—v. (Warwickshire recusants, 1592).
[64] SP 12/238, no. 126 (i).
[65] E377/15, ros. 33, 35 and 55.

recusants but had no obviously powerful Catholic squire nearby. Post-Reformation Catholicism could scarcely have survived without the country house, and there may be justice in the charge that the clergy, themselves drawn from the upper echelons of recusant society, abandoned the lower orders. But at least in the early decades and well into the seventeenth century English recusancy was more than merely a household religion, a closed world of squire and family, plus servants and tenantry, surviving rather forlornly in an alien environment.

In coming to a conclusion about the dynamics of recusant society, much turns on one's interpretation of the lamentable conflict between the secular clergy (some of them) and the Jesuits (most of them) at the end of the sixteenth century.[66]

It is the origin of the conflict which matters first: and that is perhaps easier to discover than has sometimes been supposed. In part it was simply a personality clash. The two protagonists, Robert Persons and the secular priest, Christopher Bagshaw, were ex-fellows of Balliol College, Oxford, gifted and, in their different ways, difficult men who disliked each other as relentlessly as two fellows of Balliol have ever done. In larger part the 'stirs' and 'broils' were simply another episode in that perennial rivalry between secular and regular clergy which is all too familiar to the church historian; and it was a result of the fact that the secular clergy, Marian and seminarist, were on the whole men of exceptional quality compared with the average parish clerk of pre-Reformation England or compared with the run-of-the-mill clergy in other parts of Europe. Many were mature men when they became priests, Oxford or Cambridge graduates and (remarkably often) ex-fellows. Some had overcome parental opposition, risked or undergone interrogation and many hardships (including confinement) before they got to Douai or Rome. The formation they received there was, by all reports, a good one. They returned home in the knowledge that trials and tribulations, and the possibility of a

---

[66] There is an immense literature on all this. As a short cut the reader is referred to A. Pritchard, *Catholic Loyalism in Elizabethan England* (Chapel Hill, N. Carolina, 1979), esp. chs. v to ix, and the authorities cited there.

horrible death, awaited them. They were men who had been well tested and trained; they were on the whole dedicated to preaching and administering the sacraments. Indeed, it is one of the ironies of the whole story that the Catholic clergy came nearest to achieving the clerical reformation which Protestantism eagerly sought. It was the Established Church which had to cope with the dead wood and mediocrity which it inherited from its Catholic predecessor. So the seminary priests could well ask: what exactly had the Society of Jesus to contribute? What special qualities had this new brand of regular clergy to bring to the English scene? There was no easy answer. To put it bluntly, there was no obvious pastoral or missionary reason why the Jesuits should have been there at all.

Friction, resentment and treading on toes were bound to ensue. There was no need for ideological disagreements to set the two groups at odds. When these came (as they did), they simply made things worse.

This was primarily an inter-clerical dispute. The subsequent rows about the appointment of the archpriest and the struggle by the seculars to get Rome to replace him with a bishop — these, too, were of greater interest to clergy than laity. On the whole, the slanging match probably passed most of the laity by. It passed by many of the clergy (on both sides), too. But since it has left behind a huge amount of highly coloured and vituperative writing, it has seemed very important to historians. To disputes about church government and Jesuit tactics important and passionately debated issues of principle were added. They concerned such questions as whether English Catholics should seek the patronage, and support the cause, of Philip II, Spain and the Habsburgs; whether violence (plots against the queen, armadas and so on) ought to continue to be part of the Catholic programme; whether Catholics should not strive to be more obviously loyal Englishmen and obedient subjects to whom some toleration could safely be granted.[67]

We have heard this before. These issues were not new. Moreover, they were not fought out primarily inside England.

[67] Cf. works by Bossy, cited in note 50 above; Holmes, *Resistance and Compromise.*

The main dispute was between exiled English Catholics — Cardinal Allen, Persons and their supporters (who consisted of secular priests and layfolk, as well as Jesuits) — and secular clergy, religious and laity who had to live and survive in England. The militants, as their critics bitterly observed, were conveniently out of that firing-line which they had done much to create. The issues certainly mattered to some laymen. For the most acrimonious opponents of Jesuits, lay and clerical, the only good Jesuit was an arrested one about to be deported from England's shores. But for the cooler heads the calm and sanity of, say, Henry Garnet (Jesuit superior in England at the time of the Gunpowder Plot) would have spoken louder than printed vituperation hurled by the two factions at one another across the waters.[68]

Feuds and internal tensions abounded; external pressures to conform were strong. Persecution, bloodless and bloody, always threatened. Nevertheless the English Catholic community manifestly had not died the death of spiritual malnutrition which Elizabeth had intended. On the contrary, its survival is one of the most remarkable stories of the Counter-Reformation.

---

[68] In his admirable *Seminary Priests*, vols. i and ii, Anstruther has rightly pointed out the many seculars who were not deeply engaged in the disputes or fiercely hostile to Jesuits.

8

Rival Evangelisms

England was sufficiently 'Protestant' in 1559 to produce a Parliament that passed the two foundation statutes of the restored, Protestant Church of England. It was sufficiently 'Protestant' — and increasingly so — thereafter to enable the Elizabethan Settlement to 'settle'. Alas, we cannot know how many Protestants there were, say, by the middle of Elizabeth's reign. Worse (since there were many reasons for not being a papist, not all of which were lofty ones) we cannot assess the quality of their Protestantism and measure the zealots against the politiques, the lukewarm, the mere conformists, and so on.

For the 'hot gospeller' as distinct from the 'cold-statute' Protestant, however, the message of the new creed was one of liberation from the tyranny of popish 'works' and 'merit-theology', from the undergrowth of saints' days and votive masses, purgatory, pardons and pilgrimages, monks and friars, holy water, holy oils and holy wells, mitres and cowls, scapulars and shaven heads, incense and ashes, trentals and blessed relics, schoolmen and 'filthy' canon law — and all the rest of the intricate accumulation of Catholic piety and practice. Protestantism, to change the metaphor, took a shoulder to the whole thing and heaved it over, condemning it as idolatry, magic or irrelevance, as pagan or semi-pagan fantasy and clutter that at least kept men and women in religious infancy and at worst crippled and perverted them.

Protestantism required more than personal conversion and the throwing away of what were regarded as the props and sops, the placebos and hypnotics of the old creed. It asked more than that men and women should place themselves in God's hands, for they were already there. It asked that they should stand head high and wholly on their own feet *and* acknowledge their total dependence on an inscrutable, incomprehensible deity. They had to face up to their own vile sinfulness and to the awesome fact that they were already predestined to Heaven or Hell by the irreversible and unmerited decree of God.

For those who had seen the great light the issues were clear. The path had been laid out. The struggle to build Jerusalem was on. But what about the others — probably the overwhelming majority?

The Reformation simplified everything. It effected a shift from a religion of symbol and allegory, ceremony and formal gesture to one that was plain and direct: a shift from the visual to the aural, from ritual to literal exposition, from the numinous and mysterious to the everyday. It moved from the high colours of statue, window and painted walls to whitewash; from ornate vestments and altar frontal to plain tablecloth and surplice; from a religion that, with baptismal salt on lips, anointings and frankincense — as well as image, word and chant — sought out all the senses, to one that concentrated on the word and innerliness. There was a shift from a religion that often went out of doors on pilgrimage and procession to an indoor one; from the sacral and churchly to the familial and domestic; from sacrament to word (though this is easily overstated); from the objectivity of *ex opere operato* and Real Presence, for instance, to the subjectivity of 'feeling faith' and experience.

Many pre-Reformation English men and women probably did not go to church very regularly, and some hardly ever or not at all. But even the most casual attenders at mass would have been momentarily silent and semi-attentive at the elevation of the consecrated host and wine. For those who were more serious, that was the supreme event. They had to come to adore. And, as has been said, they came to reap the spiritual and temporal 'fruits' of the mass. Now, however, there was no elevation; and there was no mass.

At mass the congregation's attention would have been drawn to the crucifixion scene on the roodscreen — the rood itself with the two figures of Mary and John on either side —

and behind them the 'doom', a portrayal of the Last Judgement on the tympanum which filled the space between the rood loft and the top of the chancel arch. All this dominated the interior of the church, drawing eyes upwards and towards the east end, and compensating, so to speak, for the fact that high altar and reredos were cut off from the layman's view by the chancel screen. But that had changed, too. Rood, doom and rood loft, as well as altar, were gone — but not the screen itself — and attention redirected towards the pulpit, now high and dominating (though there had been plenty of imposing medieval pulpits) and moved into a commanding position in the nave, which had also undergone important changes.

The late medieval parish church had consisted of a 'mysterious succession' of semi-independent spaces cut off from nave and chancel by parclose screens of stone and wood.[1] Even the humblest church had to be explored, walked round and into. It could not be taken in with a single sweep of the eye. Here again, the Reformation simplified. As the side altars and screens of guilds and chantries came down, nave and aisles were turned into a single, open auditorium in which the faithful could assemble to hear the minister proclaim the word of God, plain and unadorned.

The removal of chantry and guild altars, plus their shrouds of stone or timber, meant not only that a major part of the church had had its papistical 'clutter' stripped out but that the way was clear for introducing more pews.

Pewing had begun long before the Reformation, but it accelerated fast as a result of it, simply because there were now more open spaces to be filled which had previously been occupied by side chapels. There was much to be said for the pew, or at least some simple seating in the form of benches. They were a boon to young and old. The more elaborate types kept out draughts. They helped to make congregations more attentive and orderly. However, as well as encouraging more recollected attendance at services, they made congregations more captive and hence more subject to the minister as he read the word of God and proclaimed it

---

[1] G. W. O. Addleshaw and F. Etchells, *The Architectural Setting of Anglican Worship* (1948), p. 15. I have used this excellent book for much of what follows.

in sermon.[2] Insofar as the new order stressed the ministry of the word and insofar as layfolk were now being gathered round increasingly impressive pulpits, inside the average parish church the tables might have seemed to be turning against the average layman. Moreover, the chances were steadily increasing as the sixteenth century wore on that the minister would be a university graduate, educationally and perhaps socially removed from the majority of his flock. And if he were a zealous preacher and of the 'hotter' sort (and hence bent on disciplining laggard layfolk), he would exercise a more immediate and personal dominance over his people than did the average pre-Reformation parish priest, whose authority was *ex officio* and whose ministry was efficacious *ex opere operato*, not on account of his own qualities (not *ex opere operantis*).

That the Reformation witnessed the victory of the lay estate over the clerical is therefore true but not the whole truth. This is an important fact. Perhaps a particular case will help to develop it.

In 1538 the village of Spelsbury in Oxfordshire had, besides its two churchwardens, the following 'keepers of church lights', that is, of lights maintained mainly by confraternities in the village: Thomas Cross and Richard Ryman of one light, Leonard Carpenter of St Michael's light, William Percy and John Grey of St Anthony's, John Sourch and John Bumpas of St Christopher's, John Box and William Ryman of St Erasmus's, Robert Guy and Thomas Tryndall of St Catherine's, plus the wardens of the Hearse light, St Nicholas's and Our Lady's. Finally, there were John Winter and, be it noted, *Joan* Belcher of the Trinity light. These layfolk administered the lights, and looked after the affairs of what were (mostly, if not always) simple rural confraternities. In Spelsbury, besides the two churchwardens and a 'deacon' (parish clerk) who lived in a house owned by the parish, no less than twenty-two layfolk held positions of responsibility, handled quite large sums of money — Joan Belcher had 15*s*.

---

[2] The often rapid advance of pewing can be seen in churchwardens' accounts, Tall pews (and competition among parishioners could produce ever-higher constructions) could also hide inattention and non-conformist behaviour, Puritan and 'Church-papist', so pews were a mixed blessing. Hence Laud's insistence that they be low, of uniform height and facing the altar.

in hand at the beginning of the year, while her male co-warden had a mere 6s. 8d. — and exercised some control over what went on in those parts of the church where their lamps and maybe statues (or even altars) stood. Furthermore, they would presumably have hired clergy to say mass on patronal feastdays, on obit days and anniversaries, and to bury their dead brethren. John Winter and Joan Belcher would have had a fair amount of cash to dispense to clergy.[3]

Such folk may have been the parish elite and have excited jealousy of fellow-laity. Some of their surnames recur again and again, and not a few of those in office in 1538 had been there several years. Agreed, there were 'perks'. Keepers of lights are conspicuous among those who hired the church sheep, that is, sheep bequeathed to the church for the benefit of this or that light. The Belcher family was a prominent bidder, so Joan may have been in it only for the sheep. However, that is not exactly the point. The fact remains that the old ways gave her and a score of others an active role in the parish life, including its strictly religious life.

Spelsbury is remarkable only because its churchwardens' accounts happen to have survived and also happened to record the other wardens' business, whereas churchwardens often noted only those wardens' 'increases', that is, the annual profits paid into the main accounts. Many other parishes would have been able to match Spelsbury. Those with more sophisticated guilds would have provided lay men and perhaps occasionally women with even greater scope and influence.

So, as has been suggested, Joan Belcher and the others might have been surprised to be told that the medieval Church had reduced the laity to passivity. When the Reformation swept away lights and guilds and condemned the theology of expiation and Purgatory, how might those former wardens have reacted to the claim that Protestantism liberated the layman from clerical domination and restored him to his rightful place in the Christian community? What might Joan Belcher have said to that?

She and wardens of the humbler rural guilds would have

---

[3] F. W. Weaver and G. N. Clarke (eds), *Churchwardens' Accounts of Marston, Spelsbury and Pyrton*, Oxf. Rec. Soc., v (1925), 51–2.

hired clergy to say mass on feast days and anniversaries, and to bury the dead as need arose. But there was also a large array of non-beneficed clerics in pre-Reformation England who were permanently employed by layfolk as chantry priests, as stipendiaries serving non-perpetual chantries (the so-called 'services') and as chaplains of the more affluent guilds, both religious and craft.[4] Like the cantarists proper, these were effectively outside the control of the local bishop and in some respects almost as apart from the main parish clergy as were the regulars, the monks and friars. Moreover a striking fact about the so-called chantry certificates of 1546 and 1548 is how often the commissioners reported that chantry and guild priests were well learned and 'of good conversation'. They were no riff-raff, no clerical proletariat.

With the suppression of the confraternities, chantries, services and obits, most lost their livelihoods. As we have seen, some ex-cantarists and guild priests were re-employed as schoolmasters of former chantry and guild schools. A few were awarded annual salaries (from Westminster) to enable them to act as auxiliary clergy in parish churches and chapels of ease, i.e. were absorbed into the parochial structures. A few more were able to survive when towns recovered former endowments of guilds and chantries and so on (as we have seen already) and were able to reappoint dispossessed clergy to livings now in their gift. Thus Sheffield was able to provide for all three of its previous chaplains. Boston replaced its eighteen former guild priests with a mere two, who were to celebrate in the parish church.[5]

The rest of these clergy had to make their own way. Many full-time ex-cantarists were pensioned off. Ex-guild and 'service' priests and those who had been hired for funerals, obits and the like on an *ad hoc* basis (unless they were already curates or chaplains who eked out their meagre livings in this way) simply disappeared.

The meaning of all this is clear: an 'army' of secular clergy previously hired by layfolk and sometimes appointed by them to paid posts for life had largely ceased to exist. To put

---

[4] Cf. M. L. Zell, 'The personnel of the clergy in Kent, in the Reformation period', *Engl. Hist. Rev.*, lxxxix (1974), 513–33.
[5] *CPR, Philip and Mary*, i, 170–2; ii, 153–5.

the same thing another way: thanks to the Reformation the laity lost control over a whole class of clergy previously in their employ and subject, in varying degrees, to their oversight.

Thus we face an unexpected conclusion that, in this respect, the Reformation caused the pendulum of influence to swing *against* laymen. On the whole, as the history of the Church shows, the clerical establishment has always looked askance on confraternities and the like. They cut across official jurisdictions. The humblest had the look of an *imperium in imperio*. And might not beneficed clergy and their superiors, from archdeacons to bishops and beyond, have looked askance at brother-clergy who were lay hirelings and dependants, and owed allegiance to lay organisations? If so, the Reformation was a victory for the official clergy and canonical authority over the separate lay-dominated structures lying alongside and within the old Church (one hesitates to speak of a lay-dominated 'alternative' Church, but there was something of that about it). Secular clergy and especially secular bishops may not have shed many tears when the religious were suppressed, for exemptions and privileges of the regular clergy were never easy to live with. They may have shed even fewer when the act of 1547 carried away hundreds of lay organisations strewn across the ecclesiastical map and delivered many clergy from economic dependence on them. Incidentally, but perhaps not unwittingly, the act was a victory for episcopacy and clericalism.

On the other hand — and there almost always is one — the Reformation occasioned a massive transfer of former ecclesiastical lands and patronage into lay hands when the hundreds of livings previously appropriated to religious houses were confiscated at the dissolution of the monasteries and the lay rector appeared on the scene. To him came via the crown not only the rectorial tithes previously gathered by religious but in many cases virtually unchecked powers of appointment of the clergy (the vicars) who were actually responsible for the cure of souls: a manifest advance for the layman at the expense of the clerical estate.

So how can we reconcile these two claims, namely, that the laity both gained and lost ground? How could they do these things at more or less the same time? The answer is that the laymen concerned in these two movements were not the same. Those who gained were gentlemen well up the social scale, for it was they who acquired rectories and abbey lands, just as the clergy who were once more being appointed by towns were the creatures of urban oligarchies, not appointees of guilds whose membership could have included many of the 'middling' and lower sorts. It was these last who lost, in town and country. Power had shifted upwards, leaving those in the middle and lower ranks empty-handed.

The later sixteenth century is famous for the appearance of another species of lay-controlled cleric: the Puritan lecturer, the godly preacher often employed by towns (the lectureship being endowed by townsmen) who was to join a *corps d'élite* of protestant preachers and play a conspicuous role in the struggle to turn English men and women away from ignorance, vice, indolence and the rest. But to appreciate him to the full three things have to be noted.

First, he was commonly the creature of the governing class, whether town magistrates or affluent Puritan gentlemen. Secondly, he had interesting pre-Reformation forebears. In Coventry, for instance, a rich mercer called Thomas Bond had in 1507 founded an almshouse for ten poor men and women whose chaplain, besides ministering to the hospital inmates, was to preach in and around the city of Coventry at least forty sermons a year. He was to be a DD or BD or 'at least' an MA, and he was to be appointed by Trinity guild, to which the almshouse was also entrusted.[6] So here was a pre-Reformation preaching ministry under lay supervision. There was no 'proto-Protestantism' about this, either. Bond was a devout, old-fashioned Catholic whose concern for high-class preaching perhaps owed something to Coventry's reputation for heterodoxy. Moreover he wanted the beadsmen of the almshouse to be involved in the apostolate, too. They were to submit to so rigorous a regime of prayer and fasting on behalf of Trinity guild and the souls of all the faithful departed that, assuming most were old and infirm when they arrived, there must have been a rapid turnover of residents. So we have public preaching, prayer and fasting: the Puritan programme in miniature. Coventry had at least two other

6   E301/34, fo. 5.

pre-Reformation endowed 'lectureships'. London had received its first one a century before.[7]

The Puritan lecturers had a long ancestry. Even when (and this is the third point) larger towns had acquired several of them (say, by the end of the sixteenth century) the total number of clergy under the direct control of the magistracy, as lecturers and chaplains and the like, was probably markedly lower than the total employed by urban laity a hundred years before. The town lectureships had not restored the status quo, and the control of these clerics was now concentrated in the hands of the ruling oligarchy and not dispersed among guilds and lesser folk.

Note the word 'concentrated'. By simplifying life the Reformation concentrated things. In particular it concentrated allegiance by reducing the number and diversity of what are today called 'foci of authority'. It put an end to dual loyalty to pope and prince. It put an end to loyalty to local monastery, shrine and confraternity. It denied that the living have any responsibility for the well-being of the dead, the Church Suffering, and exonerated the Church Militant on Earth from any duty to pray for the repose of the souls of the faithful departed. Indeed, it expressly forbade such supplication, and thus forbade a present generation to evince any active religious concern for their ancestors. To that extent it cut the spiritual bonds between the living and the dead, between this world and the next. It also broke Heaven and Earth apart by ending communication between Church Militant and Church Triumphant.

In the past those on Earth had known that the 'whole company of Heaven' stood near. Intercession of saints offered access to temporal as well as spiritual favours. It gave protection, reduced the sense of helplessness, bestowed extra control over the environment. Saints, especially patronal and local ones, provided an 'alternative' patronage system, so to speak, to whom anyone could turn, however humble, and which would never ignore or betray a suppliant. The saints

---

[7] *VCH, Warks.*, viii, 351; P. S. Seaver, *Puritan Lectureships: The politics of religious dissent, 1560–1662* (Stanford, 1970), p. 75.

stood over and against temporal, earthly patrons and authority-figures, and were mightier than any of them. They were the champions of the meek and lowly, to whom the latter could appeal to intervene in the affairs of this world and for aid. So they, too, divided loyalties. They made claims that transcended earthly allegiances and gave secret strength and assurance to devotees.

Many saints were proof that ordinary men and women could matter, that the humblest could be exalted. Their *Lives*, best-sellers from early printing-presses and often garnished with extravagant tales of miracles and pious legends, told of rich men's sons exchanging silks for hairshirts, of holy virgins lambasting princes and even popes, of kings giving all they had to the poor, of the most improbable outcasts and unprivileged of folk receiving Heaven's choicest favours. The saints inverted 'norms' as profoundly as did any charivari. They made the wise look foolish and the foolish wise. They were dangerous. Even if the example of their lives ultimately redounded to the benefit of the clerical estate, that example was no less of a 'threat' to the cleric, or should have been. It was not just that a prince like Henry would have known that Becket, Richard and the others had to go, for their feastdays and shrines were a constant reproof to kings and likely to give subjects wrong ideas. The challenge of the saints went deeper and wider than that.

There were many female saints: heroines of the early Church who had defied husbands and emperors, immensely energetic Anglo-Saxon women who had built nunneries and travelled widely, holy wives and widows (admittedly usually well-to-do ones) as well as holy nuns. There were Margaret, Catherine, Mary Magdalen and Bridget, to cite perhaps the most common later-medieval patronal saints. Above all, there was Mary herself. The numerous dedications and devotions to her, as well as her shrines, show how prominent a place she had in English religious life. All this tempered male authority and (though it is admittedly impossible to measure what effect this had on daily living) asserted the dignity of womanhood. But now all that was gone, together with such outlets for female energy and independence as the religious life had offered. Albeit it at the price of celibacy, in large establishments at any rate it had given access to public responsibility and power which women would not know again for generations. And the guilds, which had allowed women membership in their own right and the chance of office, had also been swept away.

Of course, to the zealous Protestant this hacking down of Catholic complexity was deliverance from false religion. The Lord's household was being purged of man-made idols and superstition. Protestantism proclaimed man's nothingness in the face of the awesome, absolute sovereignty of an unknowable deity. Nothing else really mattered. Anything which seemed to obscure that stark fact, to soften or 'domesticate' it was the work of Satan.

For the zealot, therefore, there had been ample compensation for what had been destroyed. But Protestantism is a difficult creed to come to terms with. Its basic tenet, justification by faith alone, is not easy to grasp. The idea of man's depravity and helplessness encounters resistance which is not merely human vanity. Above all, as the history of Protestantism shows, the doctrine of double predestination, that is, that God is the direct author of both election and damnation, has repeatedly been a stumbling-block — indeed, a rock on which Protestant unity has frequently broken. In its pure form, it was an austere creed. The many who could not submit to its austerity, who had not made the leap, found themselves denied their old ways and 'world-view' and unable to partake of the consolations of the new.

They were cut off from and could not plead for their ancestors and deceased loved ones. The votive mass (for this or that purpose, temporal or spiritual) had gone. There was no appeal to any supra-national authority or to any saint; no recourse (officially) to shrine, holy relic or exorcism; no protecting statue or medal; no friar and monk to offset parson and bishop; no confraternity. People were more exposed than ever before. Simply because there was little appeal against them and no alternatives to them the surviving authority-figures were more present and immediate than ever.

There were ways of making good some of what had been lost. The stripping away of the elaborate protective cloak of holy water, special blessings, medals, relics and so on doubtless increased dependence on the professional physician, the herbalist and the cunning man — even if it also left folk more vulnerable to curses and black magic. Perhaps the disappearance of the confraternity drove people back into the family and strengthened artisan and craft guilds. Nonetheless, the effect of the Reformation was to make many people more subject to the powers that were, in fact as in theory.

Both secular and clerical authority had advanced against the middle and lower orders of lay society. We can illustrate what has happened if we return to the average post-Reformation parish church and consider the changes that took place there. First, weekly attendance at church — always an ecclesiastical obligation, but probably very imperfectly achieved — was now being enforced by both Church and state (with fines and censures) and, though much always depended on the vigilance of churchwardens and justices, probably more effectively than ever before. Secondly, once there, the rank-and-file increasingly found themselves brought under the discipline of benches and pews (though the poorest probably stood at the back or sat on the floor) and required to listen dutifully to a steady flow of sermons delivered from on high by the minister.

Pews defined as well as disciplined. There were bachelors' pews, judges' pews, pews for unmarried girls, for the parson's wife and, naturally, the squire (the manorial pew). Some churches had free pews, or at least benches, assigned according to precedence by the churchwardens. Pew spaces were sold and became an important source of income to the parish. Pews were let and bequeathed. They became family possessions. They announced social rank and wealth. A former chantry chapel might be turned into a family pew by the very family that had previously built the chantry, and some of the former stone re-used. Before long such a pew could have become an elaborate 'parlour pew' — a private room with chairs, carpets, bookshelves, even a fire and dog-kennel, roofed and curtained and perhaps with separate outside entrance so that its users would not have to come and go with the *hoi polloi* or have attendance and devotion easily observed. The final step would be to raise this ecclesiastical 'opera-box' above floor level and give it as commanding a position as that occupied by the pulpit. By then the wheel would have turned full circle: the aisles that had been cleared of medieval chapels and screens were now partly refilled by private parlour and family pews. At the back stood or sat the poor; in between, carefully graded, sat the rest. And to complete this didactic layout, on the top of the chancel screen, where previously there had stood the crucifixion scene, with a Last Judgement behind, there was now the royal coat of arms.[8]

Pilgrimages had taken folk out and about, enabled ordinary people to see and hear things which they would otherwise never have experienced. As Chaucer knew, they broke down social barriers and could end up with people of all sorts and degrees swapping stories. As for processions, they displayed rank and precedence to the onlooker but bonded the participants. Thus the ceremonies on Rogation days ('Cross-week' or 'Gangdays') enabled the community to pray for the harvest, affirm its identity by 'beating the bounds' (to mark out its territory) and, by processing with banners and bells, to engage in general jollification which, like the works outing of later times, inevitably eroded barriers of age, sex and rank. Pilgrimages and processions were levellers.

That is not why they were denounced by Protestants. The latter argued that they were rooted in pagan superstition and, in the case of Rogation day processions, revived popish prayers and ceremonies. But their disappearance removed a leveller nonetheless.

The same was true of Protestant attacks on lords and abbeys of misrule, Shrove and Hocktide carousels, Christmas disguisings, boy bishops, and the rest. The complaint was against their paganism, their irreverence and encouragement of 'scoffs, jests, wanton gesture or ribald talk'.[9] It is fashionable to argue today that this institutionalised ridicule and letting off of steam in the long run protected the status quo. That may be true, but burlesque also provided some defence against the overmighty, could curb the bully and teach the high-handed a useful lesson. It levelled, too.

Horizons were closing in. The world was becoming a more disciplined, hierarchical, authoritarian place. It was becoming

---

8 Addleshaw and Etchells, *Architectural Setting*, pp. 77ff.
9 Grindal, *Remains*, p. 142.

a more masculine and patriarchal one. And, as maypoles, morris-dancing and charivari (not to mention dicing and tippling) went down before the Puritan attack, a more earnest and serious one.

Perhaps it was always likely that larger towns would tend to welcome this — as places like Coventry, Hull, Leicester, Northampton and so on did — for magistracies often faced a pretty lawless, godless and feckless populace. The violence and drunkenness of those caught in what is called today 'the poverty trap' cried out for the discipline, and the practical this-worldliness of the Puritan who believed in self-help and godly living. This was not necessarily 'social control' in the crude sense of using religion simply to bring the lower orders to heel and keep them there. Civic pride, a sincere concern for law and order and for the problem of poverty, plus (above all) zeal for the Gospel, could also animate a magistracy. The godly town magistrates and their clergy were a sort of presbytery, of which truly reformed episcopacy would strongly approve. It was a regime which found much support from the Court of High Commission and the consistory and archdeacons' courts of dioceses over which an Edmund Grindal or Thomas Bentham or other zealous bishops presided.

It was not exclusively urban. Godly gentlemen (often county justices) and clergy came together for 'exercises', i.e. to hear sermons, talk together and to plan the betterment of mankind which required that the word of God be preached, the sacraments rightly administered and true discipline imposed in town and country. The campaign to Protestantise England brought layman and cleric together.[10] It was a joint effort of zealous clergy and zealous lay men and women (mainly of the 'better' sort) against the great mass of clergy and layfolk of all ranks.

The temptation was to push too hard, to demand too much too quickly. At the bottom of the social scale there were those who reacted against Sabbatarian discipline, frequent and lengthy sermons and the Puritan crusade against sin. At the top there were gentlemen (as one Bishop Curteys

---

[10] Cf P. Collinson, *The Religion of Protestants: the Church in English Society, 1559–1625* (Oxford, 1982), esp. ch. 4.

of Chichester discovered) who resented being hustled in public, hauled up 'in the face of' social inferiors and 'improved'. A county elite was not to be treated in this way by aggressive, intrusive episcopacy and took revenge.[11] Curteys was dismissed.

Middling people could be equally resistant. Consider what happened in Banbury, where a zealous local Puritan gentleman, Sir Anthony Cope, and a zealous Puritan vicar, Thomas Bracebridge, strove to reform the town. When Mary Green, a papist, was cited to appear for recusancy, the apparitor was 'sore beaten'. When she was excommunicated her supporters mocked the sentence with 'bragging words'. When the vicar tried to pursue a notorious sinner who profaned the Sabbath, lured people away from services and lived in adultery, the culprit turned up at church at service-time and so teased the vicar that the congregation laughed aloud — 'contrary to her majesty's Injunctions'. When Bracebridge then went after the man's daughter, who was also no angel, she and a friend lured him to an empty house on the pretext that the occupant was dying, shut the door fast and pulled a knife on him. His hand was cut and he was buffeted 'very sore about ye face and head'.[12] Eventually neighbours rescued him. Finally, when he and Sir Anthony tried to forbid churchales, maypoles, wakes, morris-dancing and the rest, and to close the taverns, the sheriff of Oxfordshire appealed to the lord chancellor and Privy Council, warning that riots would ensue. Banbury folk were to make an important point, namely, that if no ale and jollity were allowed their prosperity as a market town would suffer.[13] People would take their trade elsewhere — a sobering reminder that Calvinism and commerce were not always natural allies, and that provision of lecturers for market towns (a particular Puritan concern) for the edification of those who came there on business might not have pulled in large audiences. Protestantising the English would be a long, uphill struggle.

---

[11] SP 12/112, nos. 13, 20, 29—41. The story has been told more than once (e.g. R. B. Manning, *Religion and Society in Elizabethan Sussex*, pp. 78—90).
[12] SP 12/223, no. 47.
[13] SP 12/224, nos. 54—8.

It has more than once been remarked how much the two movements competing for the mind and hearts of the English people — zealous (Puritan) Protestantism and resurgent Catholicism — had in common, for all their profound differences of doctrine and structures.[14] Both were indeed missionary, bent on preaching the Gospel and winning souls. Both were convinced of their rightness (on somewhat differing grounds). Both owed much, in varying ways, to lay support and patronage, the household and women. Both were combative, made full use of the printing press and set such store by polemical writings, spiritual manuals, catechisms and the like that, by the early seventeenth century, each could point to a formidable library of its writings. Both Reformation and Counter-Reformation were disciplining and in some sense 'puritanical' movements. Campion, it has been observed, may have had more in common with a Protestant missionary like John Penry than either would have cared to admit. The same could be true of Edmund Grindal and, say, Charles Borromeo.

In the Catholic view of things Protestant error had apparently (but temporarily) triumphed only because of the *coup d'état* of 1558 and the subsequent persecution of the old faith by the authorities. In Catholic eyes, English Protestantism's strength lay largely in the fact that it had the weight of the state behind it.[15] To the Protestant, there were two outstanding reasons why the papists prospered. First, they profited incalculably from the winking, conniving and refusal to report neighbours and so on which made a mockery of the recusancy laws. Thus, for example, priests were smuggled in and out of the country via a score of ports, whole areas of the land remained virtually Catholic and gaols were as leaky as sieves (Winchester's had a Catholic gaoler who gave his priest-prisoners keys and allowed them to use the gaol as a lodging house while they continued to minister

---

[14] E.g. P. McGrath, *Papists and Puritans under Elizabeth I* (1967), esp. ch. 13.
[15] And because it had enriched the ruling classes with ex-ecclesiastical 'loot'. So in 1586 a papist told a minister: 'the religion now professed here in England is but a pollitical and temporary religion, or rather Machevile's religion.' (SP 12/192, no. 52 (i).) That the new order was but 'temporary' and that restoration of the old was round the corner was, of course, a familiar papist theme.

to Catholics in the locality[16]) or such active centres of Catholic missionary endeavour that scores came thither for instruction or reconciliation, and to receive the sacraments and attend mass (even mass with music and incense).[17] Popery had a second and damnable advantage: it pandered to the popular appetite for magic and wizardry, and was able to exploit a heightened fear of witches and evil spirits among common folk. Its blessed medals and grains, *agnus deis* and holy water, its saints and shrines and so on would dupe the gullible as long as fear of curse, spell and possession remained. Protestantism denounced the amulets and incantations of folklore and popular religion, and denounced Catholic 'magic', which it regarded as virtually indistinguishable from them, but put nothing in their place.[18] Thus ministers of the new Church felt at a serious disadvantage compared with their papist rivals who had 'tricks' galore, the best prophecies, the lure of pardons and, perhaps above all, the 'wicked' conjuring of exorcisms. Protestantism of course could deal with possession by evil spirits: with public prayer and fasting. But this was much slower and more cumbersome than Catholic exorcism. As early as about 1570 Edwin Sandys, later archbishop of York, was deploring in a sermon how allegedly stage-managed papistical exorcisms won over simple souls, especially women, who were thereby lured into 'breaking their faith to Christ, their loyalty to the prince and their promised obedience to their husbands'. Papists, he also observed, 'have books of Merlin and other fantastical spirits, full of doubtful sayings and deceitful dreams...all tending to this end, that alteration is near, that the state will not long continue, that religion cannot endure long.'[19]

Papists, it was supposed, ever dabbled in sorcery and magic. An official list of capital enemies of the queen drawn

[16] SP 12/273, no. 23.

[17] The best story of this kind belongs to 1633, when (allegedly) a visitor to a London prison found a priest saying mass and the gaoler himself swinging the incense censer before a great crowd of men and women (Anstruther, *Seminary Priests*, ii, 88).

[18] Cf., of course, K. Thomas, *Religion and the Decline of Magic* (1971), esp. ch. 3.

[19] Sandys, *Sermons*, PS, 2 (1841), 67–8. Cf. the appeal to Merlin by Henry Chauncy (brother of Maurice, the historian of the English Carthusian martyrs) in SP 12/151, no. 21.

up in 1586 included not just the obvious names of disaffected Catholic gentlemen but nine accused of black magic, including one Bertles 'ye great devil', the 'old witch of Ramsbury, Maude Twagood enchantresse, Mother Streaton, witch' and Christopher Wat, 'sorcerer', together with Gregory the 'taleteller' who allegedly was one of those who stole the head of the earl of Northumberland (one of the leaders of the rising of 1569) from its tomb in York.[20] A little later the government was being alerted to the news that the papists planned to bring in an Italian magician called Maximilianus whose Mediterranean virtuosity would surely dazzle the provincial English.[21]

English Catholics never missed an opportunity to claim that Protestantism was the mother of all impiety, sedition and rebellion. Protestants, however, knew that they made the best subjects and citizens. Whatever their forebears might have said in Mary's reign, whatever Theodore Beza and Calvinists in France and Netherlands might have said later, they themselves preached obedience to the prince. They preached against idleness, waste, extravagance and licence, and for thrift, sobriety and honesty. The preached extreme social conservatism, from the time of Tyndale and Latimer onwards bidding everyone to be content with, and to strive hard in, the station to which God had called him and to be obedient (servants, apprentices, husbandmen and artisans and so on — and wives) to those placed over them.[22] Could they have been more respectable and acceptable?

The 'hotter sort' of Protestant was fired by a theology of history which taught him that God would never desert his faithful people, that the English had an especial mandate and that the rule of the saints was nigh. Catholics knew that theirs was the faith of their forefathers, was what had been taught always, everywhere and by all, and was

[20] SP 12/192, no. 57. In 1590 a woman sought a conjurer to produce wax images of her husband's enemies, including one 'who lived by robbinge papistes' (SP 12/130, no. 30).

[21] SP 12/162, no. 51.

[22] See (e.g.) Tyndale, *Parable of the Wicked Mammon* in PS, 6 (1848), esp. 100–3, and his *Obedience of a Christian Man* (ibid., p. 201); Latimer's sermons constantly reiterate the same theme. See his *Sermons* and *Remains*, PS, 16 and 20 (1844, 5), esp. 214–15, 406–10, 503–4 in the first volume.

truth guaranteed by the divine, living authority of the Church.

By the end of the sixteenth century English Catholicism had made a remarkable recovery. Its flowering was due to persecution (albeit erratic), lay courage and the quality of its clergy (which is not to deny that their were some timid and mediocre priests, secular and regular, and apostates, some of whom did terrible damage to the mission by betraying former friends). Catholics were buoyed up, too, by giving the famous dictum 'extra Ecclesiam nulla salus [outside the Church no salvation]' a very literal interpretation. For many, it seems, this meant that there was no salvation for anyone who was not a member of their visible Church. As the Jesuit martyr, Edmund Arrowsmith, said to the man about to arrest him, 'Sir, it is a pity you are not a Catholic...because all are damned who die in your religion.'[23]

There was a final source of strength, the conviction that they had won the literary battle with their opponents. When, early in Elizabeth's reign, Bishop John Jewel of Salisbury had preached his famous 'challenge' sermon calling on Catholic apologists to show that such central Catholic tenets as belief in Purgatory, the papal primacy, veneration of saints and the mass could be found in the early Church, he not only forced his opponents onto the defensive but also struck at what was, at that time, the weakest part of the Catholic defence system. Formidable though the English Catholic exiles in Louvain were who sprang to take up the challenge, a fair-minded person would probably agree that Jewel won most of the initial rounds. But that person would also have to agree that the bishop overreached himself in the course of the subsequent prolix controversy. His chief Catholic critics, Stapleton and Harding, were able to catch him out too often doing discreditable things to the evidence, such as adding crucial words or phrases, deleting awkward bits and misidentifying people.[24] Jewel won battles, but he lost the war. Nonetheless, Catholics were still on the defensive.

---

[23] *Foley*, ii, 35. Cf. ibid., v, 387−8 and CRS, 54 (1962), pp. 14 and 26 for similar attitudes.

[24] Justification of this claim would require much more space than a footnote allows. Perhaps three quick examples will nonetheless show how Jewel could nod: he substituted 'etc.' for crucial words of Justinian to make the latter *seem* to claim that papal authority was an imperial concession; he claimed Pius II as a

By the end of the century they had found the counter-challenge to Jewel's and were able to take the initiative. Their weapon was not new, but it was used now with new skill and vigour. Simply put, it was the question: where were you before Luther? The Protestant was asked to show his spiritual ancestry, starting with the centuries immediately before the Reformation and tracing it back through the Middle Ages to the early Church. The tables had been turned. It was probably Robert Persons more than anyone else who gave Catholic polemics this new direction, for he was no mean historian and set himself the task not only of rebutting the work of John Foxe but also of providing his co-religionists with an account of England's Christian history. This, so he believed, showed that England had always been a Catholic country and never a 'Protestant' one until recent times. Numerous Catholic tracts appeared repeating the challenge, criticising what were regarded as pitiful attempts to meet it, revelling in the growing lack of unanimity on major issues among Protestant divines and the difficulties involved in trying to find orthodox Protestants in pre-Reformation England.[25]

There were other writings, too. But this genre buoyed up

_____

conciliarist, forgetting that by the time Aeneas Silvius Piccolomini became pope he had retracted his former views; he claimed that the martyr Eupsychius was a bishop and a married man (i.e. he inserted 'episcopus' against his name) though he was in fact a layman. (See his *Apology* and *Defence of the Apology* in his *Works*, PS, 19 (1845), p. 363; and PS, 30 (1848), pp. 187, 409). Stapleton and co. claimed that there were over a thousand significant errors in Jewel's works, some of them involving serious falsification, and that, in the subsequent exchanges, he not only failed to acknowledge them but made new ones and played fast and loose with his opponents' writings, omitting lines and even whole pages. A quick (and very skilful) guide to all this is in Francis Walsingham's *A Search made into matters of religion etc.* (1609), one of the cleverest books produced by the recusants, and both calm and fair.

[25] Of the numerous examples, I would pick out the following (apart from the book by Walsingham cited in note 24): T. Fitzherbert, *A Supplement to the Discussion of M. D. Barlowes Answere to the Judgement of a Catholike Englishman...* (1613) and his other writings; W. Wright, *A Treatise of the Church* (1616); G. Musket, *The Bishop of London his Legacy* (1623). There were highly entertaining reports by John Percy on the 'conferences' between the Jesuit Fisher and Protestant divines. All these authors made use of Persons's writings, such as *A Treatise of Three Conversions of England from Paganism to the Christian Religion* (1603, 1604).

more than did others. It confirmed what had always been a widely held view, namely, that if Catholics were allowed to be heard, given a fair chance to put their case or to meet opponents in open debate (as Campion, for example, had not been), they would be invincible.

For the zealous Catholic, therefore, it was a question of when and how victory would come, not whether. Some believed in the use of force; others hoped for a peaceful solution — the accession of a Catholic monarch or a royal conversion. Even those who wanted to sue for toleration had not necessarily abandoned hope of winning all thereby. Later on, the search for an accord with the government was often a tacit admission of failure (or at least acceptance that the re-conversion of England lay a long way away and that, until it came, Catholics would have to live on the edge of English life). But some regarded toleration as a sure way to success. Mr Skinner of Rowington in Warwickshire, who was mentioned above[26] as first raising the idea of seeking toleration from the queen, explained his motives to the local vicar very candidly. If there were no compulsion to attend the vicar's church, if men were free to choose, he asked, how many would come? 'Not passinge X of our parysshe, I warrante thee', Skinner declared. The vicar and his supporters would never be able 'to stand with [i.e. up to] us. We shalbe V to one against you.'[27] Whether Skinner's assessment was accurate is not the point. For him the bid for toleration was no white flag, no admission of defeat. It was the quickest way to victory.

Both English papists and English Protestants had allegiances which transcended national ones, but both were proudly English and, with a few exceptions in both camps, loyal subjects of the crown. Papists rejected the royal supremacy (but whether a king of Spain had much less *de facto* control of church life in his dominions than did Elizabeth or the early Stuarts is a moot point). On the other hand, caesaro-papism had no genuinely Protestant genes. The royal supremacy

26 pp. 153–4.
27 SP 12/167, no. 21 (v).

was a transplant into the body Protestant and never a complete success. The danger of rejection always lurked. And while some Protestants felt uneasy about England's Erastianism, some Catholics would eventually be ready to take an oath of allegiance to the crown which at least got them off the hook as regards the papal claim to the right to depose princes. The ecclesiastical scene was complicated and full of movement.

Both Catholic and Protestant communities had their internal tensions. Some of the most radical Protestants, despairing of monarch and bishops, were driven into the arms of the classis, i.e. Presbyterianism; others could not ignore that deep Protestant instinct for the 'gathered' church, and the ideal of the self-governing local community. The pull of sect and Separatism was strong. For their part, English Catholics oscillated between theories of loyalism and resistance, and later agonised over the papal deposing power and whether, when and exactly how a hierarchy should be re-established. And were not Jesuits accused by some of their co-religionists of 'presbyterianism'? In truth, the idea of 'ascending' authority and the atomising tendencies latent in Protestantism could be, or could seem to be, almost as menacing to the established order as Catholic ultramontanism and Jesuit theories about the popular origins of political power, the right of resistance and tyrannicide.[28] No bishop, no squire.

Protestantism was dogged by the danger that its over-eager, disciplining clergy would provoke new anticlericalism among the great mass of ungodly, unregenerate Englishmen. Puritans not only described bear-baiting as a 'filthie stinking and loathsome game' but denounced most of the favourite pastimes. They scorned female fripperies and cosmetics, as well as 'monstrous' male attire (including wigs and doublets). From the time of Latimer the zealots had proposed the death penalty for adultery.[29] Some wanted branding for fornication. Some extreme Separatists would have abolished the universities.

[28] On all this, see P. Holmes, *Resistance and Compromise*; A Pritchard, *Catholic Loyalism in Elizabethan England*; P. Collinson, *Elizabethan Puritan Movement* (1967).
[29] Latimer, *Sermons* and *Remains*, i, 244; ii, 93. Cf. R. L. Greaves, *Society and Religion in Elizabethan England* (Minnesota, 1981), p. 234.

For their part, Catholics were dogged by Spaniards. Their Spanish connections, perhaps inevitable in the circumstances, accorded ill with patriotism, allowed opponents to blacken them with the eagerly cultivated 'Black Legend' of Spanish atrocities and played into government's hands by giving it exactly what it wanted, namely, a chance to label Catholics as traitors and lackeys of Spanish imperialism, as well as to foster feuds within the English recusant community between the pro-Spanish and Jesuit 'party' and those who wanted to escape from the *damnosa hereditas* of dependence on the Habsburg cause.[30] Peace with Spain in 1604 brought no relief, because the government had found a new apple of discord, the proposed oath of allegiance.

There was, of course, a larger issue yet: the former abbey lands. Books of casuistry produced chiefly under the guidance of Persons and Allen for English Catholic confessors show that Rome's amnesty concerning former Church property granted via Reginald Pole in Mary's reign was not thereafter considered as final. The replies to questions about whether Catholics might buy or sell such lands, or alter, add to or demolish former monastic buildings and so on prove that the question of their ultimate fate was still an open one. It was for a future pope to decide. Until then, a Catholic might buy ex-monastic lands provided he intended to abide by that decision, might sell to anyone who 'he thinks will be as ready as he is to uphold the judgement of the Church when it shall decide what to do on the matter', and might improve what he had acquired (even keeping a record of expenditure with a view to claiming this back from the religious one day).[31] In 1604 the Spanish envoy in England was telling his master that ownership of ex-monastic property was a major obstacle to the conversion of inwardly Catholic laymen[32] — while Persons and other Jesuits always

---

[30] Cf. T. Clancy, *Papist Pamphleteers. The Allens — Persons Party and the Political Thought of the Counter-Reformation in England, 1572—1615* (Chicago, 1964); Pritchard, *Catholic Loyalism*, esp. ch. ix; Holmes, *Resistance and Compromise*. Hence the importance of the plans of the anti-Jesuit party, led by Bagshaw, to found an English seminary in Paris (*CSP, Addenda, 1580—1625*, p. 410) and cultivate French patronage.

[31] P. Holmes, (ed.) *Elizabethan Casuistry*, CRS, 67 (1981), 43, 96—8, 100—1, 111—14.

[32] A. J. Loomie (ed.), *Spain and the Jacobean Catholics*, CRS, 64 (1973), 41.

argued that it was precisely because they were a newly founded order and had no claims on these lands, and hence offered no threat to anyone, that they were more suited to serve the English mission than any other religious.

It is impossible to imagine today that, had England returned to the fold, Rome would not have let bygones be bygones and reiterated its former amnesty; but that is not the point. At the time, the issue (and hence the fears) were alive. They were still alive in James II's reign.[33]

Interestingly enough they were kept alive by the zealous Protestant, too. As early as 1574, the Puritan Walter Travers pointed to the especial affront of lay rectories and urged that impropriated livings be given back to the Church.[34] The Puritan petition to Parliament and the *Discourse on Ecclesiastical Government* of 1585 repeated the demand. By then issues were widening. If things once consecrated to God belonged to him for ever, as Leviticus says, why stop at impropriated livings? Abbey lands, too, were 'of this nature', i.e. could not be given by any earthly authority to profane uses. Layfolk, a Presbyterian tract warned, who thought that the attack on bishops would provide 'like pray as they had some times at the overthrowe of the Abbeys', would be disappointed. They faced not gain but the loss of what they had already seized from God.[35] These were dangerous positions, indeed. Such words played straight into the hands of Puritans' enemies, notably Richard Bancroft, bishop of London, who would make full play with the threat that the 'left' offered to the propertied classes.

Ironically, therefore, the same stick could be used to beat both 'left' and 'right'. The problem of the great spoliation would not go away. Fears may have been exaggerated and gladly exploited by the likes of Bancroft, but nothing was more likely to strengthen the centre.

That centre was Anglicanism. We can see it emerging by the end of Elizabeth's reign, receiving its most famous apologia

---

[33] Cf. N. Johnston, *The Assurance of Abbey and other Church Lands in England...* (1687).

[34] *A Declaration of ecclesiastical Discipline* (1584), p. 116.

[35] SP 12/245, nos. 89 and 90.

from Hooker and defining ever more clearly thereafter its fundamental principle: that England had its own way of doing things and that the Church of England was *sui generis*. It rejected the doctrinaire biblicism (in its eyes 'bibliolatry') of the hard-line Protestant in favour of a more broadly based appeal to tradition, reason and history — as well as Scripture.

It was unimpeachably English and patriotic. It was comprehensive (within bounds) and humane. Whitgift was rebuked for his harsh ways; austere Sabbatarianism was rejected; Banbury was allowed to keep its maypoles. To some extent the comparatively tolerant and easy-going character of the Anglican Church reminds one of the pre-Reformation Church in England. A wheel had come full circle.

Anglicanism was also safer. It accommodated the royal supremacy without scruple; indeed, that was its keystone. It was less prone (or so it seemed) to clericalism than were the competing evangelisms which stood on either side of it. Above all, it would not challenge lay rectors and impropriations or raise the ghastly question of the ex-abbey lands and so on. Anglicanism locked the door on that spectre, and made things safe for prince and squire, for bishop and lay magistrate, for the possessing classes, for law and order.

Adultery would not be punished by death. The momentous idea of 'things indifferent' (adiaphora) was salvaged. Elizabeth and Whitgift (good Calvinist that he was) stood firm against ultra-Calvinists and insisted that there was no single church polity or government laid down in the New Testament.[36] Anglicans did not see themselves as an Elect Nation engaged in battle with Antichrist. Rome was not the Whore of Babylon. A 'branch theory' which portrayed Christendom as a collection of national churches (in a sense all more or less right and all more or less wrong) had been enunciated by Stephen Gardiner in 1535 and now came to the fore again. Some Anglicans seriously hoped for a *modus vivendi* with less 'Roman' Romanists.

True enough, Archbishop Laud's assertion of divine-right episcopacy later outraged Puritans as much as it would have

---

[36] 'I find no one, certain and perfect kind of government prescribed or commanded in the Scriptures of the church of Christ', he said (*Works*, i, 184–5). It was for each church (i.e. national church) to determine its own polity, under the prince's guidance.

dismayed Whitgift, and his attempt to restore the economic well-being of the Church, while never opening up the explosive issue of ex-abbey lands, deeply worried the propertied. But perhaps we should not suppose that Laud got everything wrong. Anglicanism's reinstatement of man's freedom, the rejection of double predestination, the moderation by the High Church party of the Spartan diet of sermons and psalms,[37] the return to a more sacramental, 'mysterious' religion, to ceremony and colour perhaps had a deeper appeal to popular religious instincts than did the ways of Geneva.

If W. K. Jordan's account of English philanthropy during the period 1480 to 1660 (corrected to allow for inflation) is to be trusted, there was a marked decline in the volume of bequests and other giving to almost all causes — education, public works, and above all religion — in the middle and later decades of the sixteenth century despite the fact, which Jordan himself did not note, that the major transfer of former ecclesiastical wealth into lay hands during this period meant that the donor and bequest-making sector of society had acquired a larger share of the cake and therefore had more to give to good causes.[38]

---

[37] Perhaps one Thomas Nicholson spoke for many when, in 1615, having thrown a snowball at folk coming from a sermon, he said, 'It was never good world since ther were so many sermons.' Quoted in Palliser, *Tudor York*, p. 259.

[38] W. Bittle and T. Lane, 'Inflation and Philanthropy: a reassessment of W. K. Jordan's data', *Econ. Hist. Rev.*, 2nd ser., xxix (1976), is a reworking of the figures in Jordan's mammoth work, *Philanthropy in England, 1480–1660* (1959) and his subsequent volumes such as *The Charities of Rural England 1480–1660*, (1961) in the light of the inflation of the sixteenth century which Jordan insisted on ignoring. We now know for sure what critics at the time (like D. C. Coleman) pointed out, namely, that Jordan's figures show exactly the opposite of what Jordan himself claimed: they show that the level of giving to good causes dropped strikingly in the second half of the century and only by the 1630s was it getting back to pre-Reformation levels (in real terms). Even so, his figures have to be handled very cautiously, because he gives little information about where he got them and did erratic things like including in the figures for the 1520s Wolsey's foundations in Oxford and Ipswich resulting from the suppression of twenty-nine decayed religious houses (hardly 'philanthropy' in the usual sense). Moreover decadal totals can be so distorted by sudden large bequests or other one-off foundations (especially royal ones) that it can be misleading to deduce long-term trends from them. However, there seems to be no doubt about the decline in giving to most good causes in the second half of the Tudor century, albeit there was a telling, but short-lived, upturn in the mid-1550s, especially in Mary's reign.

Of course, the abolition of monasticism and Purgatory inevitably resulted in a decline in religious benefactions. But the decline was greater than what one could reasonably expect the Reformation to have occasioned, and affected even donations to church repairs and maintenance of clergy (to which no Protestant could object). Moreover, there is evidence that the decline in religious giving was faster at the top of the social scale than at the bottom: a drop for the gentry from about 70 per cent of all giving at the beginning of the century to some 9 per cent at the end, but for those identified as 'husbandmen' from 90 to 27 per cent.

The well-to-do were doubtless spending their money on conspicuous consumption, their families, building and wordly display, as well as more 'secular' good works. Religious giving reached its lowest point in the 1580s and 1590s. After 1600, however, there is a striking upturn. By the 1630s it has reached almost pre-Reformation levels, with the proportion of middle and upper-class giving also steadily advancing. Some of this was for town lecturers and the like, which was not to Arminian, High Church tastes. But is it not also possible that many Englishmen preferred the beauty of holiness to Protestant starkness and were prepared to pay for it?

The commotions, rebellions, the tumults and destruction, in a word, the topsy-turvydom of the middle decades of the sixteenth century had been survived. The fiercest of the ideological conflicts of the later decades of the century, which had often threatened to tear apart town, village and family, had abated, though, true enough, Laud was to drive Puritans to a frenzy. England had survived desperate war. Peace had been made with Spain. The traumas of terrible hunger and plague of the 1590s had passed. And perhaps there was the warmth of a more humane and consoling religion, of a less frightening God. Things were more like what they used to be. Another wheel had turned at least part of a circle.

Bibliography

For published books, unless otherwise noted, the place of publication is London.

PRIMARY SOURCES

Manuscripts

British Library
Additional MSS 5861, 28,533 (Ely wills and Holy Trinity guild, Sleaford, accounts)
Egerton MS 2886 (Compotus book, Blessed Virgin Mary guild, Boston)
Harleian MS 4795 (Register and calendar, Corpus Christi guild, Boston)

House of Lords RO
Original acts, 35 Henry VIII, no. 42

Public Record Office
Exchequer records: Church goods (E117), 1–14
                           Chantry certificates (E301), 1–38
                           Church inventories (E315), 495–515
                           Schools continuation warrants (E319), 1
                           Recusant rolls (E377), 14, 15
King's Bench: Ancient indictments (KB9), 544
Prerogative Court of Canterbury (PCC) wills
Roman Transcripts (PRO 31/9), vols. 1, 3, 61 and 62
State Papers: Edward VI (SP 10), *passim*
               Elizabeth I, Domestic (SP 12), *passim*
               James I, Domestic (SP 14), 14, 80

Coventry RO
MS A6 (Corpus Christi guild register)

Dorset CRO
Guild records: B3/CD 15, 16, 22, 32, 56 (Bridport)
Churchwardens' accounts: P155/CW 20—34, P204/CW 35 (Sherborne and Wimborne)

Durham, Dean and Chapter Muniments
Miscellaneous Charter 7233 (Accounts, etc., St Mary Magdalen guild, Wolviston)

Gloucester CRO
Churchwardens' accounts: P217/CW2/1 (Michinhampton)
Wills, 1541—44

Huntingdon CRO
Churchwardens' accounts: MS 2280/28, 2449/25 (Holywell and Ramsey)
Wills (Archdeaconry of Hunts.), vol. 4

Leicester CRO
Churchwardens' accounts: DG36/140 (Melton Mowbray)

Northampton CRO
Churchwardens' accounts: 94P/21, 243P/309 (Culworth and Norton by Daventry)
Wills, 1st series, vol. E

Warwick CRO
Churchwardens' accounts: DRB64/63, 87/1, 158/19, 581/45 (Solihull, St Nicholas Warwick, Great Packington, Holy Trinity Coventry)

Worcester City RO
Chamber Order Book I

Printed Works

Acts of the Privy Council, ed. J. R. Dasent, 32 vols. (1890—1970)
Amphlett, J. (ed.), *Churchwardens' Accounts of St Michael's in Bed-wardine, Worcester, from 1539 to 1603*, Worcestershire Historical Society (1896)
Anstruther, G., *The Seminary Priests. A dictionary of the secular clergy of England and Wales, 1558—1850*, 4 vols. (St Edmund's College, ware, and Ushaw College, Durham, 1968—77)
Basing, P. (ed.), *Parish Fraternity Register. Fraternity of the Holy Trinity and SS Fabian and Sebastian in the Parish of St Botolph without Aldersgate*, LRS, 18 (1982)
Bateson, M. (ed.), *Records of the Borough of Leicester, 1103—1603*, 3 vols. (Cambridge, 1899—1903)
Becon, T., *Works (Catechism, etc.)*, PS, 13 (1844)

Bell, P. (ed.), *Bedfordshire Wills, 1480—1519*, Bedfordshire Historical Record Society, 45 (1966)

Bluet, T., *Important Considerations which Ought to Move all True and Sound Catholics, etc.* (1601)

Brinkworth, E. R. (ed.), *Archdeacon's Court: Liber Actorum, 1584*, Oxfordshire Record Society, 24 (1942)

Calendar of Patent Rolls, Edward VI, 6 vols. (1924—9), *Philip and Mary*, 4 vols. (1936—9), *Elizabeth I*, 7 vols. (1944—)

Calendar of State Papers, Domestic Series, of the Reigns of Edward VI, Mary, Elizabeth I and *James I*, 12 vols. (1856—72)

Calendar of State Papers, Domestic Series, Addenda, 1547—65, 1566—79, 1580—1625, 3 vols. (1870—2)

Cirkett, A. F. (ed.), *English Wills 1498—1526*, Bedfordshire Historical Record Society, 37 (1957)

Clay, C. W. (ed.), *North Country Wills I*, Surtees Society, 116 (1908)

Cranmer, T., *Works II: Remains and Letters*, PS, 24 (1846)

Darlington, I. (ed.), *London Consistory Wills, 1492—1547*, LRS, 3 (1967)

Dickens, A. G. (ed.), *Tudor Treatises*, Yorkshire Archaeological Society, 125 (1959)

Dugdale, W. (ed.), *Monasticon Anglicanum* (1718)

Fitzherbert, T., *A Supplement to the Discussion of M. D. Barlowes Answere to the Iudgment of a Catholike Englishman, etc.* (1613)

Foley, H. (ed.), *Records of the English Province of the Society of Jesus*, 8 vols. (1877—83)

Foster, C. W. (ed.), *Lincoln Wills, 1505—1530*, Lincolnshire Record Society, 5 and 10 (1914, 1918)

Lincoln Wills III, 1530—32, Lincolnshire Record Society, 24 (1930)

Fowler, J. T. (ed.), *The Rites of Durham, being a description or brief declaration of all the ancient monuments, rites and customs belonging or being within the monastical church of Durham before the suppression, written 1593*, Surtees Society, cvii (1902)

Furnivall, F. J. (ed.), *The Gild of St Mary Lichfield*, Early English Text Society (1920)

Godfrey, W. H. (ed.), *Transcripts of Sussex Wills ... up to the year 1560*, Sussex Record Society, 41, 42, 43 (1935, 1938, 1939)

Grace, M. (ed.), *Records of the Gild of St George in Norwich, 1389—1547*, Norfolk Record Society (1937)

Green, E. (ed.), *Somerset Chantries: survey and rental*, Somerset Record Society, ii (1888)

Grindal, E., *Remains*, PS 8 (1843)

Grumbly, W. (ed.), *Obituary Notes of the English Dominicans from 1555 to 1952* (1955)

Harris, M. D. (ed.), *The register of the guild of the Holy Trinity, St Mary, St John the Baptist and St Katherine of Coventry*, Dugdale Society, xiii (1935)

Harvey Bloom, J. (ed.), *The Gild Register: Stratford upon Avon, 1406 —1535* (1907)

Hobhouse, E. (ed.), *Churchwardens' Accounts of Croscombe, Pilton, Milton, Yatton, Tintinhull, Morebath and St Michael's, Bath, ranging from* AD *1349 to 1560*, Somerset Record Society, iv (1890)

Holmes, P. (ed.), *Elizabethan Casuistry*, CRS, 67 (1981)

Hutchinson, T., *Works*, PS 4 (1842)

Jewel, J., *Works*, 2 vols., PS 19, 26 and 30 (1845, 1847 and 1848)

Kenny, A. (ed.), *The Responsa Scolarum of the English College, Rome*, 2 vols., CRS, 54 and 55 (1962, 1963)

Kitching, C. J. (ed.), *London and Middlesex Chantry Certificate, 1548*, LRS, xvi (1980)

Latimer, H., *Sermons* and *Remains*, PS 16 and 20 (1844, 1845)

Letters and Papers, Foreign and Domestic, of the Reign of Henry VIII, edited by J. S. Brewer, J. Gairdner and R. H. Brodie, 21 vols. (1862—1932)

Loomie, A. J. (ed.), *Spain and the Jacobean Catholics*, CRS, 64 (1973)

McGregor, M. (ed.), *Bedfordshire Wills proved in the Prerogative Court of Canterbury, 1383—1548*, Bedfordshire Historical Record Society, 58 (1979)

Musket, G. *The Bishop of London his Legacy* (1623)

Nichols, J. G. (ed.), *Narratives of the Reformation*, Camden Society, 1st series, cxxvii (1860)

O'Brien, M. (ed.), *Halesowen Churchwardens' Accounts (1487—1582)*, Worcestershire Historical Society (1957)

Persons, R., *A Treatise of Three Conversions of England from Paganism to the Christian Religion* (1603, 1604)

Peacock, E., *English Church Furniture, Ornaments and Decorations at the period of the Reformation* (1866)

Pilkington, J., *Works*, PS 3 (1842)

Raine, J. (ed.), *Depositions and other ecclesiastical proceedings from the courts of Durham, extending from 1311 to the reign of Elizabeth*, Surtees Society, v (1845)

Sandys, E., *Sermons*, PS 2 (1841)

Smith, L. Toulmin (ed.), *English Gilds*, Early English Text Society (1870)

Statutes of the Realm, 11 vols., 1830—52

Templeman, G. (ed.), *The records of the guild of the Holy Trinity, St Mary, St John the Baptist and St Katherine of Coventry II*, Dugdale Society, xix (1944)

Tyndale, W., *Works*, PS 6 (1848)

Travers, W., *A Declaration of Ecclesiastical Discipline* (1584)

Wainwright, T. (ed.), *Bridport Records and Ancient Manuscripts* (Bridport, n.d.)

Walsingham, F. , *A Search made into Matters of Religion etc.* (1609)

Weaver, F. W. (ed.), *Somerset Medieval Wills, 3rd series, 1531–1558*, Somerset Record Society, xxii (1904)

Weaver, F. W., and Clark, G. N. (eds.), *Churchwardens' Accounts of Marston, Spelsbury and Pyrton*, Oxfordshire Record Society, v (1925)

Whitgift, J., *Works*, PS 50 (1853)

Wright, T. (ed.), *Churchwardens' Accounts of the town of Ludlow in Shropshire, from 1540 to the end of the reign of Queen Elizabeth*, Camden Society, 1st series, cii (1869)

Wright, W., *A Treatise of the Church* (1616)

SECONDARY WORKS

Addleshaw, G. W. O., and Etchells, F., *The Architectural Setting of Anglican Worship* (1948)

Bittle, W., and Lane, T., 'Inflation and Philanthropy: a reassessment of W. K. Jordan's data', *Economic History Review*, 2nd series, xxix (1976), 203ff

Blench, J. W., *Preaching in England in the late Fifteenth and Sixteenth Centuries* (Oxford, 1964)

Bossy, J., *The English Catholic Community, 1570–1850* (1976)
  'The character of Elizabethan Catholicism', *Past and Present*, 21 (1962), 39–59
  'Essai de sociographie de la messe, 1200–1700, *Annales*, 36 (1981), 44–70

Bowker, M., *The Secular Clergy in the Diocese of Lincoln, 1495–1520* (1968)
  The Henrician Reformation. The diocese of Lincoln under John Longland. 1521–1547 (Cambridge, 1981)
  'The Commons Supplication against the Ordinaries in the light of some Archidiaconal Acta', *TRHS*, 5th series, 21 (1971), 61–77
  'The Henrician Reformation and the parish clergy', *Bulletin of the Institute of Historical Research*, 50 (1977), 28–49.

Brigden, S., 'Tithe controversy in Reformation London', *Journal of Ecclesiastical History*, 32 (1981), 44–70

Clancy, T., *Papist Pamphleteers. The Allens-Persons Party and the Political Thought of the Counter-Reformation in England, 1572–1615* (Chicago, 1964)

Clark, P., *English Provincial Society from the Reformation to the Revolution: religion, politics and society in Kent, 1500–1640*, (Hassocks, Sussex, 1977)

Cohn, H. J., 'Anticlericalism in the German Peasants' War, 1525', *Past and Present*, 83 (1979), 3–31

Collinson, P., *The Elizabethan Puritan Movement* (1967)
  The Religion of Protestants: the Church in English Society, 1559–1625 (Oxford, 1982)
Cornwall, J., *The Revolt of the Peasantry, 1549* (1977)
Cox, C., *Architectural Styles in the English Parish Church* (n.d.)
Crofts, R., 'Books, Reform and Reformation', *Arch. f. Ref.*, lxxi (1980), 21–35
Davis, J., 'Joan of Kent, Lollardy and the English Reformation', *Journal of Ecclesiastical History*, 33 (1982), 225–33
Dickens, A. G., *The English Reformation* (1964)
Elton, G. R., 'The Commons' Supplication of 1532: Parliamentary Manoeuvres in the Reign of Henry VIII', *English Historical Review*, lxvi (1951), 507–34
  'Thomas More and the opposition to Henry VIII', *Bulletin of the Institute of Historical Research*, xli (1968), 19–34
  'Politics and the Pilgrimage of Grace', in B. Malament (ed.), *After the Reformation. Essays in honor of J. H. Hexter* (Manchester, 1980), pp. 25–56
Gasquet, F. A., *The Eve of the Reformation* (1919 edn)
Greaves, R. L., *Society and Religion in Elizabethan England* (Minnesota, 1981)
Haigh, C., *Reformation and Resistance in Tudor Lancashire* (Cambridge, 1975)
  'Some Aspects of the Recent Historiography of the English Reformation', in W. J. Mommsen (ed.), *The Urban Classes, the Nobility and the Reformation*, Publications of the German Historical Institute, London, 5 (1980)
  'From Monopoly to Minority: Catholicism in early modern England', *TRHS*, 5th series, 31 (1981), 129–47
Hanlon, Sr J. D., 'These be but Women', in C. H. Carter (ed.), *From the Renaissance to the Counter-Reformation, Essays in honour of Garrett Mattingly* (1966), pp. 371–400
Heal, F., *Of Prelates and Princes. A study in the economic and social position of the Tudor episcopate* (Cambridge, 1980)
Heath, P., *The English Parish Clergy on the Eve of the Reformation* (1969)
Holmes, P., *Resistance and Compromise: the political thought of Elizabethan Catholics* (1982)
Houlbrooke, R., *Church Courts and the People during the English Reformation* (1979)
Hughes, P., *The Reformation in England*, 3 vols. (1950–4)
Janelle, P., *L'Angleterre Catholique à la veille du schisme* (Paris, 1935)
Johnston, H., *The Assurance of Abbey and other Church Lands in England etc* (1687)
Jones, N. L., *Faith by statute: Parliament and the settlement of religion,*

1559, Royal Historical Society Studies in History, 32 (1982)

Jordan, W. K., *Philanthrophy in England, 1480–1660* (1959)
  The Charities of Rural England, 1480–1660 (1961)

Kelly, M. J., 'The Submission of the Clergy', *TRHS*, 5th series, 15 (1965), 97–119

Kitching, C. J., 'The Quest for Concealed Lands in the Reign of Elizabeth', *TRHS*, 5th series, 24 (1974), 63–78

Knowles, M. D., *The Religious Orders in England, III. The Tudor Age* (Cambridge, 1959)

Kreider, A., *English Chantries: the road to dissolution* (Cambridge Mass., 1979)

Lander, S., 'Church courts and the Reformation in the Diocese of Chichester, 1500–58', in R. O'Day and F. Heal (eds.), *Continuity and Change: Personnel and Administration of the Church in England, 1500–1642* (Leicester, 1976), pp. 215–37

Leach, A. F., *English Schools at the Reformation, 1546–8* (1896)

Lehmberg, S. E., *The Reformation Parliament, 1529–1536* (Cambridge, 1970)
  The Later Parliaments of the Reign of Henry VIII, 1536–1547 (1980)

Loach, J., and Tittler, R. (eds.), *The Mid-Tudor Polity, c.1540–1560* (Cambridge, 1980)

Loades, D., *The Reign of Mary Tudor* (1979)

Luxton, I., 'The Reformation and popular culture', in F. Heal and R. O'Day (eds.), *Church and Society in England: Henry VIII to James I* (1977), pp. 57–77

MacCaffrey, W., *The Shaping of the Elizabethan Regime* (1969)
  Queen Elizabeth and the Making of Policy, 1572–1588 (Princeton, 1981)

MacCullough, D., 'Catholic and Puritan in Elizabethan Suffolk', *Arch. f. Ref.*, lxxii (1981), 232–87.

McGrath, P., *Papists and Puritans under Elizabeth I* (1967)

Manning, R. B., *Religion and Society in Elizabethan Sussex* (Leicester, 1961)

Moeller, B., 'Frömmigkeit in Deutschland um 1500', *Arch. f. Ref.*, lvi (1965), 5–31

Morris, R., *Cathedrals and Abbeys of England and Wales. The building Church, 600–1540* (1979)

Oberman, H., *The Harvest of Medieval Theology* (1963)

Orme, N., *English Schools in the Middle Ages* (1973)

Owen, D. M., *Church and Society in Medieval Lincolnshire* (Lincoln, 1971)

Oxley, J. E., *The Reformation in Essex to the death of Mary* (Manchester, 1965)

Palliser, D. M., *Tudor York* (Oxford, 1979)

'Popular Reactions to the Reformation during the years of Uncertainty, 1530—70', in F. Heal and R. O'Day (eds.), *Church and Society in England: Henry VIII to James I* (1977), pp. 35—56

Pevsner, N. (ed.), *The Buildings of England*, 46 vols. (Harmondsworth, 1951—74)

Phillips, G. E., *The Extinction of the ancient Hierarchy...* (1905)

Phythian-Adams, C., 'Ceremony and the citizen: the communal year at Coventry, 1450—1550', in P. Clark and P. Slack (eds.), *Crisis and Order in English Towns, 1500—1700* (1972)

Pogson, R. H., 'Revival and reform in Mary Tudor's Church: a question of money', *Journal of Ecclesiastical History*, xxv (1974), 249—65

'The Legacy of the Schism: Confusion, Continuity and Change in the Marian Clergy', in J. Loach and R. Tittler (eds), *The Mid-Tudor Polity, c.1540—1560* (1980), pp. 116—136.

Powell, K. G., 'The Beginnings of Protestantism in Gloucestershire', *Transactions of the Bristol and Gloucestershire Archaeological Society*, 90 (1971)

Pritchard, A., *Catholic Loyalism in Elizabethan England* (Chapel Hill, N. Carolina, 1979)

Ritter, G., 'Why the Reformation occurred in Germany', *Church History*, xxvii (1958), 99—106

Rogers, A., *The Making of Stamford* (1965)

Rowse, A. L., *Tudor Cornwall* (1941)

Scarisbrick, J. J., *Henry VIII* (1968)

Seaver, P. S., *Puritan Lectureships. The politics of religious dissent, 1560—1662* (Stanford, 1970)

Simon, J., *Education and Society in Tudor England* (Cambridge, 1966)

Spelman, H., *The History and Fate of Sacrilege* (1698)

Thomas, K., *Religion and the Decline of Magic* (1971)

Tittler, R., 'The Emergence of Urban Policy, 1536—58', in J. Loach and R. Tittler (eds), *The Mid-Tudor Polity, c.1540—1560* (1980), pp. 74—93

Trimble, W. R., *The Catholic Laity in Elizabethan England, 1558—1603* (Cambridge, Mass., 1964)

Victoria County Histories

Westlake, H. F., *The Parish Gilds of Medieval England* (1919)

Wright, T., *A Historical and Descriptive Sketch of Ludlow Castle and the Church of St Lawrence, Ludlow* (18th edn, Shrewsbury, 1929)

Youings, J., *The Dissolution of the Monasteries* (1971)

Zell, M. L., 'The personnel of the clergy in Kent, in the Reformation period', *English Historical Review*, lxxxix (1974), 513—33

'Economic Problems of the Parochial Clergy', in R. O'Day and F. Heal (eds), *Princes and Paupers in the English Church, 1500—1800* (Leicester, 1981)

Index